Custer, Cody, and Grand Duke Alexis

Custer, Cody, and Grand Duke Alexis

Historical Archaeology of the Royal Buffalo Hunt

Douglas D. Scott, Peter Bleed,
and Stephen Damm

University of Oklahoma Press : Norman

Library of Congress Cataloging-in-Publication Data

Scott, Douglas D.
  Custer, Cody, and Grand Duke Alexis : historical archaeology of the royal buffalo hunt / Douglas D. Scott, Peter Bleed, and Stephen Damm.
    p. cm.
  Includes bibliographical references and index.
  ISBN 978-0-8061-4347-7 (pbk. : alk. paper) 1. Archaeology and history—Nebraska—Hayes County. 2. American bison hunting—Nebraska—Hayes County—History—19th century. 3. Camp sites, facilities, etc.—Nebraska—Hayes County—History—19th century. 4. Material culture—Nebraska—Hayes County—History—19th century. 5. Hayes County (Neb.)—Antiquities. 6. Aleksei Aleksandrovich, Grand Duke of Russia, 1850–1908—Travel—Nebraska—Hayes County. 7. Custer, George A. (George Armstrong), 1839-1876. 8. Buffalo Bill, 1846-1917. 9. Spotted Tail, 1823–1881. 10. Hunting guides—Nebraska—Hayes County—History—19th century. I. Bleed, Peter. II. Damm, Stephen, 1981– III. Title.
  F672.H4S36 2013
  978.2'832—dc23
                                                                  2012028824

The paper in this book meets the guidelines for permanence and durability of the Committee on Production Guidelines for Book Longevity of the Council on Library Resources, Inc. ∞

Copyright © 2013 by the University of Oklahoma Press, Norman, Publishing Division of the University. Manufactured in the U.S.A.

All rights reserved. No part of this publication may be reproduced, stored in a retrieval system, or transmitted, in any form or by any means, electronic, mechanical, photocopying, recording, or otherwise—except as permitted under Section 107 or 108 of the United States Copyright Act—without the prior written permission of the University of Oklahoma Press. To request permission to reproduce selections from this book, write to Permissions, University of Oklahoma Press, 2800 Venture Drive, Norman OK 73069, or email rights.oupress@ou.edu.

Contents

List of Illustrations	vii
Preface	xi
Acknowledgments	xvii
Chapter 1. A Royal Comes to Town	3
Chapter 2. Conceptual Contexts for Camp Alexis Archaeology	11
Chapter 3. The Grand Duke's Tour of the United States	22
Chapter 4. Camp Alexis and the Royal Buffalo Hunt	38
Chapter 5. Edric Eaton and the Hunt Party Photographs	78
Chapter 6. The Archaeology of Camp Alexis	109
Chapter 7. Interpreting Camp Alexis: The Context of Military Camps and Camping in the West	134
Chapter 8. Camp Alexis Historical Archaeology: Its Context and Meaning	156
Notes	163
References	181
Index	201

Illustrations

1. Grand Duke Alexis in the dress of an Imperial Russian Army officer — 4
2. Grand Duke Alexis in civilian dress — 23
3. Arrival of the Russian squadron in New York — 25
4. The Russian cruiser *Svetlana*, on which Grand Duke Alexis served — 25
5. The New York reception committee greeting Grand Duke Alexis — 26
6. Grand welcoming parade for Grand Duke Alexis — 26
7. The welcoming parade, with New York militia units — 27
8. The Mosby Confederate Mountain Rifle from which a key to New York City was fashioned — 28
9. An invitation to a ball honoring Grand Duke Alexis at the Philadelphia Music Academy — 29
10. Grand Duke Alexis dancing at the Navy Ball — 29
11. A waltz composed in honor of Grand Duke Alexis's visit to Philadelphia — 30
12. Grand Duke Alexis during the ball in Denver — 33
13. Funeral procession in Paris for Grand Duke Alexis — 36
14. Map of Camp Alexis location in Hayes County — 39
15. Maj. Gen. William T. Sherman, planner of the royal buffalo hunt — 41

16. Maj. Gen. Philip Sheridan, hunt master and organizer	42
17. Lt. Col. George A. Custer in civilian dress	46
18. A buffalo hunt in Kansas hosted by George Custer ca. 1867	46
19. A temporary railroad bridge crossing the frozen Missouri River	49
20. A Union Pacific Railroad time card prepared for Grand Duke Alexis's trip	49
21. Former Nebraska Territorial Governor Alvin Saunders	54
22. Custer's 1867 route from the Republican River and the scout to Red Willow Creek	55
23. Grand Duke Alexis bringing down the first buffalo of the hunt	59
24. David Frank Neiswanger, who commemorated historic sites in western Nebraska	73
25. The Neiswanger Camp Alexis monument ca. 1938	73
26. The original commemorative monument at the hunt site	73
27. Sites of the John Dunning dugout, the 1930s-era baseball diamond, and the modern hunt monument	75
28. Impersonators of George Custer and California Joe Milner at the 2009 rendezvous	76
29. The imperial hunting party	79
30. George Custer and Grand Duke Alexis posed with hunting weapons	81
31. Edric L. Eaton ca. 1870	83
32. An American Indian camp, purported to be Spotted Tail's	86
33. Eaton Number 1. The mounted party	88
34. Members of the mounted party who can be identified	88
35. Eaton Number 2. Standing members of the camp	91
36. Members of the standing group who can be identified	91
37. Eaton Number 3. Grand Duke Alexis's tent	93
38. Eaton Number 4. Spotted Tail with his wife and daughter in front of their tent	97
39. Eaton Number 5. William F. Cody seated in Eaton's Omaha Studio	100
40. A variant of Eaton Number 5. Professor Henry Ward and William F. Cody	100
41. Eaton Number 6. George Custer and Spotted Tail	102
42. The Berghaus sketch of the 1867 buffalo-hunt dinner	106
43. The traditional Camp Alexis site	111

44. The monument commemorating the royal buffalo hunt	111
45. Members of the 2008 archaeological field school working in a cluster of metal finds	113
46. A topographic map of the site	115
47. American Indian iron tools	117
48. American Indian dangle	117
49. Spotted Tail at the 1868 Fort Laramie Treaty and inset of a hoop earring and dangle	118
50. Buttons and a saber-belt stud	119
51. Cut nails	121
52. Expedient iron tent stakes	123
53. Miscellaneous artifacts	123
54. Containers	127
55. Lead-foil seals from wine or champagne bottles	127
56. Bullets and cartridges	128
57. A dark-green glass bottle for ale or stout	130
58. An idealized cavalry-camp layout	135
59. Eaton Number 6 (dining tent with Spotted Tail and George Custer) overlaid on the modern landscape	145
60. Eaton Number 3 (Grand Duke Alexis's tent with Adm. Constantine Possiet, Spotted Tail, and Lt. Count Paul Shouvalov) overlaid on the modern landscape	146
61. Eaton Numbers 3 and 6 (the dining tent and Grand Duke Alexis's tent) overlaid on the modern landscape	147
62. Eaton Number 4 (Spotted Tail with his wife and daughter) overlaid on the modern landscape	148
63. A three-dimensional model of the camp superimposed on a current aerial photograph	149
64. A Seventh U.S. Cavalry field camp during the 1874 Black Hills Expedition	152

Preface

Widely heralded at the time, but usually treated as a footnote today, is the visit to the United States by Russian Grand Duke Alexis in late 1871 and early 1872. Traveling by rail and steamboat, he ranged the eastern seaboard into Canada, as far south as New Orleans, and westward to Denver. The focus of the western leg of the trip was a specially arranged buffalo hunt, now referred to as the "royal buffalo hunt." That hunt, which took place in Nebraska, was hosted by Maj. Gen. Philip Sheridan. The participants included several iconic western characters: Chief Spotted Tail of the Brulé Sioux, Lt. Col. George A. Custer, and William F. "Buffalo Bill" Cody. We became interested in the story of Grand Duke Alexis and the royal buffalo hunt because, as archaeologists, we thought that the archaeology of the site and its material culture might offer interesting insights into the events of January 1872. As anthropologists we wondered how the U.S. government had actually treated the grand duke. What was the lot of the soldiers who had accompanied the hunting party? And what could we learn about Spotted Tail's Brulé band, who had been brought to the camp both to help with the hunt and to entertain the guests? Initially we were interested in the material record of the hunt and hoped that artifacts preserved at the site would reflect the events and social groups. We also realized that among the many sites and places the grand duke visited, the Red

Willow Creek campsite was the only one likely to have remained unchanged or whose archaeological information related to his visit had been preserved. Thus of those places where Alexis, Sheridan, Custer, Cody, and others once trod, Camp Alexis might be the only tangible site that can be identified with certainty.

When friends and colleagues learned about our interest in the royal buffalo hunt, their reactions fell into a rather narrow range. Some were simply unaware that a son of Czar Alexander II came to southwestern Nebraska when the state was new. But they were a minority. The visit of the Czar's son to the wintry plains of western Nebraska in company with military leaders and famous plainsmen is well established in frontier lore. Certainly everyone in Hayes County, where the campsite is located, knows about the event. It is celebrated, among other ways, on the shoulder patches worn by the county sheriff and his deputies. The fact that many people were aware of the grand duke's visit convinced us that there was broad interest in anything we could add to the story. But among those aware of the event were some who wanted to know how a team of archaeologists could add anything to what was known of a brief, long-past hunting trip. That is a fair question, and this volume is our attempt to answer it. The challenge we faced as we investigated the royal buffalo hunt was, using the tools of archaeology, to make an original contribution to what was known of the hunt.

We found good archaeological reasons for investigating the site where Grand Duke Alexis camped in 1872. First, short-term encampments were a key element of western expansion, and Camp Alexis offered a fine place to develop methods for recognizing and researching such sites. Second, with civilians, soldiers and American Indians, the camp provides a place to investigate archaeological evidence of cultural interaction on the frontier. And third, to augment these topics, we came up with purely historical questions that deserved investigation. Accounts of the hunt and life in the camp seemed to be based on only a few sources. Virtually all were short on specifics, and inconsistencies were common in published information. That set us to searching for new records that would augment our archaeological information. Discoveries followed in part because there is a big audience for anything related to George Custer and Buffalo Bill. Archive and library holdings could be augmented with documents in private collections. There we found images and travel documents that added a new dimension to the Camp Alexis story. As we searched we were lucky enough to meet many others who shared our interest in the grand duke and his visit. Their response was encouraging, but it also showed us that the story to be revealed in the archaeology of Camp Alexis would not be a simple one. One person encouraged us to consider how bringing a nobleman to the frontier reflected the expansionism of America in the Gilded Age. Another wanted to know which hat Custer wore while on this hunt. We were pulled in many directions, presented with a raft of questions, and blessed with many kinds of information. Organizing our observations and presenting them in appropriate ways had been at least as hard as making the discoveries.

The past generation of American archaeologists wrestled with issues of how and why to study the past. Recovering material residue of past events and learning to use them as a record of the past entails a web of technical challenges. Making those records credible to other scholars has not always been easy. But beyond those challenges, archaeologists have hotly debated what we should do with the record we study. With a grounding in anthropology, most American archaeologists have used the archaeological record to investigate cultural patterns and ecological lifestyles. This approach to archaeology reveals long-term changes in the human past. Another important community of archaeologists advocated using the archaeological record as a source of information about the development of human social, economic, and intellectual conditions. Debates regarding the relative merits of these—and other—approaches enlivened archaeology and produced studies that stimulated the discipline. They also convinced archaeologists that our discipline could address big issues and grand ideas. But, as with most academic disciplines, theoretical debates within archaeology lose their steam. In the process, all approaches have had their limits exposed, and as a consequence, no single theoretical or methodological perspective has been judged ideal either for archaeological investigations or for the treatment of the human past. No "top-down agenda" seems to do justice to the richness and complexity of the archaeological record.

We began exploring Grand Duke Alexis's 1872 buffalo hunt as archaeologists. As our research led us to new sources and records, we tried to solve the challenges they presented. We never felt the need for a strongly prescriptive theoretical stance, but as we set about pulling our diverse sources together, we discovered that some archaeologists were finding it useful to approach their work as "microhistory." Notable in that regard are the papers assembled by Brooks, DeCorse, and Walton and the studies by Beaudry and Veit.[1] Microhistory seemed to describe neatly what we were doing with Camp Alexis.

Microhistory proposes that the past be studied neither in simple specific terms nor in trivial descriptive detail. Rather, it is an "exploratory stance" that encourages anthropologists, historians, and archaeologists to acknowledge the specific grounding of their research.[2] In addition to making it clear that research is treating a specific topic, microhistory encourages researchers to acknowledge the nature and peculiarities of the records they are using to study their topic. Attention to the record is, of course, familiar to modern archaeologists, but all research into the human past must use some kinds of record—written, recalled, recorded, graphic, constructed, landscape, or material. More than simply acknowledging the peculiarities of a given record, microhistory suggests that its nature and content be acknowledged. No record is perfect. All have strengths. All expose distinctive sides of the past. All carry real or potential error. And because different records make diverse interpretive demands, different records tend to have their own audiences. Recognizing the distinctive qualities of records encourages the use of multiple records and synthetic consideration of past events. Use of multiple records significantly expands the audience even for specific research. Complementary use of records offers broadened views and the potential for correcting shortcomings and errors. And microhistory recognizes that the specific data associated with topics do not marginalize those topics. To the contrary, advocates of microhistory suggest that paying close attention to records can reveal connections between concrete events and broad developments. Finally, part of the appeal of microhistory for us is that it is still a fresh enough discipline to be free of dogma. Rather than directing research in a particular direction or to a predictable conclusion, we are comfortable using microhistory to explore relationships and follow the available records where they lead.

Employing the inclusiveness of microhistory in our study of the imperial buffalo hunt, we determined to mine Russian archives. In our field they are an unexplored, potentially rich source of information. With support from the Nebraska Humanities Council we were able to pursue this course. As often happens with studies of the past, unexpected new evidence took us in a slightly different direction.

One aspect of our search was to determine if any archives held copies of photographs taken by Omaha photographer Edric L. Eaton at the camp on Red Willow Creek. When we started our work, Eaton was known to have taken photographs, but no copies were known to exist. However, through a set of marvelously intricate and interconnected events we learned that two other researchers also were looking for Eaton photographs. One published photograph that was found purported to be of Spotted Tail's camp on Red Willow Creek. That it existed helped establish the likelihood that other Eaton images still existed.[3] A stereograph of Custer and Spotted Tail came to our attention in 1999, and five more stereographs of the camp and its participants came to light in 2000. With all the publicity surrounding the grand duke's visit, which involved Custer and other prominent men of the time, and with the intense historical interest in the hunt, it seems ironic that it has taken nearly 140 years for the significance of these photographs to be recognized. Thus our microhistory approach includes a variety of records to compare and contrast, to parse and corroborate. The historical record we have assembled includes letters, contemporary newspaper and magazine articles, personal recollections, recent and older historical assessments, local and regional hunt lore, material from Russian and U.S. archives—all the meat of historical inquiry. A second type of record is the contemporary photographs of the campsite and the campers. These we treat both as a historical source and as a record of material culture. The third record is that of the archaeology of the camp, mainly the artifacts and the context in which they were found. Woven together they become a strong fabric that uses the whole to develop a richer story of our frontier past.

A note on references for the reader. We employ a modified scientific referencing format in this work. We bend to the conventional endnote method of referencing, but the individual endnotes use the scientific referencing scheme we are familiar with and prefer. We believe this hybrid approach accomplishes our goal of systematic and extensive referencing called for in scientific publications but does not clutter the pages with in-text citations.

Acknowledgments

A great many people have aided our research efforts and study of Camp Alexis and the buffalo hunt. We are grateful to each. We wish particularly to thank Wayne and John Mintling and Mark and Scott Clifford for granting us access to their family properties to conduct archaeological investigations. Both families have cared about and cared for the campsite since they acquired the properties in the late nineteenth century. Without their cooperation and support we could not have accomplished the field investigations. Lyle Hutchens and David Chalfant generously shared the information and the artifacts that they had acquired while metal detecting on the site. The students of the 2008 and 2009 University of Nebraska Department of Anthropology archaeological field schools did the yeoman work of metal detecting and recording artifacts found on the campsite.

The Nebraska Humanities Council grant enabled us to research the Russian archives, and Kristen Nute and Elena Testekova of the Baltic Russian Information Center kindly provided us translations and interpretations of Russian documents. Jim Potter, John Carter, and the staff of the Nebraska State Historical Society research room directed us to many sources and provided helpful comments and suggestions. To them we are especially grateful. John Doerner and Sharon Small of the National Park Service, Little Bighorn Battlefield National Monument, generously provided information and copies of a variety of images from their files. Professor Jim Carr of the University of Nebraska, Lincoln, Chemistry Department identified the silver content of our recovered ear bob. The University of Nebraska Interlibrary Loan staff did yeoman work in finding many an obscure reference during our research. Andrew Ireland of the W. Dale Clark Main Library, Omaha Public Library, found and provided copies of significant locations in Omaha that played a role in the hunt story. Melissa Mead of the University of Rochester Rhees Library archives was helpful in finding and supplying a copy of an image of Henry Ward and Bill Cody for analysis. The staff of the Kansas State Historical Society archives provided help and direction in finding Kansas-related materials. The library staff in the University of Nebraska, Lincoln, Center for Great Plains Studies dug out several obscure references from their holdings. We are grateful to Eli Paul of the Missouri Valley Room, Kansas City Public Library, for bringing the James Forsyth Papers to our attention. The Center for Great Plains Studies generously gave us a small stipend to facilitate our research in the James Forsyth Papers in the archives of the University of Washington. Wendi Lindquist, Ph.D. candidate in the History Department, University of Washington, conducted research for us in the Forsyth Papers. Author Jeff Barnes brought the Frank Thomson archive to our attention, for which we are extremely grateful. Robert Sieczkiewicz and Brian Stewart, archivists at Drexel University, were instrumental in our research in the Thomson Papers, which they hold and for which we offer them a special thanks. Maria Fitzgerald, of the Beinecke Rare Book and Manuscript Library, Yale University, kindly provided information on an Eaton image from the James Forsyth Papers in their collections. Research in the James Forsyth-related holdings in the William Clements Library, University of Michigan, was facilitated by the able staff. We extend our thanks to each staff member, archivist, and researcher in each of these fine repositories.

Professor Lee Farrow of Auburn University at Montgomery very generously shared her research on the grand duke's U.S. sojourn and offered us encouragement and advice. Sincere thanks are due to Jeremy M. Johnston, editor of the William F. Cody papers, McCracken Research Library, Buffalo Bill Historical Center, in Cody, Wyoming, for his gracious assistance in finding several obscure sources related to Cody's role in the hunt. The staff of Chicago's Oakwood Cemetery were helpful in our efforts to locate the Eaton family graves, which were instrumental in our completion of the Eaton genealogy. Likewise the staff of the Chicago Historical Society archives, particularly Anne Marie Chase, were helpful in guiding us to copies of the city directories. Deborah Hull-Walski, collections manager, Department of Anthropology, Smithsonian Institution, and intern Katherine Birmingham scoured the National Anthropological Archives and the Museum of American History archives for Eaton images and for Gustavus Fox's files. We owe them a special debt of gratitude. We want to thank Steve Haack of Lincoln for his analysis of the time of day when each Eaton photograph was taken.

We gratefully acknowledge the editorial work of John Drayton, Alice Stanton, and Emmy Ezzell of the University of Oklahoma Press for their guidance. Their hard work is truly appreciated.

There are two individuals without whose generosity we could have never completed this study. Western photograph collectors Larry Ness and Jim Crain allowed us nearly unlimited access to their collections and shared their vast knowledge. Jim and Larry loaned us their original Eaton images of Camp Alexis for study and analysis. For this we can never fully thank them. Those images, together with the archaeological discoveries, afforded us a true perspective of the camp and the people who once walked that ground.

Custer, Cody, and Grand Duke Alexis

1

A Royal Comes to Town

On the chilly morning of January 13, 1872, a special train pulled onto the Union Pacific siding at North Platte Station. Its progress to and through Nebraska had been watched carefully both in communities it passed and by newspaper readers across the country because its principal passenger was His Imperial Highness, Grand Duke Aleksei Alexandrovich of the House of Romanov, third son of Czar Alexander II of Russia. Grand Duke Alexis, as his name is anglicized, was a handsome twenty-one-year old midway through a goodwill tour of the United States. With much fanfare he had seen the cities and sights of the East—New York, Washington, and Niagara Falls—and now he was about to enjoy a western adventure, a grand buffalo hunt on the plains of Nebraska.

The grand duke had been in North America for more than a month, during which time he had been involved in a series of carefully scheduled events. Most of his days, and even some nights, had been spent on trains. During the weeks preceding his arrival at North Platte, his base had been a group of five Pullman cars that offered storage space, dining areas, and sleeping facilities both for dignitaries and for the grand duke's retinue. And one drawing room or parlor car was for use by the grand duke only. The cars were richly equipped and well heated, but even so, the grand duke's home was less than ten feet wide and was filled with people. Likely the

Figure 1. Grand Duke Alexis in the dress of an Imperial Russian Army officer. Douglas Scott collection.

opportunity to spend loosely scheduled time in the open plains was particularly appealing.

The grand duke's hunting companions were a new and varied social set. His host was Lt. Gen. Philip Sheridan, commander of the U.S. Army Department of the Missouri. General Sheridan had met the grand duke in Omaha and there had attached his two Pullman cars to the royal train. Sheridan also brought a retinue of senior military leaders to help the grand duke enjoy fine meals and conviviality as they crossed the plains. Notable in this group was the dashing Civil War hero and Indian fighter Lt. Col. George A. Custer.

In addition to the grand duke's official and personal staff and the visiting military leaders, the group that disembarked at North Platte Station included several participants. Railroad staff members, notably the train manager Frank Thomson, of Civil War railroading fame, were on board to make sure that everything went smoothly. At least one reporter had joined the group to keep newspaper readers across the country informed of the grand duke's activities through telegraph dispatches. An adventurous Omaha photographer, Edric L. Eaton, was accompanying the party to capture images of the event. The famous frontier scout William F. "Buffalo Bill" Cody was to serve as scout and local liaison. And waiting to serve as a military escort was a company of U.S. cavalry.

With martial efficiency the group boarded army wagons and mounted cavalry horses that had been assembled for their use and set out on a military road that led into southwestern Nebraska. Soon they were crossing largely unsettled land that American Indians used regularly as hunting territory. After more than eight frigid hours, the party reached a south-facing terrace above a fork of Red Willow Creek where a tent camp had been pitched by a company of Second Cavalry troopers who had preceded the travelers. The grand duke and his companions were met by the musical strains of the Second Cavalry band and a champagne toast to celebrate their safe arrival. Awaiting them were well-pitched tents, most fitted with stoves to ward off the January chill, three with wooden floors. Once settled into their field accommodations, the party enjoyed the first of several sumptuous meals. The next afternoon a band of Brulé Sioux led by Chief Spotted Tail joined the temporary community, which was called Camp Alexis. For two days this party of royalty, military leaders, Indians and Indian fighters, journalists, and a soon-to-be showman hunted buffalo, ate and drank expansively, and experienced the free and limitless life of the open frontier.

By the morning of January 16 the hunt was over. The grand duke and his traveling companions mounted their horses, and the military wagons that had brought them into the plains returned them to the world of modern transportation and electronic communication. Back on his special train, the grand duke resumed his travels, to Denver, back to Kansas, on to New Orleans, and then overseas. After the hunters had departed, troopers of the Second Cavalry stayed long enough to strike the tents that had formed Camp Alexis. They cleaned the campsite, disposed of the waste and litter, packed their wagons, and then, just days before a serious blizzard swept across the region, returned to their bases at North Platte and Fort McPherson. With the hunt over and the tents removed, Camp Alexis was once again a bit of windswept grassland. Its history, however, was far from over.

By January 16, stories about the hunt and life in Camp Alexis had appeared in eastern newspapers. Within the next few days, information in these unsigned accounts was recycled in other papers, often with embellishments, reorderings, and details calculated to make the grand buffalo hunt the subject of great popular interest.

Stories published during the rest of the grand duke's journey invariably mentioned the hunt. Photographs of the hunters were taken and distributed. In particular, pictures of Custer and the grand duke dressed in hunting clothes documented their adventure and helped cement Custer's romantic image as a western adventurer. Buffalo Bill, who was about to begin his career as a showman, strove to have his role in the hunt emphasized. Some accounts describe him as the hunt coordinator and place him near the center of every activity. Cody seems to have been adept at working with the media even at this early stage of his career as showman.

Several publications that appeared in the years following the grand duke's trip enlarged on activities in the camp on Red Willow Creek. Among these were Buffalo Bill's accounts, in which he added specific details, including spicy tidbits, about what went on at Camp Alexis. Not surprisingly, these accounts emphasized Cody's role in events that took place during the hunt. Recollections of the hunt appeared in enough frontier memoirs and recollections to indicate that other participants in the hunt also had found it of interest. Several of these recollections are, however, secondary, setting down what the writer had heard others say about the grand hunt. Notable in this regard are Elizabeth Custer's descriptions of camp features, which she must have heard from her husband. In addition to participant accounts, settlers who followed the buffalo hunters by only a year or two provided information and lore about the grand hunt. Recollections by people who had been present when the hunt occurred or by ranchers and travelers familiar with the area were of great local interest. Some of these accounts, appearing in print by the early years of the twentieth century, provided yet another body of information on the hunt. Indeed, so much has been written about the grand hunt and so much of it is compelling that it has become a fixture of western lore, with treatments in movies, television programs, and even comic books.

Two aspects of the published sources on the grand duke's buffalo hunt deserve comment. First, although the literature on the hunt seems large, it is actually remarkably narrow. Most of what is known about the hunt comes from recorded observations by just a few individuals. These accounts deserve close reading but should be augmented with perspectives and sources that add substance to what is known to have happened at Camp Alexis. Second, even a cursory consideration of what has been written and claimed about the grand hunt reveals material that is implausible or simply incredible. Sources that offer a concrete basis for evaluating conflicting accounts would significantly enhance understanding of the grand duke's western adventure.

The goal of the research behind this volume has been to assemble new information and untapped sources that offer a basis for rooting out the less-than-credible information that has grown around the grand duke's western adventure. This search revealed four untapped sources. Newspaper accounts began to appear within days of the hunt. These have not been used widely. They might be less than perfect, but they are unsullied by the accretions that taint many sources. The photographs taken by Edric Eaton on January 14 and 15, 1872, are an important second source of information. Rediscovered only recently, they have not received much attention, but they depict the party members and the camp. Documents in Russian state archives, not easily accessible until the 1990s, provide a third important perspective on those who participated in the hunt. Finally there is the archaeological record. Relics collected by private efforts together with artifacts recovered during the systematic archaeological investigation provide tangible evidence of where the site and its associated features were located. Using these sources, we hope to refine what is known about the buffalo hunters and the processes that brought them to the wintry plains of the Nebraska frontier.

The site of Camp Alexis is primary among the underutilized and overlooked sources of information about the grand duke's hunt. Historical sources on the grand duke's hunt multiplied rapidly, but physical development of the campsite evolved slowly. One hundred forty years have changed the campsite, but of all the places that Grand Duke Alexis visited in 1871 and 1872, only Camp Alexis retains an ambience and physical appearance that the buffalo hunters would recognize. Only at Camp Alexis can a modern observer stand where the grand duke stood and see the country, the horizons, and the landscape that could support a western adventure.

The campsite is on land that was opened to homesteading by 1873, and by the mid- to late 1870s several ranches and small farms had appeared along Red Willow Creek. An east-west section line that would have been entirely invisible to the hunters divided the campsite into separate holdings. In the late nineteenth century, Rufus Mintling acquired the southern portion. The northern portion became the property of William Clifford. The Clifford and Mintling families still own the land and preserve the site. Because the terrace, which was expansive enough to accommodate a large hunting camp, is too small and irregular to hold a center-pivot irrigation system, it has been used as grazing land since it was homesteaded. As a conveniently flat piece of the plains with a famous history, the campsite came to have a variety of uses. By the 1920s it was being used as a meeting area for gatherings of "Old Settlers" and other social events at which the grand hunt was recalled. A baseball field with a chicken-wire backstop was set up on a part of the site. Rodeos were organized there. In 1931 a handsome locally crafted red-sandstone monument was set up near the southern end of the campsite to commemorate the 1872 hunt. In 1988 that marker was moved to a place of honor in the Hayes County courthouse. The excellent replica that replaced it is the only readily visible evidence of the hunt on the campsite. Because accessing the campsite entails crossing active agricultural fields, public visitation is limited, but residents continue to hold commemorative celebrations at and near the site.

We became interested in the buffalo hunt because, as archaeologists, we thought the campsite might preserve material culture that would offer insights into the events of January 1872. On our initial visits to the campsite, in 1997, we met the landowners and others in southwestern Nebraska who care about the in the site and the great hunt. Initially we could ask no more than general questions about the site and events that transpired there. From the beginning we were struck by the unspoiled quality of the campsite and the fact that it is very much the place visited by Grand Duke Alexis, George Custer, Phil Sheridan, Spotted Tail, and, yes, Buffalo Bill. As anthropologists we also appreciated that Camp Alexis was an intercultural community whose occupants were both elite and common and Euroamerican and native. Easily available accounts suggest how the U.S. government treated the grand duke, but we had to ask about the lot of the soldiers who accompanied the hunting party. Where had they slept? How had they been arrayed? And what about the members of Chief Spotted Tail's band who had been brought to the camp to both help with the hunt and entertain the guests? How had their camp related to the military and royal tents? Archaeological evidence should show how the various groups present at Camp Alexis related to one another.

Facing such questions, we were surprised that the campsite

seemed devoid of archaeological materials. Early twentieth-century visitors to the site reported extensive litters of broken champagne bottles and caviar tins, but our initial visits convinced us that any archaeological signature would be, at best, subtle. As we considered methods that would expose the archaeological potential of the campsite, we realized that even this problem offered positive potential. With its extensive history, Camp Alexis could show us how to study the archaeology of short-term tent camps. As the army and others explored and occupied the American West, they created such camps in the thousands. These sites have attracted little archaeological attention precisely because they are hard to recognize and investigate. Insights from Camp Alexis might help to bring such short-term and ephemeral sites into focus.

As we scanned historical accounts of the great hunt for insights that might help us understand its archaeological traces, we were struck by the inconsistencies and doubtful assertions in published accounts. The archaeology of Camp Alexis might be meager, but historical sources, although ample, were flawed. Investigation of both Camp Alexis and the grand duke's buffalo hunt of 1872 seemed ideally suited to the interdisciplinary perspectives of modern historical archaeology. Archaeological investigation of western battlefields and military sites offers a good basis for interpreting materials left at Camp Alexis. The synthetic interests of anthropology also pointed to documentary sources we had overlooked in our investigation of the grand duke's adventure. We began to believe, for example, that tapping into the interests and expertise of collectors could reveal sources and information that had not been available for scholarly research. We also thought that an archaeological approach would enable us to assess what had been reported about the grand duke's hunt. The specific chronology, material limitations, and practical realities inherent in archaeological research provide a concrete basis for evaluating written sources. Finally, systematic investigation of western military sites has helped establish a broad research agenda and a series of general questions about how the U.S. Army operated on the western frontier. In light of that research, synthetic investigation of Camp Alexis should be able to move beyond descriptions of the campsite and how the royal hunting party was treated. How and why, for example, did military leaders organize the hunt? Why was southwestern Nebraska chosen as hunting territory? What were the longer-term impacts of this three-day jaunt?

The impact of Grand Duke Alexis's buffalo hunt far exceeded the three days he spent in the field. Reports of the adventure appeared in newspapers across the country during and after the hunt. Indeed the entire American public followed newspaper accounts, not only of his western adventure, but also of his entire journey through the United States. The grand duke's visit was a triumph for Russian diplomacy. Russia had supported the federal government during the American Civil War. Czar Alexander II, who saw the freeing of the serfs as parallel with the emancipation of the slaves, felt a strong bond with the United States and particularly with President Abraham Lincoln. The Russian court was also grateful to Andrew Johnson's administration for the purchase of Alaska and the cash influx that the transaction brought to the imperial coffers. Good feeling between the countries was at a high point, and most U.S. citizens viewed the grand duke's visit in a very positive light.

Here, using varied but intricately bound sources of information and data, we construct the story of the royal buffalo hunt. Our method of approach is holistic. We use primary written records and accounts to build a story of the hunt, the camp, and its occupants; we analyze photographs of the camp, evaluating them as documents containing evidence of the people and camp life; and we record archaeological artifacts left by hunt participants as evidence of their behavior. These complementary but distinct data sets are the stuff of which modern historic archaeological research is made. From them we develop a new appreciation and a new understanding of the events of January 13–16, 1872. As the sole surviving site associated with the Grand Duke Alexis's stay in the United States that can be documented archaeologically, this place achieves a significance in history that deserves to be chronicled, interpreted, and preserved as the representative site of a major diplomatic event in American history.

2

CONCEPTUAL CONTEXTS FOR CAMP ALEXIS ARCHAEOLOGY

General Sheridan had promised the grand duke a successful buffalo hunt. Fulfilling that promise entailed a long list of needs. There must be supplies and equipment for a base camp. There must be soldiers to transport the equipment and create the camp. And there must be additional personnel to support the hunt and staff the event. The hunt also required adventurous participants, companions suitable to a royal visitor being scrutinized by American and Russian audiences. Then, to assure success, the hunting party needed to know where the bison were to be found and easily hunted.

Sheridan solved many of his logistical problems by ordering elements of the Second Cavalry stationed at Fort McPherson and North Platte Station, Nebraska, to find the buffalo and establish a field camp. Sheridan knew that buffalo were wintering not far from Fort McPherson, Nebraska. In September and October 1871 he had taken a hunting party, mostly prominent New Yorkers and Chicagoans, south from Fort McPherson to that same area hunting and camping and then had concluded at Fort Hays, Kansas. The men who accompanied Sheridan on that hunt were so prominent and wealthy that it came to be known as the "millionaires' hunt." Fort McPherson's commander sent his chief scout, William F. Cody, to find the wintering herds and to help select a suitable campsite. Cody had done the same for the Sheridan during the September–October hunt. Sheridan also called upon prominent members of his staff and George Custer to provide convivial associates for the grand duke and his entourage.

As archaeologists seeking new and worthwhile information on camp activities that provided logistical support for the hunt, we too had a list of needs. Archaeologists need to find the material-culture record: items left behind that document past behavior. Without physical remains and their associated context, archaeology has little to say about the past. We needed materials left by the grand duke and his hunting colleagues. Beyond that, we needed information about those materials. We needed to be sure they were linked to the 1872 hunt. To interpret them as a record, we also needed to know where and how they were distributed on the landscape, how they were treated before and after having been discarded, and how they were used when the camp was occupied. Finally, for a full understanding of the materials, we needed ideas, a theoretical baseline, about conditions that contributed to the event. These ideas are critical to any interpretation we might offer, and making them explicit and concrete is a vital step in modern archaeology.

Before delving into an evaluation of the historical record and the recovered material-culture record of Camp Alexis, we present conceptual contexts for the assessment of the camp and its artifacts. Placing the physical manifestations of the camp and its inhabitants' behavior in context of the historical record allows us to evaluate the record of the hunt, the hunters, and the processes that brought them to the wintry plains of the Nebraska frontier.

Hunting for Sport:
A Context for the Royal Buffalo Hunt

The story of the royal buffalo hunt starts with an understanding of the views of sport hunting in the nineteenth century and, concomitantly, the alleged role of the army in the destruction of the Great Plains buffalo herds. The history of hunting stretches far into the human past. Archaeologists have developed techniques for recording how Stone Age hunters took game animals and used their meat, sinews, skins, bones, and organs as food or raw materials.[1] In these analyses, the role of hunting as a subsistence activity has been a primary focus, but ornaments and trophies made from teeth, antlers and tusks make it clear that hunting was always more than a simple economic activity. Conversely, hunting by elite classes of early civilizations and premodern states, marked by specialized weaponry and legal bases, was probably never entirely recreational.[2] What is clear is that in Europe and elsewhere recreational hunting developed as an important pastime of the landed elite by medieval times, after agricultural production was well established, political units were clearly defined, and social categories fixed. These values informed nineteenth-century American notions of sport hunting.[3]

At the time of contact, Europeans considered American Indians subsistence hunters, although this concept ignores the fact that Central and South American cultures, and some in North America, were organized hierarchically. European settlers in the new world rejected the concept of royal reserves, holding to the view that unclaimed lands were open equally to Indians, settlers, and pioneers for subsistence hunting. The idea that hunting could be an outdoor leisure activity developed in America only after large areas had been settled. Frederick Paxson viewed hunting within the context of a growing American celebration of the natural wilderness.[4] To Paxson, outdoor sports, including hunting, began to manifest themselves in North America in the second quarter of the nineteenth century. Before that time, hunting had been largely a subsistence activity. Paxson felt that sport hunting arose out of the belief that some sectors of American society felt it worthwhile to keep the mind and body well toned and exercised. To Paxson, this sentiment developed from the Puritan religious and social ethic of hard work and religious observance as the means to moral and spiritual salvation. Frivolity was unacceptable as a purely recreational activity; every activity must have a moral or spiritual purpose. Toning the mind and body was certainly a popular emphasis of mid-nineteenth-century America. There was widespread belief that outdoor exercise, exposure to fresh air and strenuous activities, was beneficial to the human body and mind. Sport hunting embodied these outdoor concepts, and included the added advantage of taking game as meat, which then (as today) was deemed a positive alternative to the domestic production of meat. To many the consumption of wild game was, somehow, healthier.

In nineteenth-century North America, sport hunting developed together with policies on the management of wild areas. Modern society, by contrast—especially in urban areas—is largely opposed to sport hunting and particularly trophy hunting. The same concept does not hold true in more rural areas of the United States, where hunting both for subsistence and recreation is still held as a near-inalienable right. Modern opponents of hunting largely ignore its role in modern wildlife management and environmental conservation.[5] Even within the wildlife-management arena, where hunting is widely promoted and strictly regulated, wildlife biologists often ignore humans as part of the ecosystem they are regulating, forgetting that we are predators (even if bound by culture) and part of a natural ecosystem.

In reviewing the role of firearms in the fur trade in North America, James Hanson clearly and unequivocally demonstrates that firearms were indispensable tools from earliest colonial times both for colonists and for American Indians.[6] From the early days of what became the United States to the present, firearms have been ubiquitous. Clayton Cramer's[7] study of the role of firearms in the United States includes a chapter on guns and sporting prior to the mid-nineteenth century. He argues that in the early Republic, firearms were common, as was knowledge of their use. His literature review also shows that in that era firearms were primarily a subsistence and defense tool, and that although target shooting and other recreational uses of firearms did exist before 1850, they were not a major activity. Reinforcing the rise of the middle class in the second quarter of the nineteenth century and the concomitant development of leisure sports and recreation, Cramer shows how the use of firearms in that era moved from strictly subsistence and defense to the center of outdoor recreational pursuits.

The development of sport hunting in the trans-Mississippi West parallels its development elsewhere in North America and, indeed, the world. That recreational hunters sought large game avidly throughout the nineteenth century is perhaps best illustrated by Theodore Roosevelt's worldwide safaris undertaken for personal pleasure and to gather scientific specimens for various North American museums.[8] In his work on British sportsmen in the West from 1833 to 1881, John Merritt does not consider the rise of recreational hunting and sport, but his descriptions of eleven hunting expeditions in the West parallel that development.[9] With the publication of Larry McMurtry's successful Berrybender Narratives, which trace the adventures of an English hunting party on the Great Plains frontier, elite sport hunters have also entered popular western literature.[10]

By the time the royal buffalo hunt took place, the decline of the immense bison herds was well under way. Less than a decade after the 1872 hunt, bison would be hunted nearly to extinction. Hide hunters took a tremendous toll on the vast herds in their effort to supply robes, tongue and hump meat, and leather for the drive belts that ran America's manufacturing machinery.[11] One scholar alleged that the army command, including Sherman and Sheridan, actively promoted buffalo sport hunting, encouraging large-scale destruction of the herds as a means of diminishing American Indian dependence on bison as their primary source of meat.[12] The premise of this controversial theory is that having eliminated the bison, the army could more easily subdue the tribes, move them to reservations, and make them dependent on domestic livestock as the primary meat resource. The distribution of domestic beef as a means of introducing Indians to a more sedentary lifestyle—in combination with practical training of their children in government schools—would acculturate the Indians into mainstream society. This overt buffalo-destruction scenario, however, was refuted.[13] The prevailing theory regarding the loss of the herds is grounded in a combination of factors: changing climates in the grasslands, expansion of disease vectors, and overhunting both by Indians and by Euroamericans.[14] In any event it is unlikely that Sheridan or Sherman considered Grand Duke Alexis's buffalo-hunting foray to be part of this purported grand scheme. As suggested by Albert Bierstadt, the hunt was no more than a grand entertainment gesture.[15]

Hunting and Tourism in the 1870s

We decided to place our study of Camp Alexis and the royal buffalo hunt under the academic rubric of early tourism. Tourism was once seen as a privilege of the elite or at least those with leisure time.[16] Some historians see tourists and the entrepreneurs who encouraged their ventures as elites who strove to eliminate or reduce to insignificance the role of laborers such as those who built the transportation networks and tourist facilities. Historians have studied tourists and tourism for decades.[17] Mid-twentieth century historians, for example, used the views of foreign travelers in the nineteenth-century United States as a means of assessing commentary on our social and economic systems. The general theme recounts how others viewed America through its growth. The Wild West was judged to have romantic appeal as well as scenic beauty. Some saw America and the West as vast new places of economic growth, social egalitarianism and both cultural and natural change and challenge. More modern historical analyses of the role of tourism are taken largely from the context of economic value or impact and the effect on cultural and natural resources, both positive and negative, as more and more people come to see and participate in ecological tourism.[18] Hal K. Rothman reduces the historical perspective on American tourism to three distinct and sometimes contradictory concepts, the sublime view of the West as part of the romance and romanticism of the West, the power of conquest as a part of Manifest Destiny, and the conception of empiricism which he sees as the heart of post-Darwinian science.[19]

The historical record and historians' analyses of tourism are a valuable jumping-off point for our analysis of the royal buffalo hunt and of Camp Alexis. We embrace the anthropological constructs of tourism as a means to understand both the why of tourism and the process. The process of tourism has been a topic of anthropological inquiry for more than thirty years.[20]

From an anthropological perspective modern tourism represents one of the largest movements of human populations outside wartime and is a force for culture contact and change. The form and goals of tourism are culturally derived and determined, shift through time, and vary between cultures.[21] William Hunt recently developed an anthropology-based archaeological model of tourism based on his work in Yellowstone National Park.[22] Yellowstone, the first national park, was established in 1872, only a few months after Grand Duke Alexis's hunt in Nebraska. We use Hunt's model to inform our investigations of the grand duke's travels in the West.

Millions of people travel the world every year, and during the past two centuries tourism has been a major force in culture contact and social change. These short-term demographic changes produce tremendous forces in support of acculturation. Tourism creates activities that lie outside those of normal, everyday existence. In fact, some anthropologists view a tour as similar to a religious pilgrimage. They have determined that pilgrimages and tours both are marked by stages or conditions of existence that are out of the ordinary. These stages are *separation, advance, sojourn, return,* and *aggregation.*[23]

The beginning is marked by physical *separation* from one's normal everyday activities and social structures. Following separation is *advance,* the portion of the trip in which the traveler moves toward the focal point (destination). At the third phase, the *sojourn*, the traveler has reached the focal point of the trip. To a greater or lesser degree, the sojourn is marked by a kind of "liminoid" realm of existence. "Liminality" in the anthropological sense refers to the state and process of transition, as in a rite of passage. This psychological condition is based on strongly held mystical or philosophical convictions. In the pilgrimage, religious mysticism is the philosophical motivation behind the trip, and the mystical point of focus for the pilgrim is the sacred site located at some distance from the normal place of residence and daily labor. For the tourist, the philosophical perspective appears to be Romanticism, and the liminoid state is encountered at some location perceived as a "natural area," more or less free from human development.[24]

The Romantic philosophical movement of the late-eighteenth and nineteenth centuries rejected rationalism, formal rules and restrictions in art and society, and the urban civilization created by the Industrial Revolution. Complementing this rejection were the promotion of the subjective (imagination and emotion), an appreciation of less formal art and music, and a spiritual affinity for nature as a source of purification and renewal. Prominent among the beliefs of romantics—early and modern—is the value of all life forms and natural areas for their own sake rather than for their economic utility. The liminoid quality of tourism is particularly evident where travel to and enjoyment of a natural resource or environment is involved.

The final phase of tourism is *aggregation*, when tourists return home and are reunited with their previous socioeconomic environment. Upon returning, travelers regale their companions with events of the trip, wonders beheld, and personal transformations in body and/or spirit that the vacation or pilgrimage wrought.

William Hunt's model employs these broad-ranging components to establish a series of research questions about tourism and the archaeological signature left from such behavior.[25] He presents a detailed context and developmental model based on the interaction of three primary socioeconomic spheres of influence from which he identifies potential research topics for Yellowstone National Park: cultural landscape, economics, the tourist system, architecture, subsistence, ethnicity, and health and sanitation.

The grand duke's American tour and buffalo hunt occurred during the earliest tourism period at Yellowstone (1872–82), which

Hunt names Nascence. During this period, Hunt observes, tourism in Yellowstone was primitive in all senses of the word. And because few facilities or organizational structures existed, the park had few visitors. Hunt identifies two general groups. The larger consisted of people from a variety of social classes residing in the Yellowstone region. The smaller comprised extra-regional travelers of American or foreign extraction, usually of some social prominence, with the necessary wealth and leisure time to allow opportunities for recreating at great distances from their home—a profile that fits Grand Duke Alexis.

External facilitators such as transportation affected access to Yellowstone in the Nascence period. Routes consisted of roads and trails largely informal in character; conveyances were relatively limited: railroads, steamboats, wagons and buggies, stagecoaches, and horses. The grand duke's buffalo hunt followed this same general pattern. Railroads and river steamers were an expedient and efficient means of movement for the party, and to a certain extent they dictated the grand duke's itinerary. Even the buffalo hunt needed to take place near a railroad and telegraph lines. For Alexis these were lifelines as well as transportation networks. The hunt party and camp follow the Yellowstone tourism model in that the party followed a trail, not a formally established or maintained road, to the campsite, and they enjoyed comfortable but primitive tent camping.

Support and supply in the early days of Yellowstone tourism was primitive. With the exception of a few crude log-cabin hotels and bathhouses, camp locations were unique to each individual or group, and weather conditions dictated daily events. Once inside the park, tourists had to rely on their own resources. Those seeking supplies—including food other than meat—had to travel for several days, carrying all supplies to the park via pack train or wagon. Fresh meat was acquired by hunting game, a practice not yet discouraged by park management. The buffalo hunt was well furnished with luxuries for the dining table, but it follows Hunt's model with most supplies being transported to the camp by army wagon from remote supply centers. The purpose of the camp was not sightseeing but hunting, which supplemented the transported table fare.

Hunt's model of early tourism in Yellowstone National Park neatly describes Grand Duke Alexis's buffalo hunt and his general travels in the United States. The grand duke might have been part of a diplomatic mission, but his hosts showed him the sights of the young nation and entertained him on its frontier. From an anthropological perspective, Alexis's travels in the United States mirror those of a tourist or pilgrim of the same era.

The royal buffalo hunt can also be placed in the category of adventure travel. Adventure travel or tourism is not new, but the label and the concept are modern and are defined as a type of tourism, involving exploration or travel to remote, exotic, and possibly hostile areas.[26] Adventure travel usually includes physical activity or a cultural exchange or interaction and engagement with nature. Modern adventure tourism attracts specialized travelers by allowing them to step outside their comfort zone. Today those activities range from experiencing culture shock or through the performance of acts requiring significant effort and involving some degree of risk (real or perceived) and/or physical danger.

Once again the profile of adventure tourism describes Grand Duke Alexis's foray into the West. His hunt included all the criteria required to qualify as adventure tourism in the modern sense. Hunting the American Bison constituted a real and strong engagement with nature. Camping on the Central Plains in the winter months and riding the prairies in search of the prey involved plenty of physical activity. And witnessing an American Indian camp and the hunting prowess of the Brulé group under the direction of Spotted Tail was a form of culture shock.

Military Field Camps

In Hunt's tourism model, the basic elements of support and supply during the Nascence period are primitive camps. Such ephemeral sites might seem beyond the scope of archaeology, but military camps offer models for finding such sites and developing means for studying them. Military camps are perhaps the most common archaeological site type associated with the military in the West. A soldier's moments in battle were brief compared to his time in camp or fort, where daily events formed the core of an individual's military experience. Establishing camps, maintaining camps, constructing buildings, obtaining wood, and drill are what soldiers did most. The material-culture depositional process leaves behind traces reflecting patterned human behavior, whether camp activities or battles.

Deposits of ordnance, small-arms projectiles, and personal items make battlefields relatively easy to find. The camp, however, especially the short-term camp, is difficult to locate and interpret.

In his seminal work on Civil War campsite archaeology, Joseph Balicki states that camps are likely the most common Civil War sites rather than battlefields.[27] He creates an archaeological typology of camps for the Civil War, and he identifies three basic types, permanent or long-term camps, winter quarters, and surface or very short-term camps, noting that the archaeological signature of each camp type should differ from that of the other camp types. Permanent camps are associated with long-term occupation, such as a garrison at a fort. In general, soldiers lived in barracks or modified their quarters to be more permanent and hospitable.[28] Winter quarters are characterized by "huts" or "shanties" that were built by the soldiers. Camp layout and organization were established by doctrine, but because hut features were not prescribed in military regulations or manuals of the era, hut architecture shows variability. The manner in which soldiers created or developed comfortable winter shelters within that context showed real ingenuity.[29]

Surface or short-term camps generally were temporary, like the primitive camp in Hunt's tourism model. In military contexts these camps are likely the most common site type—and the most difficult to identify. Balicki suggests that their archaeological signature will be primarily a scatter of artifacts and occasional small features such as hearths. He asserts that because surface features are absent and because current field methods make locating these sites difficult, many go unrecognized and unrecorded.[30]

Military-encampment archaeology, in Balicki's view, is challenging. The combination of indistinct artifact and feature distributions with the cultural processes affecting these distributions produces archaeological signatures that are difficult to identify and interpret. Several factors increase the likelihood of locating encampments. Among the fastest and most cost efficient and effective is simply to ask where the encampments are.[31] Opening a dialogue with landowners and relic hunters is not always in today's professional toolkit, but archaeologists such as James Legg and Steve Smith advocate keeping these lines of communication open: "With rare exceptions, all reasonably accessible battlefields, field fortifications, and campsites in North America have been collected for several decades by numerous individuals. This condition extends to even the most obscure skirmishes and bivouacs, thanks to the rigorous historical research conducted by thousands of collectors." They go on to suggest that archaeologists who develop relationships with local historians, collectors, and relic hunters are the most successful at locating and investigating military sites.[32]

Balicki emphatically notes that systematic shovel test surveys—standard procedure for many archaeologists attempting to locate archaeological sites—are inappropriate for most historic military sites and early tourism campsites.[33] Excavating small (50 cm or less) test units at standard intervals has gained such acceptance that it is often thought to be the most cost efficient and effective field method. In reality, however, this methodology almost guarantees that military sites will not be found.[34] Balacki's comparison of metal-detection and shovel-testing methodologies clearly illustrates the deficiency and irrelevance of a field strategy relying solely on shovel testing. None of the sites he reviewed would have been recognized had the field methods relied only on shovel testing. He correctly notes that metal detecting and other remote-sensing techniques are the best tools for finding military camps. Likewise metal detecting, coupled with traditional excavation and testing, is the best methodology for studying the archaeology of a camp once it is located.

In the next several chapters we employ the anthropological and archaeological concepts of tourism, tourism archaeology, and the archaeological expression of the nature and structure of transient camps as the bases for our study and evaluation of Camp Alexis.

3

The Grand Duke's Tour of the United States

The grand duke's sojourn in the United States was both Russian diplomatic outreach and in-service training for Alexis as an Imperial Russian Navy officer. As a member of the ruling house of Romanov, Alexis was not just a naval officer in training; he represented the government and rulers of Russia. His world tour was designed to build his naval and diplomatic skills so that he could take his rightful place in the ruling Romanov hierarchy upon his return to his homeland.

Grand Duke Alexis Romanov was born in Saint Petersburg on January 14, 1850 (January 4 under the Russian Orthodox calendar). Alexis was the third son and fifth child of Czar Alexander II and Czarina Maria Alexandrovna. His older brother became Czar Alexander III of Russia. Alexis also had two younger brothers.[1]

As third in line for the throne, Grand Duke Alexis was intended to have a prominent role in court life, and the Czar determined that a naval career was most appropriate. At the age of seven Alexis received the rank of midshipman. The next year a senior naval officer, Adm. Constantine Nikolayevich Possiet, was appointed his tutor in naval affairs. Alexis was given both theoretical and practical training in seamanship and the role of an Imperial Russian officer in the Czar's navy. Between 1858 and 1870 he spent summers on at least five different ships of the Russian navy.

Figure 2. Grand Duke Alexis in civilian dress. Photograph by Mathew B. Brady. Douglas Scott collection.

One frequently cited reason that Grand Duke Alexis was sent on the world cruise in 1871 and 1872 was to forget a love affair with a commoner, to which the Czar was strongly opposed. In 1869 and 1870, Alexis had an affair with an Alexandra Zhukovskaya, the daughter of the poet Vasily Andreyevich Zhukovsky. Alexandra was eight years older than him. They were parents to a son, Alexis, born on November 26, 1871, during the grand duke's stay in the United States.

Some historians assert that the marriage was morganatic and that the Russian Orthodox Church annulled it, but others dispute this claim.[2] There is no definitive evidence that Alexis married Alexandra, but there is no disputing the parentage of his son. The consensus seems to be that Alexis did not marry Alexandra because, as the daughter of an illegitimate son of a Russian landowner, she was an unsuitable match for royalty. Czar Alexander II refused to grant Alexandra a title, which would have officially recognized the grand duke's paternity, even though he was illegitimate. Other European courts also refused to grant her a title. However, in 1875 Alexandra was made Baroness Seggiano by the Republic of San Marino, and she received the right to transmit the title Baron Seggiano to her son, Alexis, and his firstborn male descendants. In 1883, Czar Alexander III, the grand duke's elder brother, granted his nephew the title of Count Belevsky, and in 1893 he approved the count's coat of arms.[3]

Russia's support of the Union during the American Civil War had lasting and positive effects for both countries.[4] Americans, including Mark Twain, traveled to Russia in 1867 on the first U.S. flagged tourist ship to visit Russia. In the same year, Adm. David Farragut sailed an American squadron to Russia as a gesture of good will. The Russian government envisioned a reciprocal visit and, after lengthy negotiations, decided that Grand Duke Alexis would head the Russian delegation.[5] The good will tour, which was to take two years, would circumnavigate the globe and would include visits to several countries. The U.S. press and the general public viewed the impending visit as evidence of the strong relationship between the United States and Russia. But, owing to diplomatic issues and political agendas on both sides of the Bering Strait, the inner circles of the two governments were less certain.

The Russian squadron, under the command of Admiral Possiet, included the frigates *Bogatyr, Svetlana,* and *The Admiral General;* the corvette *Ignatiev;* and the gunboat *Abrek.* The grand duke served as lieutenant aboard the *Svetlana.* The squadron set sail from Kronstadt on August 20, 1871, and made several ports of call before arriving in the United States. The Russian squadron was met by an American squadron under the command of V. Adm. Stephen Clegg Rowan on the frigate *Congress.* Adm. Samuel Phillips Lee, commander of the North Atlantic Squadron, also attended, on his own flagship, the *Severn.* The other ships of the squadron, the *Iroquois* and the *Kansas,* were attended by several tugs.[6]

A reception committee formed in New York during the planning for the grand duke's arrival was chaired by William Henry Aspinwall. Members of this committee Included Gen. Henry Dodge, Cyrus Field, Moses H. Grinnell, Gen. Irwin McDowell, Samuel F. B. Morse, Theodore Roosevelt, Sr., R. Adm. S. W. Godon, John Taylor Johnston, Albert Bierstadt, Lloyd Aspinwall, and other prominent New Yorkers.[7] After a short delay occasioned by the weather, on November 21, 1871, the Russian squadron anchored in New York harbor, where the grand duke was greeted by Gen. John Adams Dix. A grand military parade took place in the city to welcome Alexis.

Figure 3. Arrival of the Russian squadron in New York as depicted in *Harper's Weekly*, December 9, 1871.

Figure 4. Russian cruiser *Svetlana*, on which Grand Duke Alexis served during his world tour. Russian Naval Archives.

Figure 5. The New York reception committee greeting Grand Duke Alexis aboard the *Svetlana*, *Harpers Weekly*, December 9, 1871.

Figure 6. Grand welcoming parade for Grand Duke Alexis as depicted in *Harper's Weekly*, December 9, 1871.

Figure 7. The welcoming parade, with New York militia units. Douglas Scott collection.

The grand duke then attended a Thanksgiving service at the Russian chapel.[8]

At some point during his welcome to New York City, the grand duke purportedly received a bronze key to the city. That key is thought to have been made from a rare Confederate mountain rifle captured by the Fifth New York Cavalry in 1863 from the noted ranger Col. John Singleton Mosby. The war trophy purportedly had two inches of its muzzle cut off to make the key. The gun now resides in the 45th Infantry Museum in Oklahoma City.[9]

On November 22 the grand duke left for Washington on a special train placed at his disposal by the New York and Philadelphia Railway and paid for by the Russians.[10] The grand duke's cars were elegant Pullmans, consisting of a baggage car, commissary car, two sleeping cars, and a drawing-room car.[11] The drawing-room car, described by one reporter as a parlor car, was "simply magnificent." It was carpeted with Brussels tapestry, and its woodwork was finished in black walnut with gilded trim and accented with tulip

Figure 8. The Mosby Confederate Mountain Rifle from which a key to New York City was fashioned using two inches of bronze cut from the cannon barrel. Photograph by Douglas Scott.

wood, bird's-eye maple, French walnut, and laurel. The chairs were covered in Russian leather and monogrammed "P.P.C." for the Pullman Palace Car Company. Other seats were described as covered in crimson velvet. The entire unit was lit by oil lamps.[12] This was the height of American Victorian elegance.

On November 23 the grand duke was received by President Ulysses S. Grant, members of the Cabinet, and Mrs. Grant and daughter Julia. The visit to Washington was overshadowed by a political imbroglio arising from the Russian refusal to recall Constantin Catacazy, minister plenipotentiary of Russia to the United States.[13] The visit in Washington lasted only one day, and no formal entertainment was provided for the grand duke. The next day he left by train for Annapolis, where he visited the Naval Academy, and then returned to New York.[14]

In New York City the grand duke was the honored guest at various balls and entertainments. He visited the Military Academy at West Point and saw many other points of interest. On December 3, 1871, he left for Philadelphia. Once again his schedule was full of well-reported engagements. These invariably featured high-profile social events—balls, banquets, and public welcomes—as well as visits to industrial and military facilities. In Philadelphia his party

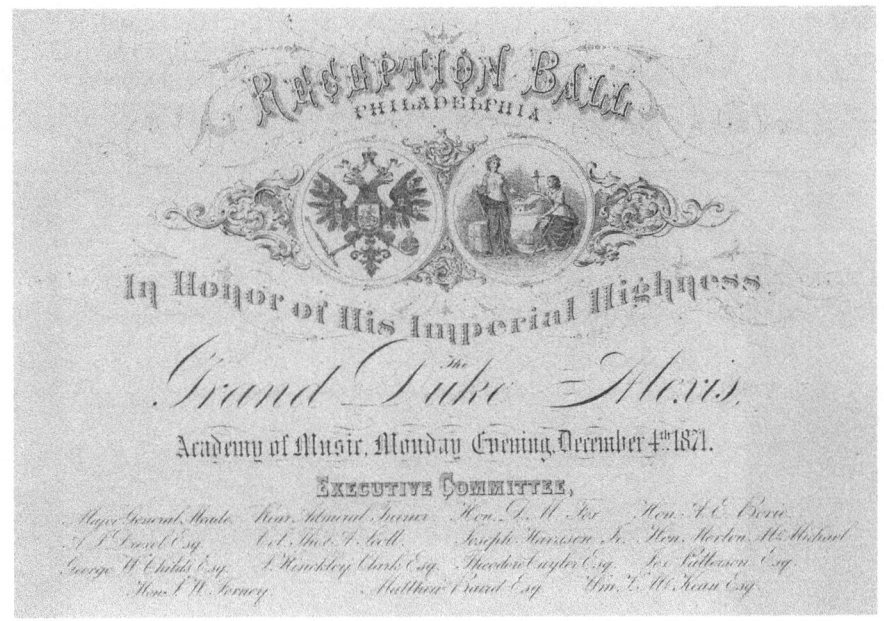

Figure 9. An invitation to a ball honoring Grand Duke Alexis at the Philadelphia Music Academy. Douglas Scott collection.

Figure 10. Grand Duke Alexis dancing at the Navy Ball, as depicted in *Harper's Weekly*, December 16, 1871.

Figure 11. A waltz of uncertain quality composed in honor of Grand Duke Alexis's visit to Philadelphia. Douglas Scott collection.

visited both the Baldwin Locomotive Works and the Philadelphia Navy Yard. As an expression of the public interest, a waltz was composed in his honor.[15]

The grand duke was back in New York by December 7, when he headed to Boston. On the way he made two stops. The first was a brief visit to the Union Metallic Cartridge Company factory in Bridgeport, Connecticut. The company had filled many ammunition orders from the Russian government and was the base of operations for Alexander Gorlov, a colonel (and later a general) in the Russian army who was overseeing Russian military procurements and actively studying American manufacturing methods. Gorlov led the grand duke on a well-organized tour of the facilities. At the end of the tour the company presented Alexis with a custom-made silver snuffbox in the form of the cartridges they were making for the Russian army. The visit was not all about business relations and industrial innovations, however. Machines were hung with flowers and ribbons, and either on their own or with management encouragement, young women working in the plant had dressed in their finest clothing. They seem to have been interested in attracting the eye of the handsome young celebrity. For his part, Alexis could only express amazement that women tending machines were so well turned out.[16]

After Bridgeport the grand duke's party continued quickly to Springfield, Massachusetts. Here the agenda was a "wholly informal reception" at the Smith & Wesson pistol factory. After walking through the shop, the grand duke received a custom-finished pistol with pearl grips, gold-enhanced with the American and Russian coats of arms, and with the inscription "From S&W to A. A." The visit to the pistol factory lasted less than two hours, hardly enough time for serious industrial negotiations, but Smith & Wesson had invested heavily in the Russian arms market and, shortly after the visit, began filling a major contract from the Russian army for pistols chambered for a new, longer .44 S&W round that became known as the .44-caliber Russian cartridge.[17] This pistol would be called the Russian Model or No. 3 Smith & Wesson revolver.[18]

The grand duke and his party were in Boston December 8–14. While there, Alexis visited Harvard University and the suburb of Cambridge. Other highlights of the visit were the battlefield of Bunker Hill and the shipyards of Charlestown.[19]

On December 17 the grand duke left by train for Canada. He stopped in Montreal and visited Lachine, Quebec, and then passed through Ottawa and Toronto, reaching Niagara Falls on December 22. The next day Alexis left by train for Buffalo, New York, where he spent Christmas.[20]

Frank Thomson, Superintendent of the Eastern Division of the Philadelphia and Erie Railroad, who managed all of the grand duke's rail travel, continued as manager of the train for his western travels.[21] E. S. Sanford, President of the Adams Express Company, was in constant touch with Thomson, giving him whatever he needed in the way of rolling stock and even assigning him a telegraph operator with instructions to support his logistical operations.[22]

Grand Duke Alexis arrived in Cleveland on December 26, where he visited the iron mills and other factories in Newburgh Heights. He then stopped in Detroit on his way to Chicago, where he arrived on December 30. The city was beginning its recovery from the great fire. He visited the destroyed part of the city and, impressed by the reconstruction, gave $5,000 to aid the homeless. On January 2–4 he visited Milwaukee, and on January 5 he arrived in St. Louis, where he stayed more than a week.[23]

Late in the morning of January 12, the imperial party arrived in Omaha, where they were met by former Nebraska Territorial Governor Alvin Saunders, local dignitaries, General Sheridan, and army officers from both the Division of the Missouri and the Department of the Platte, including Colonel Custer. The party was wined and dined at the Saunders home and then, at 3:10 p.m., departed Omaha for North Platte Station. The special train arrived at North Platte Station at about 7:00 p.m. on January 13.[24] (The details of the hunt are described in chapter 4.)

On the afternoon of January 16, following the hunt, the party returned to North Platte Station, and that evening they departed for Cheyenne. During the hunt, Frank Thomson was not idle. While participating in the hunt he worked via messenger to coordinate the next stage of the western trip.[25] On January 15, Thomson received a telegram from John Evans, former Colorado territorial governor and railroad financier, stating that he had made arrangements to have the train moved to Denver after their arrival in Cheyenne and that he was making hotel arrangements. A January 17 telegram informed Thomson that the governor of Colorado and a committee of legislators would meet the train and welcome the grand duke on his arrival in Denver. That same day, lawyer and leading Colorado citizen Henry Teller communicated with Thomson, stating he would place a locomotive at Thomson's disposal to take the grand duke on the Colorado Central Railroad line to Clear Creek Canyon to see the sights of Colorado's foothills and mountains. January 17 was a rather full day. A minor accident in the Cheyenne rail yard partially derailed the grand duke's car and entirely derailed Sheridan's. The latter, nearly upset, came to rest at a precarious angle. Apparently Thomson, who was already in Denver preparing for the next leg of the journey, offered to replace Sheridan's car. Sheridan, however, decided to stay with his car until it was righted. He insisted the grand duke continue on to Denver and that he would follow, which he did some four hours later.[26]

On January 19 the grand duke and party arrived in Denver amid pomp and circumstance. As with his travels in the eastern states, the Denver stay involved a ball given in his honor by the territorial governor and prominent members of Denver society.[27]

Hearing that buffalo had been sighted on the eastern plains of Colorado, the grand duke expressed a desire to hunt once again. A train was made up, and on January 20 the party traveled to Kit Carson to engage in a buffalo hunt in that area.[28] The *Daily Rocky Mountain News,* January 21, and the *New York Herald,* January 22,

Figure 12. Grand Duke Alexis as the center of attention during the ball in Denver. *Rocky Mountain News*, January 19, 1872.

reported that the party arrived at about 8:00 a.m. and, as General Sheridan had arranged previously, were met by a cavalry escort and horses from Fort Wallace.

Fort Wallace was a semipermanent home station on the Kansas Pacific Railroad, and its troops guarded the line in a series of small encampments associated with the stations along the route. The post garrison consisted of three companies of the Third Infantry and Company B of the Sixth Cavalry.[29] An element of Company B brought the horses from Fort Wallace for use by the hunt party. Local citizens also supplied wagons and light conveyances.

At about 11:00 a.m. the grand duke, Sheridan, and about thirty others on horseback, followed by a number of wagons filled with armed men, began the hunt. The grand duke reportedly brought down the first buffalo, a large bull. By the end of the day about fifty buffalo had been killed, with Alexis bringing down five, Custer three, and Sheridan two. The hunt party returned to Denver by 6:00 p.m.

Several later accounts of the Colorado hunt appear exaggerated and embellished. One account is near fiction. Former New Mexico governor Miguel Otero conflates the Nebraska and Colorado hunts into one and suggests he was an eyewitness.[30] He might have been present on the Colorado hunt as one of the wagon drivers as he says, but his account is mostly fiction. The hunt took place in the vicinity of Kit Carson and probably along Big Sandy or Sand Creek. Some suggest that the hunt ranged as far south as the Sand Creek Massacre site, but, given the approximately seven hours available to the hunters, it is unlikely that they ranged more than five or ten miles from the train. If they ranged ten miles, they would have been at least three miles from the massacre site. Chalkley Beeson's account is typical of such overstatement.[31] He asserts that more than two hundred buffalo were killed and that a group of Kit Carson citizens and others availed themselves of the fine food and liquor on board the hunt-party train. When these citizens became drunk and rowdy, Custer employed lively epithets to demonstrate their displeasure with the citizens. The story undoubtedly contains a grain of truth, but it is typical of the lore and myth that has grown up around the grand duke's travels in the United States and particularly in the West. Neither the train crew nor the party managers would have granted the local citizens unlimited access to the train and especially not to the dignitaries' cars. Contemporary newspaper accounts, which seem to be the most reliable in describing the Colorado sojourn, mention no such flagrant discourtesy and state that about forty buffalo, not two hundred, were killed.[32]

From Denver the party went to Topeka, where they attended a joint session of the Kansas Legislature. During the brief overnight stop in Topeka, J. Lee Knight photographed the major figures of the hunting party. (See chapter 5 for details.) The next day the party continued by rail to St. Louis, where Custer and the grand duke spent the day exploring the gateway city and were photographed once again, this time in their hunting attire and with buffalo-tail trophies from the hunt. The Missouri leg of the trip included a six-hour layover in Jefferson City, where the grand duke briefly addressed the joint houses of the Missouri General Assembly and then sat in the galleries while the usually fractious state house actually passed two bills. Before entraining for St. Louis, Alexis lunched with the governor and local dignitaries.[33]

Sheridan's cars were uncoupled from the imperial train in Topeka, and with most of his staff he returned to Chicago and army affairs. On January 25, Sheridan telegraphed the secretary of war reporting that the hunt "was very successful, much above my expectations for this season of the year. . . . I think I may safely say it gave more pleasure to the Grand Duke than any other event which has occurred to him since he has been in our country."[34]

One individual who did not decamp with Sheridan was George Custer. Apparently because Sheridan placed him in charge of the retinue for the remainder of the trip, Custer accompanied the grand duke and his entourage to New Orleans.[35] The men seem to have bonded: the grand duke expressed sincere grief upon learning of Custer's death at the Little Bighorn in June 1876.[36]

Adams Express Company president E. S. Sanford seems to have been pleased with Thomson's performance as the imperial train manager. He telegraphed Thomson at Jefferson City, congratulating him on having bagged two buffalo in Kansas. Never one to let business idle, Sanford also noted that Thomas Scott, president of the Union Pacific Railroad, was in New Orleans arranging for the final stage of the grand duke's sojourn in the United States.[37]

The grand duke was scheduled to make a short visit to Cincinnati on January 26, but to the great disappointment of the citizenry, the visit was canceled. On January 28 he left by train for Louisville, where he visited Mammoth Cave. At Louisville, Elizabeth Custer, together with Nina Sturgis, daughter of the Seventh Cavalry commander, Col. Samuel Sturgis, joined Custer for the remainder of the journey to New Orleans.[38] The Louisville portion of the trip was not without incident: Custer forgot to invite Gen. Alfred Terry and his staff to the Louisville ball held in the grand duke's honor. And Terry was further embarrassed when Alexis's staff forgot an appointment at which Terry and his staff were to be presented to the grand duke.[39]

The Mammoth Cave excursion helped cement Alexis's reputation as a ladies' man and hard partier. The party consisted of Colonel and Mrs. Custer, two other couples, and at least five single ladies. Lt. Col. James Forsyth reported that the cave visiting party was "darn eternal lively" and that "both Ladies and Gentlemen were tight on Champagne wine, etc. etc." Alexis did not escape unsullied. The party was late in returning to the imperial train, arriving after dark, and when the grand duke's carriage door was opened "a pair of nude female legs [and a] high head of hair capping a flushed and excited lady's face" were observed. As a consequence of the apparent overindulgences of the Mammoth Cave adventure, Frank Thomson had to wire for a resupply of wine and spirits.[40]

The party continued the trip by river steamer, arriving in Memphis aboard the *Great Republic* on February 2, 1872. Six days later the party left aboard the *James Howard* and, after a stop in Vicksburg, arrived in New Orleans. In New Orleans, Grand Duke Alexis attended the 1872 Mardi Gras celebration and, as guest of honor, reviewed the inaugural Rex parade. From New Orleans Alexis traveled to Pensacola, where he met the Russian fleet and set sail on February 22, 1872.[41]

The next stop for the Russian squadron was Havana, Cuba, which it reached on February 29. There a reporter quoted Alexis as having said, "I should like to live in America altogether, dividing my time from May to January between New York and the prairies, and spending the remainder in New Orleans."[42] Alexis and the fleet then sailed to Rio de Janeiro, arriving on June 3, 1872. Then, sailing eastward, the squadron stopped in Cape Town, Batavia, Singapore,

Figure 13. Funeral procession in Paris for Grand Duke Alexis. Douglas Scott collection.

and Hong Kong and arrived in Japan on October 15, 1872.[43] On November 26 the Russian squadron set sail for Vladivostok, reaching the Russian Pacific Fleet base on December 5, nearly a year and a half after it had left from Kronstadt.[44]

In 1873, Grand Duke Alexis was appointed head of the Imperial Naval Guards. He was also appointed a member of the section for shipbuilding and naval artillery of the Russian Naval Technical Committee.[45] Alexis returned to the United States briefly in the spring of 1877 while on a Russian naval cruise.[46] During the Russo-Turkish War (1877–1878) he was promoted to commander of the Russian Naval Forces on the Danube, and on January 9, 1878, he was awarded the Order of St. George–Fourth Degree. After the accession of Czar Alexander III to the throne, Alexis was appointed head of the Naval Department, and in 1883 he was also appointed General Admiral of the Russian Imperial Fleet. Though his control over the day-to-day affairs of the military was limited, Alexis was involved in naval and military planning. He was instrumental in modernizing the Russian Navy, but following the defeat of the Russian Pacific Squadron at the Battle of Tsushima Strait, during the Russo-Japanese War, Alexis was relieved of his command. In 1905 he retired.[47] Alexis's nephew, Grand Duke Alexander, places Alexis's life and accomplishments in a negative light, referring to his uncle as a Beau Brummell and "a case for fast women and slow ships," alluding to Alexis's reputation as a ladies' man and as architect of the Tsushima Strait disaster.[48]

After the assassination of his brother, Grand Duke Sergei, in February 1905 and his retirement in disgrace from the navy in June that same year, Alexis chose to spend most of his time in Paris. His penchant for comfort and good living eventually took their toll, and he died of pneumonia in Paris on November 27, 1908. After a lavish state funeral in Paris, the grand duke's remains were shipped to St. Petersburg and buried in the royal crypt in the cathedral.

4

CAMP ALEXIS AND THE ROYAL BUFFALO HUNT

The U.S. government invitation to the grand duke to participate in a western buffalo hunt during his stop in the United States was a seemingly simple gesture, but implementing the hunt became a complicated effort. The results justified the effort, however. The hunt was a great success, and in the ensuing years Alexis remembered it fondly.[1] Gen. Phillip Sheridan and a host of 1870s luminaries, including Lt. Col. George Custer, were among the party that traveled in reserved railroad cars from Omaha to North Platte Station and then by wagon to Red Willow Creek in Hayes County, Nebraska, for what became known as the royal buffalo hunt.[2]

The royal buffalo hunt is well known among western Indian Wars and buffalo-hunting researchers. William F. Cody's accounts of the hunt are among the most colorful and frequently cited, but they are full of exaggerated self-promotion and a good deal of embellishment that recurs in similar versions in other Cody autobiographies.[3] Early and even modern chroniclers, relying on this account, give Cody the honor of having organized the hunt for General Sheridan and of having found Spotted Tail and his band and brought them to the camp. In fact, as other primary documents demonstrate, Cody's role was far more pedestrian. Sheridan did know Cody from the September and October "millionaires' hunt," but Cody was in charge of

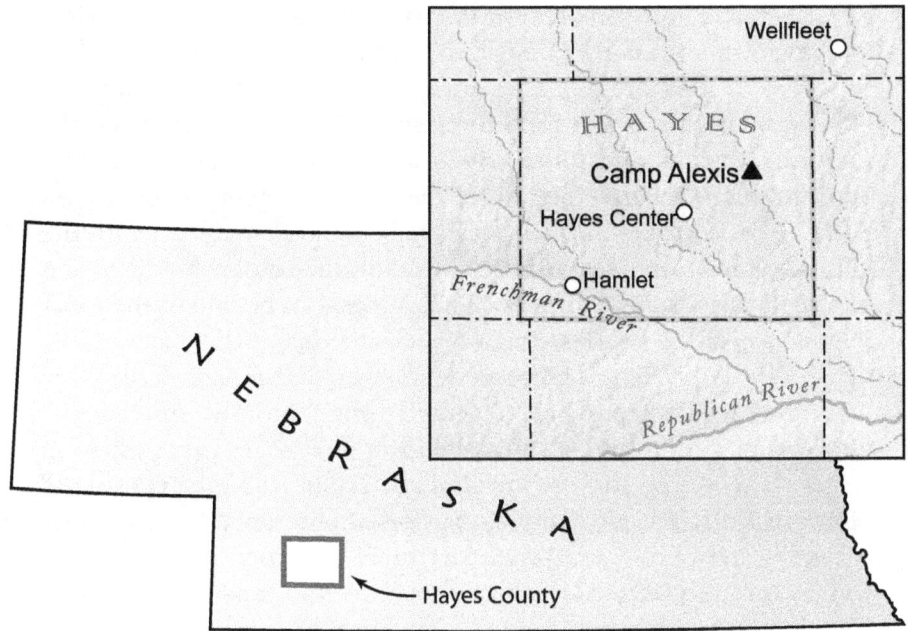

Figure 14. Location of Camp Alexis in Hayes County. Map by Tom Jonas. Copyright © 2013, University of Oklahoma Press.

nothing more than finding buffalo for the party to shoot and adding color to the camp.[4]

One source often used as a primary document for the grand duke's American sojourn is William Warren Tucker's *His Imperial Highness: The Grand Duke Alexis in the United States during the Winter of 1871–1872*. This limited-issue volume was privately printed without author attribution by the Riverside Press of Cambridge, Mass., in 1872 and was intended for distribution to hunt-party members as a memento. Only a few copies are known to exist. Jeff Dykes's 1972 reprint found wide acceptance and is now a collectors' edition. In 2004, Eliborn also reprinted the volume. The Library of Congress scanned a copy of the 1872 edition, which is available on their American Memories website. Tucker's introduction notes that he assembled the work from contemporary newspaper accounts and suggests he smoothed them out and added elements to create a flowing narrative.[5] Tucker's work is valuable both as an early account of the grand duke's visit to America and as a recounting of the buffalo hunt, but in reality it is a secondary source. Tucker was not with the party at any point, and he assembled the disparate newspaper accounts without consulting the participants or correcting errors of fact.

Today many more resources are available to retell the hunt story. Contemporary newspaper accounts, several recently discovered primary documents, and some private document collections allow a new and more accurate picture of the hunt to emerge. Recently reports by participants in the hunt have become available in both the U.S. National Archives and Records Administration holdings and in the Russian State Archives. What appears to be one of the most reliable sources is a series of newspaper accounts filed by an unidentified *New York Herald* correspondent who accompanied the hunt party. He filed the reports via telegraph during the hunt, and the content was picked up and used in one form or another by newspapers across the country, such as the *Chicago Tribune* and the *Cleveland Morning Daily Herald*. Employing these contemporary newspaper accounts and public and private archival documentary sources as well as carefully vetted later accounts allows an expanded and more complete view of the hunt and the hunt camp.

Russian historian Zoia Bleykova places the beginning of the hunt on November 23, 1871, at an official dinner in Washington at which General Sherman, seated next to the grand duke, learned of his interest in the American West and his desire to see "Red Skinned Indians."[6] As a result of an impasse involving Russian diplomatic personnel stationed in Washington, this dinner never occurred. In fact, planning for Grand Duke Alexis's visit to the United States actually began long before the unlikely dinner conversation. Grand Duke Alexis's U.S. stopover was part of the original itinerary developed through formal diplomatic channels and had been rumored as early as 1869. Russian Foreign Minister Alexander Gorchakov informed the minister to the United States, Constantin Catacazy, in February 1871 that Grand Duke Alexis would tour the world. Gorchakov suggested that the itinerary include a stop in New York then a tour of selected areas of the United States.[7]

Upon learning of the impending tour, Albert Bierstadt assembled leading New York citizens to plan for the royal visit.[8] Thanks to his Russian connections, Bierstadt became a major figure in planning for the grand duke's visit, and he seems to be the one who first broached the idea of a buffalo hunt to General Sherman. The artist might have learned of the grand duke's interest in hunting when they met while Bierstadt was visiting Russia.[9]

Figure 15. Gen. William T. Sherman, planner of the royal buffalo hunt. Douglas Scott collection.

In a letter dated July 3, 1871, Bierstadt, stated: "You are doubtlessly aware that the Grand Duke Alexis of Russia is to be here in October, and I have learned that he is quite desirous of witnessing a Buffalo Hunt. As his visit partakes of a somewhat national character, would it not be well to give him one on a grand scale, with Indians included, as a rare piece of American hospitality?" Bierstadt went on to suggest that the Indians entertain the Russians through dancing and by demonstrating their buffalo-hunting skills, all within a reasonable distance of the railroad line. He urged Sherman to participate in the hunt but suggested that General Sheridan, as an officer of appropriate rank, host the event. That same day Bierstadt also wrote Secretary of War William W. Belknap broaching the idea to him as well. The secretary's reply assured Bierstadt that the War Department would have no difficulty in procuring a hunt or other similar amusements in which the grand duke might take an interest during his sojourn in the United States.[10] Apparently both governments also discussed the itinerary: a revised itinerary proposed dropping several West Coast and inland stops but included a buffalo hunt and a run to Salt Lake, possibly a visit to San Francisco, and then a swing through the South to include New Orleans.[11]

Figure 16. Maj. Gen. Philip Sheridan, hunt master and organizer. Douglas Scott collection.

Sherman began general planning for such a hunt but stopped when the grand duke's arrival dates shifted. Planning appears to have gone back into full swing in October before the grand duke's arrival in New York.[12] Because Sherman planned to sail for Europe on November 11, 1871, a few days prior to the grand duke's arrival in New York, he could not participate in the hunt, but he appointed Philip Sheridan, commander of the Division of the Missouri, to host the hunt.[13] On November 1 Secretary Belknap authorized Sherman to write to Sheridan informing him that he could expend army funds to support entertaining the grand duke on a buffalo hunt.[14]

That same day Sherman wrote to Sheridan authorizing him to move ahead with planning for the hunt and expending the necessary funds.[15] Sheridan's reply is unknown, but on November 2, Secretary Belknap wrote to Secretary of State Hamilton Fish telling him that Sheridan would extend all courtesies to the grand duke during his western sojourn.[16]

When Bierstadt learned of Sheridan's appointment as hunt leader, he invited him to participate in the New York festivities honoring the grand duke on his arrival in the United States.[17] Sheridan declined but said:

> If His Royal Highness desires the Buffalo hunt I will place myself at his service and can take him to large herds south of McPherson on the Union Pacific R Road, say from fifty to sixty or seventy miles. Spotted Tails band of Sioux &

Whistlers band are in the neighborhood & I can give them such inducements as will cause them to join us at least I think so.

It will be cold probably but not half so cold as Russia.

I cannot manage for more than twelve (12) persons in the suite of the Grand Duke & would like to have it a little less if possible.

Should he desire to take this hunt, he can kill buffalo to his hearts content but must be willing to rough it a little. . . .we ought to start for McPherson by the 10th of December at least.[18]

Bierstadt later received the Imperial Russian Order of St. Stanislaus. This neck badge in gold and enamel was awarded for his efforts in organizing the New York functions in honor of the grand duke, the hunt, and other services to the czar.[19]

Planning apparently proceeded apace, but the grand duke's schedule in the East precluded an early western departure. By late November Sheridan wrote Adj. Gen. Edward. D. Townsend saying that the hunt could go forward but that the grand duke needed to be aware of the potential for bad weather on the plains: "It is now so late in the season that there is no possibility of giving him a hunt unless he is willing to undergo the inclemency of the weather at this season on the plains. There are plenty of Buffalo from fifty to one hundred miles south of Fort McPherson and if the Grand Duke is willing to take the chances of a storm, etc. I could send out all the Camp and Garrison Equipage in advance, have the camp pitched and let him go rapidly from McPherson to it in ambulances or on horseback. At this season his party should not exceed ten persons, whom I think I could make pretty comfortable." Townsend forwarded the letter to Secretary of State Fish showing that all formal chains of command were being observed and kept aware of hunt plans.[20]

Sheridan continued putting his plan into effect. Through channels he requested that the Department of the Interior and the Office of Indian Affairs ask Spotted Tail and some members of his band to participate in the hunt per earlier correspondence with Albert Bierstadt. While awaiting a reply he was not idle but sent dispatches to Fort McPherson inquiring about the weather and an invitation to Spotted Tail, forwarded via the Department of the Interior Office of Indian Affairs, to participate in the hunt. The *Beatrice (Nebraska)*

Express of December 23, 1871, reported that Sheridan received the following note from Fort McPherson: "Dec. 10, 1871. Dear General: I enclose you a note from Mr. Todd Randall, agent for Spotted Tail. The weather is delightful here now. The days are almost as warm as Indian summer. Yours Truly, E. M. Hayes, Lieutenant, U.S.A."

The enclosed note read "Blackwood, Dec. 5, 1871. Sir: Spotted Tail will meet the party coming at the crossing of Wilson [Willow] creek. Please inform me when the party will be there, and I will have them in readiness. The Indians are all doing well and are perfectly satisfied. Todd Randall, U.S. subagent."

Randall, who was married to Lakota warrior Yellow Hair's sister, was not the government's first choice for a subagent to the Brulé.[21] Agent J. M. Washburn had appointed Stephen Yates, a trader, to the position, but Spotted Tail refused, and Randall was appointed by Agent James Wham. The statement that the Indians are "perfectly satisfied" refers to Sheridan's offer to provide 10,000 rations of flour, sugar, and coffee and 1,000 rations of tobacco to members of Spotted Tail's band who attended the hunt. The rations were sent from Fort McPherson to the camp on Red Willow Creek. Ethnographer and historian George Hyde suggests that a total of six hundred Brulés camped on Red Willow Creek with the hunt party, but the number varies according to the source.[22]

Sheridan telegraphed General Townsend that Spotted Tail had accepted the invitation to join the hunt. He also noted that the buffalo were plentiful and the weather fine and expressed his hope that the grand duke would accept the hunt invitation but noted that he needed at least ten days' advance notification to proceed.[23] The hunt plans were temporarily derailed when Secretary of State Fish sent Secretary of War William W. Belknap a letter stating that the travel schedule for the Russian delegation could not be altered and that the grand duke could not participate in the western hunt.[24]

Grand Duke Alexis was in Chicago, apparently enjoying a relaxing new year's eve, when General Sheridan and George Pullman arrived at the Tremont house and presented their cards to Adm. Constantine N. Possiet. They were invited to the grand duke's suite, where Sheridan spent the afternoon convincing the grand duke to add a slight detour to his schedule so that the buffalo hunt could proceed. The *Chicago Tribune* of January 1, 1872, reported that the grand duke relented and plans for the hunt were to move forward with the group to assemble in Omaha on January 10. In the meantime Alexis would not change his schedule and was to go on to Milwaukee, St. Louis, and then Omaha via Kansas City. However, in case of bad weather on the Great Plains during the hunt dates, the party would go through to California on the train before returning eastward. Sheridan moved quickly and kept the telegraph wires humming as he sent out directives and requests. Among the first telegrams he sent was one to Lt. Col. George A. Custer, then on reconstruction duty in Kentucky, asking that he join the party.[25]

George Custer, like Sheridan, was an avid hunter and outdoor sportsman. Undoubtedly this is one reason he was included in the royal buffalo hunt. Custer had a long history of sport hunting, and he particularly enjoyed the chase and taking of big game on the Great Plains, including elk, bear, and, of course, buffalo.[26] Custer hosted many hunts on the plains, especially during his stay in Kansas, between 1867 and 1869. His first encounter with a buffalo was nearly his last. In his own, somewhat self-deprecating story, he tells the tale of running his first buffalo and as he was about to fire a ball into the bull's shoulder with his Savage revolver, his horse shied and the bullet hit the horse in the head, killing it instantly and sending Custer head over heels into the path of the bull. Luckily, the startled buffalo chose to wander away rather than gore the prostrate Custer.[27]

Of the hunts that Custer hosted, several before and after the hunt with Grand Duke Alexis included European royalty. In 1869 Custer hosted Lord Waterpark and Lord Paget during a large hunt on the Kansas plains. Later, during the 1873 Yellowstone Expedition Custer allowed two English gentlemen who were on a western hunting expedition of their own to join the Yellowstone command for their protection, and one of the gentlemen later became Lord Clifford of Uxbridge.[28] Custer's exposure to European nobility, hosting various hunting parties of his own, and his enthusiasm for the hunt were perhaps among the reasons that Sheridan selected him to join the Nebraska hunt.

On January 3, Sheridan telegraphed General Townsend, notifying him that the grand duke had agreed to participate in a hunt, that the hunt was planned for January 12–20, and that, through their agent, Todd Randall, the Indians had promised to be present.[29] He requested that the War Department ask the Indian Department to direct the agents to have the Indians come to the army camp on Red Willow Creek, and he added that he would issue flour, sugar, coffee,

Figure 17. Lt. Col. George A. Custer in civilian dress in an image believed to have been taken in Omaha just before the hunt. Kansas State Historical Society.

Figure 18. A buffalo hunt in Kansas hosted by George Custer ca. 1867. Little Bighorn Battlefield National Monument.

and tobacco rations to the Indians while they were with the hunt party. Interior Secretary Charles Delano immediately responded that he had directed the proper agents of the Indian Department to have Spotted Tail and some of his warriors join the hunt party near Fort McPherson.[30] That direction took the form of a telegram sent to Todd Randall on January 4, 1872. The missive stated: "Todd Randall, in charge Spotted Tail Hunting Party, care of Commdg Officer, Fort McPherson, Nebraska. Grand Duke Alexis's Buffalo Hunt will take place from 12th to 20th of this month off McPherson. Make arrangements to have some of your party present. Coffee, Sugar, Flour, and Tobacco will be issued to Indians by Military during the hunt. H. R. Clum, Actg Commissoner."[31]

On January 3, 1872, the *New York Times* reported on plans for the hunt, noting that Sheridan and some members of his staff would take the grand duke to Fort McPherson and thence to a camp some fifty miles to the south to hunt buffalo. The article also mentioned that Spotted Tail and his band would join the hunt and collect their winter rations there, which seems to be a misrepresentation of the facts of the ration issue.

While Sheridan was completing plans for the hunt, sending telegrams to various government officials, others were wiring instructions for the transportation and logistical support of the grand duke's party. The available telegrams sent to and from train manager Frank Thomson are not only an archive of the trip, but also provide a glimpse into behind-the-scenes operations of the imperial party's overland train travel.[32] Railroad executives were anxious to participate, providing locomotives and other necessities, and ensuring his train had right-of-way on the tracks. On January 5, 1872, Theophilus E. Sickels, the Union Pacific superintendent in Omaha, telegraphed Thomson that a temporary railroad bridge spanned the Missouri at Omaha and that the hunt party train was welcome to use it. He also informed Thomson that the Union Pacific planned to make the 291-mile trip from Omaha to North Platte in twelve hours. On the same day, Sickels telegraphed Thomson asking to be informed of the day and hour the imperial train would leave Omaha so that the Union Pacific could prepare special timecards and suggesting that 3:00 p.m. would be a pleasant hour to depart. William Sanford sent Thomson a telegraphic note suggesting, tongue in cheek, that he advise Russian Consul-General Waldemar Bodisco to keep in mind that "hunting the Buffalo is exciting sport but when the Buffalo hunts you it becomes a little too exciting and also that false hair is exceedingly expensive according to the last Indian Circular."[33]

Although Sheridan and Thomson had the situation well in hand, with plans and personnel already in place, there was a good deal of public confusion as to the details of the hunt. Even as late as January 11 the *New York Times* was reporting that the hunt would occur in Kansas rather than near Fort McPherson, Nebraska, as Sheridan was planning.

In his autobiography, Cody reports that he led Lt. Col. George A. Forsyth and Dr. Morris Asch, of General Sheridan's staff, together with Capt. Edward Hayes, Fifth U.S. Cavalry, and wagons loaded with camp baggage, provisions, and tents, to Red Willow Creek and there helped them select the camp ground:

> These officers had been sent by General Sheridan to have all the necessary arrangements perfected by the time the Grand Duke should arrive. They learned from me that there were plenty of buffaloes in the vicinity, and especially on the Red Willow, sixty miles distant. They said they would like to go over on the Red Willow and pick out a suitable place for the camp; they also inquired the location of the camp of Spotted Tail, chief of the Sioux Indians. Spotted Tail had permission from the Government to hunt the buffalo with his people during the winter, in the Republican River country. It was my opinion that they were located somewhere on the Frenchman's fork, about one hundred and fifty miles from Fort McPherson.
>
> General Sheridan's commissioner informed me that he wished me to visit Spotted Tail's camp, and induce about one hundred of the leading warriors and chiefs to come to the point where it should be decided to locate the Alexis hunting camp, and to be there by the time the Grand Duke should arrive, so that he could see a body of American Indians and observe the manner in which they killed buffaloes. The Indians would also be called upon to give a grand war dance in honor of the distinguished visitor.
>
> Next morning General Forsyth and Dr. Asch, accompanied by Captain Hays, who had been left at Fort McPherson in charge of the Fifth Cavalry horses, taking an ambulance and a light wagon, to carry their tents and provisions sufficient to

Figure 19. A temporary railroad bridge (like that the Sheridan and imperial party trains may have used) across the frozen Missouri River. Omaha Public Library.

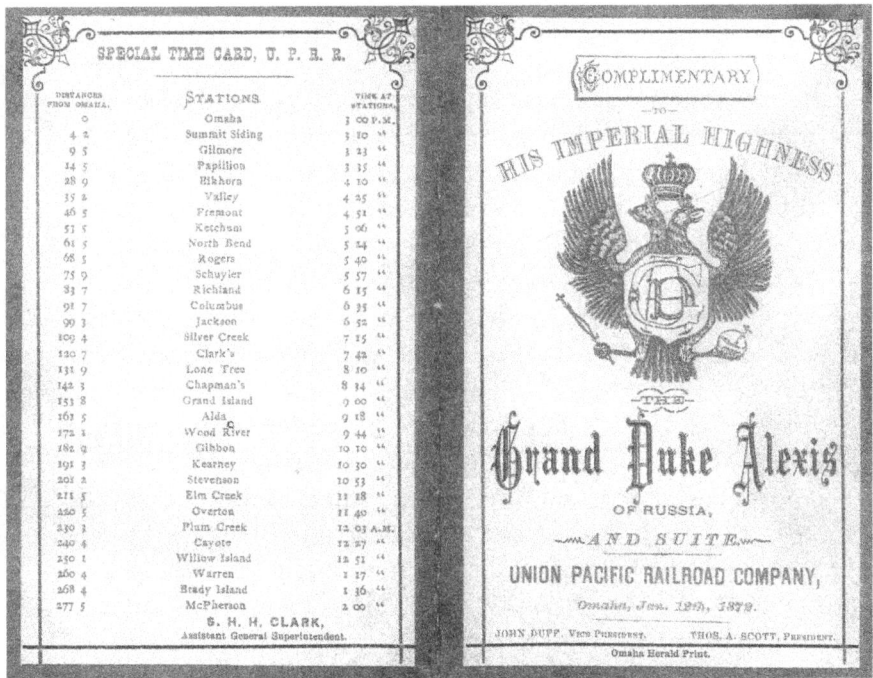

Figure 20. Union Pacific Railroad time card prepared for Grand Duke Alexis's trip to North Platte Station. Jim Crain collection.

last them two or three days, started, under my guidance, with a small escort, for Red Willow creek, arriving there at night. The next day we selected a pleasant camping place on a little knoll in the valley of the Red Willow.[34]

Cody stated that the party retuned to Fort McPherson the next day but charged him to find Spotted Tail and bring him and one hundred of his best warriors to the campsite to assist in the hunt and put on a show for the dignitaries.

The weather was very cold and I found my journey by no means a pleasant one as I was obliged to camp out with only my saddle-blankets; and besides, there was more or less danger from the Indians themselves; for, although Spotted Tail himself was friendly, I was afraid I might have difficulty in getting into his camp. I was liable at any moment to run into a party of his young men who might be out hunting, and as I had many enemies among the Sioux, I would be running considerable risk in meeting them.

At the end of the first day I camped on Stinking Water, a tributary of the Frenchman's fork, where I built a little fire in the timber; but it was so very cold I was not able to sleep much. Getting an early start in the morning I followed up the Frenchman's fork and late in the afternoon I could see, from the fresh horse tracks and from the dead buffaloes lying here and there, recently killed, that I was nearing Spotted Tail's camp. I rode on for a few miles further, and then hiding my horse in a low ravine I crawled up a high hill, where I obtained a good view of the country. I could see for four or five miles up the creek, and got sight of a village and of two or three hundred ponies in its vicinity. I waited until night came and then I succeeded in riding into the Indian camp unobserved.

I had seen Spotted Tail's camp when he came from the North and I knew the kind of lodge he was living in. As I entered the village I wrapped a blanket around my head so that the Indians could not tell whether I was a white or a redman. In this way I rode around until I found Spotted Tail's lodge. Dismounting from my horse I opened his tent door and looking in, saw the old chief lying on some robes. I spoke to him and he recognised me at once and invited me to enter. Inside the lodge I found a white man, an old frontiersman, Todd Randall, who was Spotted Tail's agent and who had lived a great many years with the Indians. He understood their language perfectly and did all the interpreting for Spotted Tail. Through him I readily communicated with the chief and informed him of my errand. I told him that the warriors and chiefs would greatly please General Sheridan if they would meet him about ten sleeps at the old Government crossing of the Red Willow. I further informed him that there was a great chief from across the water who was coming there to visit him.

Spotted Tail replied that he would be very glad to go; that the next morning he would call his people together and select those who would accompany him. I told Spotted Tail how I had entered his camp. He replied that I had acted wisely; that although his people were friendly, yet some of his young men had a grudge against me, and I might have had difficulty with them had I met them away from the village. He directed his squaw to get me something to eat, and ordered that my horse be taken care of and upon his invitation I spent the remainder of the night in his lodge.

Next morning the chiefs and warriors assembled according to orders, and to them was stated the object of my visit. They were asked: "Do you know who this man is?"

"Yes, we know him well," replied one, "that is Pa-he-has-ka," (that being my name among the Sioux, which translated means "Long-Hair") "that is our old enemy;" a great many of the Indians, who were with Spotted Tail at this time, had been driven out of the Republican country.

"That is he," said Spotted Tail. "I want all my people to be kind to him and treat him as my friend."

I noticed that several of them were looking daggers at me. They appeared as if they wished to raise my hair then and there. Spotted Tail motioned and I followed him into his lodge, and thereupon the Indians dispersed. Having the assurance of Spotted Tail that none of the young men would follow me I started back for the Red Willow, arriving the second night.[35]

Cody placed Spotted Tail's camp on Frenchman Fork of the Republican, about one hundred fifty miles from Fort McPherson and perhaps one hundred miles from the campsite. It took Cody two days to reach Spotted Tail's camp, and he purportedly waited until dark to enter because he feared that some of the band might kill him before he found Spotted Tail. Cody's purple prose describes the meeting and records that, after he had spoken with Spotted Tail via his agent interpreter, Spotted Tail agreed to come to the Red Willow camp in ten days, as promised. Forsyth and Asch were sent to Fort McPherson and North Platte Station no sooner than January 2 and, because they left from Chicago, arrived January 4 at the earliest. Sheridan staffers had to work with the Second Cavalry commander, Col. Innis N. Palmer, in Omaha and with his subordinates at Fort McPherson, to arrange for camp equipage, tents, rations, horses, wagons, and escorts. Likely the earlier aborted planning alleviated some logistical issues, but the site-selection team left for the Red Willow area no earlier than January 5 to find a suitable campsite. Assuming Cody accompanied the site-selection group, he could not have ridden to the Indian camp and coaxed Spotted Tail to join the party ten days later. There were not ten days between the camp selection and the arrival of the hunting party at North Platte Station. Nor could Cody have gone to St. Louis, as reported, to meet the grand duke.[36]

What is abundantly clear in a careful parsing of the Cody account is that it is nothing more that self-glorification. Spotted Tail was summoned by means of a telegram from official government sources, not by a lone Cody sneaking into the Brulé camp. It seems more plausible that Cody was the bearer of the January 4 telegram from Acting Commissioner H. R. Clum to Randall ordering the agent to have Spotted Tail and some of his band at the hunt. And it seems unlikely that Cody had to sneak into the camp to deliver the message.

What is known with certainty is that on January 8, Capt. James Egan, with First Lt. Joshua L. Fowler and approximately sixty-four men of Company K, Second Cavalry, from the Post at North Platte Station, left for Red Willow Creek to prepare the camp. Accompanying Egan was First Lt. Edward M. Hayes, Regimental Quartermaster, Fifth Cavalry, who was on detached service in charge of horses at Fort McPherson and acted as quartermaster for the hunt. The *Omaha Tribune and Republican,* January 15, 1872, reported that Egan's party took thirty tents for the soldiers and servants, three wagonloads of commissary stores, extra horses for the hunt party, and twenty-five wagonloads of provisions to be distributed to the Brulé. Among the camp and garrison equipage sent to Camp Alexis were four head of beef weighing some 1,600 pounds to feed the Second Cavalrymen who escorted the hunt party. The cattle were purchased from John Bratt and Company for only $160.[38] And they took horses to be left as a relay at Medicine Creek, about the halfway point, so that the hunt party could travel on fresh horses throughout its journey to the camp.

Captain Egan was no stranger to the west. An Irish immigrant, he first enlisted as a private in the U.S. Army and the Second Cavalry in 1856, was discharged in 1858, and then reenlisted in 1860 in the First (later designated the Fourth) Cavalry. He rose to the rank of corporal by 1861 and then sergeant. He fought at Bull Run, in the Peninsular Campaign, in the siege of Yorktown, at Antietam, and at the battle of Franklin, where he suffered a saber blow to the head that left him deaf in the left ear and a wound to the left hand so extensive that he never regained full use of that hand. He also fought at Middleton, where his horse fell and permanently injured his right knee, which caused him to limp the remainder of his life. Egan was commissioned from the ranks and appointed a second lieutenant in the Second Cavalry on August 10, 1863. While he was serving with Sheridan's cavalry corps at Cold Harbor, a minié ball fractured his right arm, which was partially disabled, and as with his left hand, Egan never regained full use of the arm. He was promoted to first lieutenant on October 15, 1864, and after returning to active duty with his regiment at Fort Riley, Kansas, in 1866, he was appointed captain on February 5, 1868. Egan served most of the remainder of his career in the West, was involved in numerous fights with the Indians, and was on General Crook's famed starvation march during the Great Sioux War. In 1878 he suffered another injury, this time to his hip. Never fully recovering his stamina, he asked to be retired in 1879. On May 9 he retired from active service, but his later years were unhappy because he fell into debt and perhaps had a problem with depression and alcohol. Egan died on April 14, 1883.[39]

General Sheridan, accompanied by Lt. Col. James Forsyth, Lt. Col. George Forsyth, Lt. Col. Michael Sheridan, and Lt. Col. George Custer, arrived in Omaha via Chicago on the morning of January 11. The group likely arrived in Sheridan's personal cars, a dining and sleeping car, which were to be coupled with the grand duke's cars for the hunt portion of the trip.[40] In the late morning of January 12 the imperial party arrived in Omaha, where, as reported by the *New York Herald* of January 12, 1872, they were met by Former Territorial

Governor Alvin Saunders, local dignitaries, Sheridan, Custer, and army officers from the Division of the Missouri. A room was prepared for the grand duke's use at the Grand Central Hotel, but if it was used at all it was only to enable Alexis to freshen up before dinner with Saunders.[41] The party was wined and dined at the Saunders home and at 3:10 p.m. departed Omaha for North Platte Station. Among those traveling to North Platte Station from Omaha, but not part of the hunt party, were S. H. H. Clarke, Union Pacific superintendent, and J. J. Dickey of the Western Pacific Telegraph Company, who was acting as telegrapher.[42] The train, whose engine, draped with American and Russian flags, was pulling the five Pullman cars of the imperial suite and Sheridan's two private Pullman cars, traveled at a rate of about twenty-five miles per hour, and during the evening the grand duke invited Sheridan and his party, as well as a group of Union Pacific Railroad officials traveling on the special train, to dine in his car. The *Beatrice (Nebraska) Express* of January 20, 1872, reported that dinner was served in the best style the Pullman line could produce and that Sheridan sat at the grand duke's table.

The special train arrived at North Platte Station on the morning of January 13 at about 7:00 a.m. After taking breakfast on the cars, the hunt party detrained and took their places in horse-drawn

Figure 21. Former Nebraska Territorial Governor Alvin Saunders. From Edmunds, *Pen Sketches of Nebraskans*, 1871.

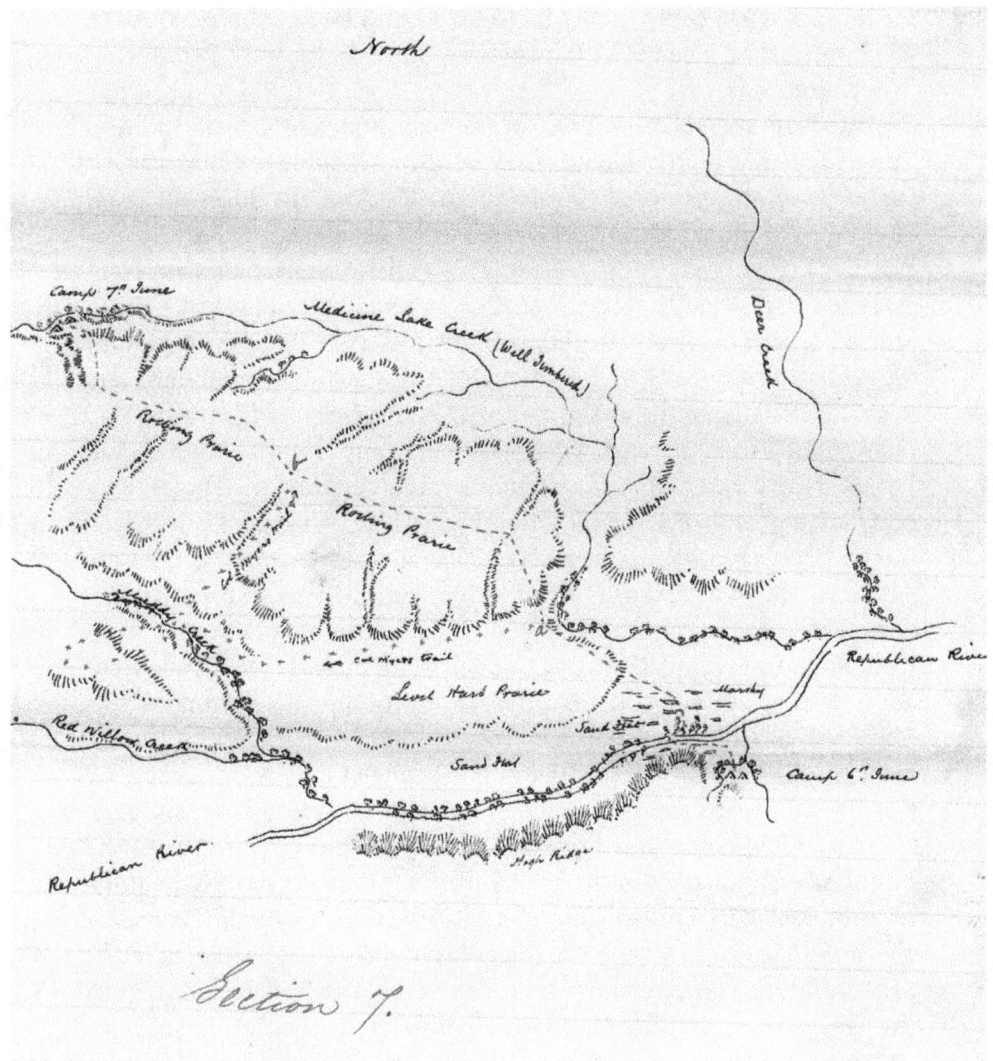

Figure 22. Custer's 1867 route from the Republican River and the scout to Red Willow Creek. Courtesy Jeff Broome.

ambulances. Sheridan and the grand duke occupied a four-horse drag, or open carriage. Cody appeared on horseback, attired in his fur-trimmed buckskin suit, and was presented to the grand duke. Then, acting as guide, he took the lead and began the trek to the camp on Red Willow.[43]

The weather was cool, the high the day before at Grand Island being about 46°F.[44] The Russian party who mounted the carriages for the drive to Camp Alexis included Grand Duke Alexis, V. Adm. Constantine N. Possiet, Counselor of State William T. V. Machin (tutor and mentor), Count Alexander Olsenfieff (aide-de-camp), Consul-General at New York Waldemar Bodisco, Naval Lt. Karl Tudeer, Secretary to the Russian Legation Vladimir Shirkoff, naval surgeon and personal physician Dr. Vladimir Koudrin, Lt. Paul Shouvalov (aide-de-camp), and perhaps five servants.[45] The American party consisted of Frank Thomson, imperial train manager, General Sheridan, Aides-de-Camp Lt. Col. Michael Sheridan and Lt. Col. James Forsyth, military secretary Lt. Col. George Forsyth, Assistant Surgeon Morris Asch, Department of the Platte commander Gen. E. O. C. Ord, Second Cavalry Colonel Palmer, Second Cavalry Maj. Nelson Sweitzer, Seventh Cavalry Lieutenant Colonel Custer, and Fifth Cavalry and camp quartermaster First Lieutenant Hayes. Second Cavalry and regimental adjutant First Lt. William Philo Clark might have accompanied Palmer or been sent ahead to the camp. The *Lincoln (Nebraska) Daily State Journal,* January 16, 1872, reported that the party was escorted to the camp by a detachment of Company E, Second Cavalry, under the command of a "Lieutenant Stevens." Other sources identify the company commander as "Lt. Stover." In fact, the officer was Second Lt. Edgar Zell Steever. He was with the Third Cavalry but had been detailed to act as Second Cavalry Company E commander in the absence of its other officers. Company E was stationed at Fort McPherson but at the time of the hunt had only thirty-four men fit for duty.[46] Unfortunately the muster rolls for Companies E and K and for the band of the Second Cavalry are not present in the National Archives. As a consequence the exact number of men who provided the escort and entertainment in the camp cannot be clearly identified. Informed speculation suggests that one hundred twenty-five is a likely number if all effective men of both companies—the band, the officers, the hunt party, and the teamsters—are included. During January 1872, Fort McPherson had a wagonmaster, an assistant wagonmaster, and ten teamsters on the civilian-employee roster. The Quartermaster Department employed thirty-one civilians, including a scout (probably Cody). And during the same period, North Platte Station employed two teamsters.[47]

The route to the camp on Red Willow Creek was not trail blazing in any sense of the word. In fact—although others had traversed the area earlier—Lt. Col. George Custer and the Seventh Cavalry blazed the trail during the 1867 summer campaign. Originally part of Gen. Winfield Scott Hancock's Kansas campaign, Custer and the Seventh Cavalry scouted for hostile Indians most of the remainder of the summer in Kansas, Colorado, and Nebraska. Between June 1 and July 13, 1867, Custer's men pioneered a trail between Fort Hays, Kansas, and Fort McPherson, Nebraska, and back to Fort Wallace, Kansas.[48] Custer experienced several firsts on this scout, including a high desertion rate among his command and his first actual skirmish with Indians, near today's Benkelman, Nebraska. During the scout to Fort McPherson the command crossed the ridge separating Medicine Creek (noted on Lt. Henry Jackson's map of the expedition, as Medicine Lake Creek) from Red Willow Creek. During the June 7 march the command spotted Indians moving to the west, and Custer sent Lt. Edward Myers and Company E in pursuit, but to no avail. Myers's pursuit took him almost due west from Medicine Creek to Muddy Creek, which he crossed. Then, moving slightly west northwestward, he crossed a high ridge overlooking Red Willow Creek and, quite possibly, the future site of Camp Alexis. Custer's command camped near Fort McPherson June 11–17. Then, moving southward, along their previous line of march, the command camped on Medicine Creek on June 18 and reached Fort Wallace on July 13. Earlier, on July 12, the column had found the remains of Lt. Lyman Kidder and his small command. They had been sent to deliver dispatches to Custer but had been annihilated by Cheyenne and Lakota warriors.[49]

The trail Custer blazed between Fort Hays and Fort McPherson continued to be used over the next few years. Lt. William Forbush, of Maj. Eugene Carr's Fifth Cavalry, scouted the route in May 1869, and it was clearly delineated on military maps of the period.[50] *The Official State Atlas of Nebraska* of 1885 shows this same road in existence at that time. General Sheridan traversed this same trail just a few months prior to the January 1872 hunt. During the September and October 1871 millionaires' buffalo hunt, Sheridan traveled and camped along the now well-known route between Fort McPherson and Fort Hays. The region was familiar to him at the time of the royal buffalo hunt.[51]

About midway and midday on the trek to the campsite, the party halted at the prearranged location on Medicine Creek for lunch and a change of horses. There the party met First Lt. Joshua Fowler of Company K, who would escort them to the camp. The lunch reportedly consisted of sandwiches and champagne.

After lunch and a change of mounts, the party continued its journey to the camp, arriving just before sunset. The *New York Herald* reporter stated: "As we ascended some rising ground, we came in full view of a splendid military camp. The Stars and Stripes were seen flying from a towering flagstaff on a broad plateau. A cheer arose from every member of our party as this scene burst upon our sight. A few moments more and the band of the Second Cavalry was playing the Russian hymn."[52] The correspondent went on to note that the party gathered around a large campfire to warm themselves but found a few of their number missing. Among the missing were General Ord, Colonel Palmer, Lieutenant Colonel Custer, and Lieutenant Shirkoff. Sheridan was about to send out a search party when "Custer carrying his buffalo rifle on his shoulder, came striding down the hill, followed presently by the others, Palmer being the only missing man who did not finally come in afoot."[53] Their ambulance had broken down and forced the party to walk perhaps five miles.

The camp was described thus: "This Camp Alexis embraces about four acres of ground, and is situated on a low grassy plateau from which the snow has been removed at the junction of the Red Willow with one of its small but now frozen tributaries. The camp faces south, and looks out on Red Willow Creek."[54] The *Lincoln (Nebraska) Daily State Journal*, January 13, 1872, noted: "The camp consists of two hospital tents, ten wall tents, and "A" tents of the servants and soldiers. Three wall tents are floored, and the duke's is carpeted. Box stoves and Sibley stoves are provided for the hospital and wall tents. The hospital tents are used as dining tents. An extensive culinary outfit also is taken along." The *New York Herald*, January 16, 1872, described the dining area as two large marquese [sic] and as "handsomely festooned inside with flags." Dinner that evening consisted of choice wines and several courses of local game, including a prairie chicken shot in the head by Custer. Apparently the grand duke wanted to taste the American fowl.

Early on the morning of the fourteenth (the grand duke's twenty-second birthday), Cody departed the camp to scout for buffalo.[55] Before 10:00 a.m. he returned with information that a herd was grazing about fifteen miles away on the divide between Red Willow and Medicine Creek. Sheridan was somewhat indisposed and could not join the hunt but assigned Custer the task of instructing Alexis on how to hunt American Bison.

During the ride to the divide the grand duke availed himself of the opportunity to learn from Custer, and when they reached the herd, he was given the honor of the first kill.[56] Custer charged through the grazing herd, scattering them but singling out a large bull for the grand duke. Then he gave a signal to Alexis, who rode up firing his revolver (likely his new Smith & Wesson) into the bull's side. The wounded animal started down a ravine, where it was finished off with pistol and rifle, the first kill of the hunt. Alexis immediately drew his hunting knife or hunting sword and took the tail as a trophy.

The hunt continued until late afternoon, when the party returned to the camp, having killed four buffalo. Some accounts state that as many as twenty or thirty bison were killed, but given that other elements of these articles appear overstated, those numbers might be exaggerated.[57] The *New York Herald* of January 16, 1872, notes that yells announced the return of the successful hunters and that the camp responded in kind. When the party arrived in camp, they found Spotted Tail and his band already encamped in the valley of Red Willow Creek. Spotted Tail had arrived earlier in the day bringing with him between four hundred and six hundred of his band,

Figure 23. Grand Duke Alexis bringing down the first buffalo of the hunt. From *Frank Leslie's Illustrated Newspaper*, February 3, 1872.

including the warriors and the subchiefs Two Lance, Whistler, War Bonnet, and Black Hat. The evening passed with dinner and a recounting of the day's stories.

The morning of January 15 dawned cold but sunny. This day's hunt included Sheridan, Ord, Palmer, Custer, at least one of the Forsyths, Michael Sheridan, Alexis, Bodisco, and six or seven other officers. Assisted by an individual identified only as Shorty, Cody again acted as scout.[58] About thirty soldiers, Spotted Tail, and eight Brulé warriors accompanied the hunt party, making quite an entourage. Once again the party traveled about fifteen miles before encountering a buffalo herd. The party ranged over rougher terrain than on the previous day but with greater success. The grand duke is reported to have killed two buffalo, Sheridan two, Spotted Tail and his group eight, and the others varying numbers for a total of fifty-six. Grand Duke Alexis had the head of one buffalo and a buffalo calf brought back to camp so that they could be preserved and sent to Russia. Upon their return to the camp, the grand duke and others announced their arrival and success by firing their weapons into the air, and those in the camp replied.[59] The Tucker volume quotes an unattributed newspaper account saying that loaded firearms were not allowed in the camp, so they were discharged into the air on their return, and that instead of acknowledging the party by returning fire, the camp took up a cheer.[60] Michael Sheridan's horse foundered and had to be led back to camp, and according to the *Lincoln (Nebraska) Daily State Journal*, January 18, 1872, Custer's horse had been ridden so hard that it collapsed and died after he reached the camp.

That evening General Sheridan asked Spotted Tail to his tent, where he gave the Brulé leader a dressing gown, a general officer's belt, and a scarlet cap ornamented with beads. Both parties made speeches seeking good will between them. A war dance was then held for the grand duke and the hunting party, at which the younger warriors recounted their war honors in traditional style.[61] The *Herald* reported a mild flirtation with Spotted Tail's daughter by several of the assembled officers, including Lieutenant Clark and Lieutenant Colonel Custer. At the conclusion of the evening's festivities, Grand Duke Alexis presented the warriors with $50 in silver half-dollars, twenty blankets, and some ivory-handled hunting knives.

Aside from the buffalo-tail trophies and the buffalo calf and buffalo head that were to be mounted, Grand Duke Alexis received as a gift from a warrior, reported to be Two Lance, an arrow with which the Indian had brought down a buffalo earlier that day.[62] Some sources suggest that Chief Spotted Tail also gave or sold Alexis an Indian tepee and a bow and arrows. The grand duke reportedly took them back to St. Petersburg. Other sources suggested that the arrow, together with the bow and the tepee, were housed in a museum in the Russian city of Tver'.[63]

The Russian Point of View

The grand duke's hunt trophies and mementos might or might not still survive. Certainly we found no trace of them. Nor is Alexis known to have published his views of the buffalo hunt or of his world tour.[64] There is, however, a suggestion that he planned to do so. An *Appleton's Journal* note of January 10, 1874, states that a St. Petersburg correspondent to the *Baltic Gazette* had seen advance copies of a soon-to-be-issued first volume of the grand duke's account of his voyage.[65] This volume, which was to focus on his visit to the United States, included a warm expression of gratitude toward George Custer and for the Nebraska hunt. If the book was published, however, there is no record of it. Recently the grand duke's personal journals were found among the Yusopov family papers in the Russian State Library. The authors commissioned the Russian Baltic Information Center (BLITZ), of St. Petersburg, Russia, and San Diego, Calif., to research the journals for comments regarding the grand duke's American trip. The journals begin in 1869 but are sporadic and contain no entries for the world voyage despite a page having that title. Apparently there are no recollections from the grand duke himself regarding the trip.

When we began our research in the late 1990s, we realized that the archives of Russia were a potentially significant source of data regarding the royal buffalo hunt. Earlier attempts to penetrate the Communist bureaucracy had been for naught, but with the fall of Communism a new opportunity presented itself. A grant from the Nebraska Humanities Council enabled us to hire a Russian historian/researcher, Elena Tsvetkova, to delve into the various Russian state archives to see if any new information might come to light.

Tsvetkova did not find the grand duke's letter describing the hunt (although it appears that one did exist and is now lost), but she did find a number of interesting tidbits. Her research uncovered the diaries of Admiral Possiet (the grand duke's advisor and mentor during the trip) and letters from some participants, including the grand duke himself. These previously unavailable documents provide some insight into the attitudes and feelings of the Russians toward the people of the United States in 1871–72.

Alexis recorded some of his impressions of America and Americans, and he shared them in his letters home. He remarked on his visits to New York, Washington, Boston, Philadelphia, Detroit, and Denver, covering topics ranging from theater attendance to the hunts in Nebraska and Colorado.

Tsvetkova also transcribed and synopsized Admiral Possiet's files and handwritten diaries, or pocket notebooks, which now are in the Russian State Naval Archives.[66] During his travels he recorded his impressions and described the events of the trip. His diaries also contain entries pertaining to the grand duke's plans for and participation in the buffalo hunts.

According to a draft letter to the czar, during the planning process, Admiral Possiet excluded a trip to California from their program, which would have excluded the proposed hunting trip as well. He was concerned that winter was rather early that year and that the weather on the western "steppes" was expected to be poor. (He was concerned, too, with the safety record of western trains, which, he had heard, derailed rather often.) When a winter thaw occurred, however, General Sheridan renewed his invitation to Alexis to join the buffalo hunt. The original plan was to spend three or four days for the hunt and to return to North Platte Station before January 1, 1872, but when circumstances prevented the earlier trip, the middle January dates were settled upon.[67]

In his diary, Admiral Possiet described something of the trip and the hunt, which is synopsized as having arrived from St. Louis. General Sheridan and five of his officers accompanied Alexis during the hunt and then to Topeka. (From there, Sheridan and his officers returned to Chicago.)[68] The admiral's description of the view from his railroad-car window—small groves of trees at the outset and then no trees or bushes—is consistent with the changes that occur in landscape and vegetation between eastern and western Nebraska and on the Great Plains in general.

Possiet went on to say that they arrived at North Platte Station and went by "four in hand" to the small camp, named Alexis, that had been arranged especially for this hunt. There they spent three days in the tents. The weather was clear but cold, -5°C (23°F) at nights. Noting that Alexis said he had described the buffalo hunt in much detail in his letters to his father, Possiet decided not to repeat the hunt stories but limited himself to describing the effect of the hunt upon Americans. He observed that in the western states there were countless bison, that the size of a herd seemed incredible, and that because Americans were very interested in everything connected with the Great West, including buffalo, the imperial hunt appealed greatly to the American public.

Possiet also reported that Alexis showed himself to be a good shot. This fact, together with his pleasant manners and appreciation of the military, won the favor of Sheridan and his staff. Apparently impressed by the speed with which information on the grand duke's tour was disseminated, he noted that the telegraph sent messages all over the country at almost the same time that Alexis fired his first shot.

After the Nebraska hunt, Possiet accepted Sheridan's invitation for a new buffalo hunt during the visit to Denver.[69] He reported that they found a lot of buffalo not far from the railroad. When the hunters arrived at the Kit Carson station, at 9:00 a.m., they were supplied with horses from the nearest military post. Fifteen individuals galloped southward from the railroad, and they returned from the hunt before sunset. Alexis returned with Sheridan at 5:30 p.m. The party found several hundred buffalo, and Alexis returned with four tails. The diary entry notes that both the grand duke and Sheridan were delighted with the opportunity afforded by the second hunt. Heartened by the success of two hunts and encouraged by Sheridan, the grand duke wounded one more buffalo with a shot from a railroad car during their trip to Topeka. Thereupon the train was stopped and some of the party pursued the herd. The wounded buffalo fell behind the others, and with three additional shots, Alexis put an end to its suffering.

Among the most informative sources found in the Russian archives were the letters Alexis wrote to members of his family: Maria Fyodorovna, wife of his brother Alexander Alexandrovich, future Czar Alexander III; Empress Maria Alexandrovna, Alexis's mother; and Emperor Alexander II, his father. According to Possiet, a letter from the grand duke to his father contains a detailed description of the hunt and a letter to Grand Duke Vladimir Alexandrovich, dated January 24, 1872, also mentions the detailed description. Unfortunately this letter with a description of the hunt was not found. However, the few available letters and telegrams that Alexis sent to his relatives reveal that he felt the full range of emotions most travelers away from home feel from time to time.

On January 14, 1872, when Alexis turned twenty-two, he reported: "I spent my birthday on the hunt in the camp and nobody knew about it. I mean Americans." On the same page in this file is the telegram (in French) that Alexis sent to his father: "The courier arrived yesterday. Thank you from the bottom of my heart for the letter and wonderful gifts. I shot five buffaloes during the third hunt. I will write on Wednesday next time. Alexis."[70]

In a January 25 letter addressed to the Grand Duchess Maria Fyodorovna, Alexis wrote: "I often remember our evenings in the Green room and our theatrical performances at yours. I hope you have a good time attending balls. I remembered you during the hunt. You would be glad to ride along these immeasurable steppes." And then, probably referring to the gala thrown for him in Denver: "I danced with two young ladies, who killed two buffaloes themselves."[71]

One of the letters containing a more extensive description of the buffalo hunt was written to his brother Vladimir on January 24: "I wrote to Papa about the buffalo hunt. But I have to tell you that I was so happy to be on the buffalo hunt again. I had such emotions that it is even funny to remember. If you could be with me your soul would have begun to shake. What a pleasure! I also hope to have a bear hunt during our voyage along the Mississippi." The grand duke also sent a photograph of himself with General Custer, most likely one of the Sholten images taken in St. Louis. In the letter Alexis asks his brother to pay attention to the nine tails and buffalo head pictured in the photograph. At the end of the letter he tells Vladimir: "Hang [the photograph] up in the water closet in Tsarskoe Selo."[72] The statement is thought to be a joke or bit of humor.

Several telegrams in French from Alexis to his father are of general interest regarding his feelings about being in America and on the hunt. A telegram dated December 31, 1871, refers to a ball held in his honor in St. Louis and the impending trip to Omaha. Alexis noted that the "weather is excellent."

On January 16, after the Nebraska hunt party had returned to North

Platte Station, Alexis sent a telegram to his father. In it he notes that he camped on the prairies and killed buffalo, but he also expressed a bit of homesickness: "I am too sad because of my loneliness."

The next day he seemed much more positive when he sent another telegram to his father thanking his parents and family for the birthday salutations. He mentions that he has returned from the hunt, where he killed three buffalo, and that Indians had accompanied the party. He notes that the party is departing for Denver. Apparently his birthday gifts were delayed. He does not acknowledge their arrival, by courier, until a telegram of January 23, 1872, in which he mentions that five buffalo were killed on the Colorado hunt.[73]

Another informative collection found in the Russian State Naval Archive is in the form of diary notes and copies of letters written by V. K. Ienesh, warrant officer of the frigate *Svetlana*, to his relatives.[74] One letter in particular gives some insight into the feelings of some Russians toward America and its inhabitants. Many Russians might not feel too different today.

> It was necessary to spend the night in tents while roaming about the steppes and mountains. They [the grand duke and his companions] killed a buffalo. The Grand Duke and the youth [young men who accompanied him] were pleased, because privations were nothing for them. Though they did not suffer from too much comfort, the Grand Duke had comfort everywhere.
>
> The trip was rather expensive because everything in the hinterland is more expensive than in New York. And the sellers charged exorbitant prices knowing that the Grand Duke cannot bargain. Yes, much Russian money was given to our American friends. Though, after this they will not be considered our friends. All of us and the Grand duke personally saw how these people are. Almost all Russians say, without justification, that we (Russians and Americans) are close friends and ready to help each other.
>
> Where on earth did this friendship come from? And could it be between two people who are so different by their nature and the way of governing, etc.? We hope that this trip acquainted Russia with America, previously known through novels by [James Fenimore] Cooper. It must save us from vain dreaming about some unknown foreign friendship.

I repeat once more that I am more and more convinced that Russia is a good country and that Russian people are good and the present way of governing (especially under the present sovereign) is good for Russia.

Ienesh's concerns regarding the cost of the trip were not his alone. Admiral Possiet had earlier communicated to the czar his concerns regarding the cost of the American stay, reaching some $1,500 per day. Those expenses included not only board, room, and transportation but also gifts that the Russians assumed must be distributed liberally to dignitaries at the various stops.[75]

Government-to-government relationships between Russia and the United States were fraught with diplomatic pitfalls during this period, and the grand duke's visit was intended to help reinforce those ties. Generally the two governments enjoyed a positive relationship throughout most of the latter half of the nineteenth century. The conservative reaction to the assassination of Czar Alexander II and to the Jewish pogroms created a more critical view of Russia both in the government and among the general populace.

At the beginning of the twentieth century, however, after nearly fifty years of good will, a less-generous mood would descend on Russian-American relations, a mood that has far outlasted the era of good will.[76]

The End of the Hunt and the Beginning of Tall Tales and Lore

At about 9:00 a.m. on January 16 the hunt party departed the camp to return to North Platte Station.[77] As they had done on the trip to the camp, they ate lunch and changed horses at Medicine Creek. The party arrived at North Platte at about 5:00 p.m. and then dined in their rail cars. Immediately upon their return, Sheridan telegraphed Secretary of War Belknap, stating: "I returned here today with the Grand Duke and party. We had a very successful buffalo hunt. Killed Twenty-four yesterday. The weather has been delightful."[78] After dinner Alexis presented Cody with some money and a valuable scarf pin. The train pulled out at about 10:00 p.m. headed to Cheyenne and the next stage of the trip.[79]

Cody's account of the return trip has Sheridan giving him the reins of the grand duke's rig, telling him to shake him up a bit:

> The conveyance provided for the Grand Duke and General Sheridan was a heavy double-seated open carriage, or rather an Irish dog-cart, and it was drawn by six spirited cavalry horses which were not much used to the harness. The driver was Bill Reed, an old overland stage driver and wagon-master; on our way in, the Grand Duke frequently expressed his admiration of the skillful manner in which Reed handled the reins. General Sheridan informed the Duke that I also had been a stage driver in the Rocky Mountains, and thereupon His Royal Highness expressed a desire to see me drive. I was in advance at the time, and General Sheridan sang out to me:
>
> "Cody, get in here and show the Duke how you can drive. Mr. Reed will exchange places with you and ride your horse."
>
> "All right, General," said I, and in a few moments I had the reins and we were rattling away over the prairie. When we were approaching Medicine creek, General Sheridan said: "Shake 'em up a little Bill, and give us some old-time stage driving."
>
> I gave the horses a crack or two of the whip, and they started off at a very rapid gait. They had a light load to pull, and kept increasing their speed at every jump, and I found it difficult to hold them. They fairly flew over the ground, and at last we reached a steep hill, or divide, which led down into the valley of the Medicine. There was no brake on the wagon, and the horses were not much on the hold back. I saw that it would be impossible to stop them. All I could do was to keep them straight in the track and let them go it down the hill, for three miles, which distance, I believe, was made in about six minutes. Every once in a while the hind wheels would strike a rut and take a bound, and not touch the ground again for fifteen or twenty feet. The Duke and the General were kept rather busy in holding their positions on the seats, and when they saw that I was keeping the horses straight in the road, they seemed to enjoy the dash which we were making. I was unable to stop the team until they ran into the camp where we

were to obtain a fresh relay, and there I succeeded in checking them. The Grand Duke said he didn't want any more of that kind of driving, as he preferred to go a little slower.[80]

This story is surely a tall tale, although the newspaper accounts do mention that some springs were broken during the trip and that one ambulance carrying Consul Bodisco, Dr. Asch, Lieutenant Tudeer, and some others upset and rolled over coming down a hill. No one was injured, but it took a bit of repair work to get the wagon back on the road.[81] However, there are no contemporary records that Cody "shook up" the grand duke. Along with the flirtation with Spotted Tail's daughter, Cody's rough ride is really the first of many hunt-lore tales that appeared following the departure of the grand duke from North Platte Station.

Cody might legitimately have highlighted his hunting adventures with the grand duke to promote his Wild West Show, but he never did so. Beginning in 1892 a team of "Russian Cossacks" performed with Cody's Wild West Show. These trick riders, who actually were Georgians, performed in both Europe and North America for many years. They introduced very popular riding tricks and were featured prominently in the show posters and literature. But Buffalo Bill seems never to have mentioned his 1872 hunt with Grand Duke Alexis as his reason for having included the "Cossacks" in his show. He seems to have been happy to present royalty in promotional materials, but the grand duke and the hunt of 1872 never received that treatment.[82]

Initially the popular press followed the hunt avidly. As time passed, the story became less newsworthy, although the February 3, 1872, issue of *Leslie's Illustrated Newspaper* did devote a short story to the hunt. A week later, *Leslie's* was lampooning the Nebraska and Colorado hunts, depicting the grand duke, some Russians, and a few U.S. officers hanging from telegraph poles along the rail lines to protect themselves from an enraged bison. And then, on February 24, 1872, a reversal: *Leslie's* featured another cover page and story on Grand Duke Alexis's trip and the hunt, reporting the stay in the United States in a favorable light.

Embellished stories of the hunt began almost as soon as the party left the area. For example, by the time the grand duke had left the United States the story of Custer's "mild flirtation" with Spotted Tail's daughter had already grown to a tall tale. And the various editions of Cody's autobiography exaggerated the hunt story and his role in it. In fact, to promote himself and his Wild West shows, he used not only local booksellers but also peddlers associated with his shows to sell his books. Similarly, in the 1890s and early 1900s, peddlers associated with the show sold copies of the biography by his sister, Helen Cody Wetmore. Cody's posthumously revised autobiography originally appeared serialized in William Randolph Hearst's international magazine from August 1916 to July 1917. When the articles were edited and published as the posthumous autobiography, Cody's accounts were embellished even further.

Over the years the desire for recognition and association with the grand duke's visit resulted in stories and recollections that can be categorized only as imagination at work. Louisa Cody said she had hosted a dinner for the grand duke and other hunt-party dignitaries at her home at Fort McPherson.[83] But the party never visited Fort McPherson. Mrs. Cody invented the tale as spice to be added to her tales of her famous husband.

Similarly, research reveals that many old-timers' recollections of the hunt and of the grand duke's sojourn in the area are only poor imitations of past events. For example, William McDonald recalled his parents' description of the grand duke as tall and good looking and dressed in gray trousers and a green-trimmed jacket sporting buttons with the Russian coat of arms.[84] He also recalled them saying that the grand duke wore a close-fitting turban and carried both a Smith & Wesson revolver with U.S. and Russian seals and a large hunting knife. This description is almost certainly taken from contemporary newspaper accounts, as is his account of the remainder of the hunt. He mixes up the arrival of Spotted Tail and his band, the Indian dance, and the grand duke's birthday, and he provides a dinner menu taken from Davies's account of the millionaires' hunt of 1871 or from one of Cody's autobiographies.

Mayme Watts Langford recalled her parents' story that the army was short of wagons and wagon drivers for the hunt and asked local ranchmen to bring their roundup mess wagons to support the hunt.[85] Mrs. Langford recalled how after the hunt her father brought the hunt-party dignitaries to their home and her mother fed them a dinner of fried buffalo. Apparently staying in town that evening, Watts and Cody arranged for a banquet in the grand duke's honor at M. C. Keith's Union Pacific hotel dining room and that all the leading North Platte citizens attended. The kindness shown to the grand duke by the Wattses was repaid when he had a buffalo robe embroidered with Russian beadwork and sent to the family as a gift. The historical record does indicate two local men were employed as wagoners, but no contracts for the use of wagons during the hunt have been found. The grand duke's party did not stay in North Platte, nor did they have dinner there after the hunt. Rather, they ate on the train cars. And it seems unlikely that the buffalo robe was a present from the grand duke.

Yet another tale of the hunt is that of Ena Raymonde, an early settler in the North Platte area. A crack shot, she allegedly was the lone woman to participate in the hunt. Aside from the fact that Spotted Tail's band included families, and his daughter and wife were photographed at the camp, Ena Raymonde did not arrive in the area to visit her brother, William Herbert Palmer, until July 1872, some six months after the hunt.[86]

W. H. Palmer, who also went by the name William "Paddy" Miles, had a dugout on Medicine Creek in 1872. His humble home might have been the site of the horse exchange and lunch stop the army set up for the hunt. D. Jean Smith recounts the undoubtedly apocryphal tale that Paddy Miles (who might well have met the hunting party during their stop on Medicine Creek) purloined a revolver from the grand duke.[87] The only source for the story is Miles's 1894 autobiography, which is bits of fact laced with a great deal of fantasy and is corroborated by no other account, contemporary or otherwise.[88]

A bit more spice was added to the story by placing black soldiers in the camp as servants. The unidentified author added a bit of racist dialogue when one of the soldiers purportedly comes up to his colonel, salutes, and says, "Ah begs leave to report, sah, dat another of dem kings has done fallen off his horse." This statement, with its minstrel-show dialect, was published by Bayard Paine and repeated by others.[89] Paine loosely attributes the source to Helen Cody Wetmore, but research revealed no such statement in any of her works on her famous brother. The earliest-known source is an unattributed article in the *Columbus (Nebraska) Daily Telegram*, April 29, 1931, which leads off with a story about the recent finding of the campsite and then tells an invented tale of the hunt. The historical record clearly shows that no African American units were serving in the area at that time, but the account has helped obscure the real story. Since the 1930s most writers have relied on one or another of Cody's accounts and to a lesser extent on Miguel Antonio Otero's

My Life on the Frontier, 1864-1882, uncritically employing them in their retelling of the buffalo hunts in Nebraska and Colorado.[90] Other accounts employ the same sources but compound the problem by introducing additional errors, such as the assertion that the Union Metallic Cartridge Company rather than the Smith & Wesson Company supplied revolvers to the Russian government.[91]

Herschel Logan, an American firearms doyen, relies on Cody's autobiography for the story of the buffalo hunt, but he has an accurate historical perspective on the story of the Smith & Wesson revolver that the grand duke might have carried on the hunt.[92] Charles Pate's research revealed that the pistol was elaborately engraved and had ivory or pearl grips upon which were engraved the coats of arms of Russia and the United States.[93] The pistol and case cost Smith & Wesson $400, an immense sum for a gun at the time. Although it cannot be ascertained with certainty, the revolver likely was a Russian model just going into production. Photographs of the grand duke and Custer taken by Sholten in St. Louis show that the pistol butt had a lanyard ring, a feature called for in the Russian contract. Admiral Possiet was presented a nickel-plated Smith & Wesson Number 3 revolver, and other members of the party received other revolvers. During the visit to the Smith & Wesson factory the grand duke also visited the Union Metallic Cartridge Company factory and witnessed the fabrication of metallic cartridges being produced for the Russian military under contract.[94]

T. F. Drummond's account of the hunt is among the few that attempt to utilize multiple primary sources. His story is laced with quotes attributed to James Hadley's account of the hunt and to Chalkley Beeson's account of the Colorado hunt.[95] Hadley, however, was not a member of the royal-hunt party. He was not even in Nebraska at the time of the hunt. He relied on newspaper accounts but implied that he had met and become friends with the Russians, which is unlikely.

Even the usually reliable United States Geological Survey fell into the trap. A 1915 guidebook places the hunting party's starting point in Nebraska at Willow Island, between Cozad and Lexington, instead of at North Platte Station.[96] Alleged association with the grand duke was not limited to the buffalo hunts. New Orleans' Mardi Gras also has Alexis myths.[97] And the story that actress Lydia Thompson and actor Lawrence Barrett socialized with the Grand Duke Alexis is wishful thinking at best.[98]

Commemorating the Hunt Site

The hunt story and the campsite remained well known in the local lore of what became Hayes County, Nebraska. In the early 1880s, several early Hayes County pioneers homesteaded the campsite. Portions of the campsite were patented by Joseph Paxton (on July 6, 1881), John Ryan (on May 18, 1883), and Samuel Tate (on January 1, 1888). Two other early homesteaders filed on other portions of the campsite—Henry Sassman in 1878 and Andrew Chambers in 1884—but both filings were canceled within months of their respective filings.[99] The multiple filings likely represent the fact that the land was not good farmland and that Red Willow Creek and its tributary made access difficult. The campsite lay at the periphery of each of the original homesteaders' claims. As ranches grew and property was aggregated to make it more profitable, two families, the Mintlings and the Cliffords, split ownership of the campsite, and they still own it. Perhaps as early as the late 1880s, local homesteader Joseph Keepers began an annual Civil War veterans reunion at Paxton Grove, just north and west of the campsite.[100] In August 1931, when the veteran population had diminished substantially, early Nebraska settler D. F. Neiswanger purchased a monument to place at the site and the annual gatherings became the Camp Duke Alexis Picnic or Old Settlers' Picnic, and this continued until the advent of World War II. The Old Settler's Picnic included a carnival with rides, sideshows, and concessions in the creek bottom. At one point a concrete dance floor was constructed in the Red Willow Creek bottom. A baseball diamond and a rodeo ground were placed on the second terrace above the creek, directly on the campsite. With the beginning of the Old Settler's Picnic, there seems to have been a renewed interest in the buffalo-hunt story.

The Second Annual Picnic was held on August 13–14, 1932. The Dukes, a baseball team from Hayes Center, Nebraska, played teams from Holyoke, Colorado, and White City, Kansas. Speeches were the order of the day, with the usual array of local and state politicos addressing an estimated eight thousand attendees.[101] Judge Bayard Paine, whom the *Hayes Center Times Republican* ordained one of the best public speakers of his day, gave an address on the history of the royal buffalo hunt that was printed in toto in subsequent issues of the paper.[102]

Figure 24. David Frank Neiswanger, who commemorated historic sites in western Nebraska. Taken by Elbert Taylor in 1938, Nebraska State Historical Society T-239-1.

Figure 25. The Neiswanger Camp Alexis monument ca. 1938. The individuals are unidentified. Image by Elbert Taylor, Nebraska State Historical Society T-239-2.

Figure 26. The original commemorative monument at the hunt site, now in the Hayes County Courthouse. Photograph by Douglas Scott.

The author of several additional pieces on Camp Alexis, Judge Paine was among the earliest writers on the hunt to conduct research and sort out conflicting stories.[103] His first research relied heavily on the William Cody accounts.[104] Later, however, his efforts to determine the exact location of the camp led him to other sources. Among his finds was a letter published in the *Indianola (Nebraska) Reporter* on January 29, 1931, from Cody to Mrs. John Longnecker, who had inquired of him as to the actual site of the camp in 1894. The editor of the *Reporter* and D. F. Neiswanger had been looking for the site on Red Willow Creek. When a local landowner reported that he had homesteaded the land in the spring of 1872, shortly after the buffalo hunt, and had found many tin cans and some pegs driven into trees, the pair visited the site and found it appealing. Upon their return to Indianola, however, they learned of Cody's response to Mrs. Longnecker's inquiry. In the letter, which was dated summer 1894, Cody wrote: "Do you know where the old government road running from Ft. McPherson to the Republican crossed the Red Willow some twenty-five miles above the mouth of the Red Willow? Well, it was about one mile above where the road crosses the creek on the east side of the creek. Alexis camped there for several days in January 1872. The article says 73 but it was a mistake of the printers. P.S. As I am going to visit the old camping grounds some day, if you will let me know where you live I would be pleased to call on you and I would like to know how you like the country, etc."

In 1931, Neiswanger erected a red Colorado sandstone marker on the site of the camp as indicated to him by John Dunning, an early settler. When it was dedicated, on August 16, the story attracted newspaper attention across the state. As a consequence the hunt story, drawn from one of Cody's accounts, was resurrected and retold.[105] In 1988 the red sandstone marker, extremely weathered, was replaced by a granite marker and is now in the Hayes County courthouse.[106]

John Dunning carried the mail, twice weekly, between Indianola and Carrico in the spring of 1882. Three days each week he spent at a dugout in the midst of the campsite, and he walked the area many times. According to Bayard Paine, Dunning told him that in 1882 he could see lines where the tents had been banked, and he pointed out the site of the flagpole and the locations of six or eight of the larger tents.[107] At that early date he found pieces of old army wagons, great piles of glass from champagne bottles and beer bottles, a few cartridges, and many cartridge cases. Dunning also told Paine that he had found beads, flint arrowheads, and spears in the area. In 1932, however, when Dunning took Paine over the ground, there was no sign of an artifact.

Dunning undoubtedly misremembered some of his time on the site fifty years earlier. He might have seen glass from champagne and beer bottles, and he likely did pick up cartridges and cartridge cases. The banked tent lines, however, were a product of his imagination. The Eaton photographs show clearly that the tents were not banked. On the other hand, creating a platform for a tent might have entailed some leveling, and this might be what Dunning saw. (See chapter 5.)

Figure 27. Sites of the John Dunning dugout, the 1930s-era baseball diamond, and the modern hunt monument shown on an aerial photograph. Graphics by Douglas Scott.

In his 1935 book, *Pioneers, Indians and Buffaloes*, Paine republished portions of his 1932 address, including the Dunning story, but he also added a section on the story of the grand duke's visit to the United States and the hunt. For the hunt story, Paine had new primary sources, including contemporary newspaper accounts of the hunt preparations and the hunt itself. Using the newspaper and other sources, Paine spent several pages debunking Cody's and Helen Cody Wetmore's accounts by pointing out discrepancies between the newspaper accounts and the Codys' clearly exaggerated records.[108]

Paine's might have been the first attempt to separate hyperbole from truth in Cody's tales. Regrettably, few researchers who cite Cody's works have used or seem to be aware of Paine's critical analysis.

Interest in the hunt story and the location of the campsite appears to have waned after World War II. Several popular western writers kept the story alive throughout the postwar years, but strong popular interest in the site was absent for many years. However, the

Figure 28. Impersonators of George Custer and California Joe Milner at the 2009 rendezvous. Photograph by Douglas Scott.

story and the site got a second wind beginning with the replacement of the sandstone monument by the granite replica that was dedicated on October 12, 1988.[109]

The royal buffalo hunt story came to public attention again in the 1990s after the collapse of the Soviet Union. Several exhibitions of Russia's imperial past were shown in select cities across the United States. A 1997 exhibition titled *Jewels of the Romanovs: Treasures of the Russian Imperial Court* commemorated the 125th anniversary of Grand Duke Alexis's visit to the United States. The exhibit focused on the jewels of state and the many dazzling artifacts from Russian museums, but one small portion of the exhibit and its catalog featured the story of the grand duke's visit and mentioned the buffalo hunt.[110] A combined Russian and American exhibit that focused on Czar Alexander II and President Abraham Lincoln featured the buffalo hunt. A section of the exhibition catalog is devoted to the hunt story but is fraught with errors.[111]

Between 1999 and 2011 an annual reenactment and festival was held at Camp Hayes Lake on Red Willow Creek a couple of miles above the campsite. The festival celebrated the hunt story and the pioneer history of Hayes County. The celebrations included reenactors (portraying Sheridan, Custer, Cody, Grand Duke Alexis, and Spotted Tail), military-style tents and American Indian tepees replicating a period campsite, food (featuring buffalo), and tours to the campsite itself.[112]

5

EDRIC EATON AND THE HUNT PARTY PHOTOGRAPHS

An enterprising Omaha photographer took five and possibly six photographs while the hunt party was in the field. These remarkable images provide a vital source of information on events and activities at the hunt camp. Several images taken in Topeka and St. Louis immediately following the hunt add further background on the hunting party. Beyond technical details of the camp organization, these images present members of the hunting party in human terms and suggest much about how the hunters were clothed and behaved in the field. They indicate that participants in the journey were eager for photos that documented their experience, and they reveal popular curiosity in Alexis's activities. Photography truly seems to have been part of the adventure.

THE IMPERIAL PARTY PHOTOGRAPH

On January 22, 1872, as the hunt group was returning from Colorado, members of the imperial hunting party sat for a group photo in Topeka, Kansas. This was one of the last photographs taken on the grand duke's western sojourn, but because it shows the participants in clear detail, it helps interpret the stereographic images taken at camp. It was taken and copyrighted by J. Lee Knight, a former Civil

War captain and politically active photographer and graphic artist based in Topeka.[1] Because the backdrop is similar to that seen in other Knight photographs, the photo seems to have been taken in Knight's studio. Prints of the picture were offered by the State Record Printing House, Topeka, Kansas. That they are found in several public and private collections suggests that the picture was widely distributed. So that the participants could be identified easily, their names were printed at the bottom of the photograph. The participants are formally attired in anticipation of joining the governor and other state officials at a banquet and a joint session of the Kansas legislature that was scheduled during the stop in Topeka. The photograph shows only individuals who were actively involved in the hunt.

Figure 29. The imperial hunting party in Topeka, Kansas, January 22, 1872. Standing, L. to R., Frank Thomson, train manager, Dr. Vladimir Koudrin, Lt. Col. George Forsyth, Count Alexander Olsenfieff, Dr. Morris Asch, Bvt. Brig. Gen. Nelson B. Sweitzer, Lt. Karl Tudeer; seated, middle row, L. to R., Consul Gen. Waldemar Bodisco, Counselor of State W. T. V. Machin, Maj. Gen. Philip Sheridan, Grand Duke Alexis, Adm. Constantine N. Possiet, Lt. Col. George A. Custer; seated on floor, L. to R., Lt. Col. James Forsyth, Lt. Paul Shouvalov, and Lt. Col. Michael V. Sheridan. Courtesy Little Bighorn Battlefield National Monument.

Seated on a settee at the center of the image are the three senior officers. The grand duke is in the center with General Sheridan and Admiral Possiet flanking. Two Russian officials, Consul Bodisco and Counselor of State Machin, are seated to the left, and Lt. Col. George A. Custer is to the right, looking pensively downward with a heavy coat and a cape draped over his shoulders. Seated on the floor in the foreground are the next three ranking officers, Lt. Col. James A. Forsyth, Lt. Paul Shouvalov, and Lt. Col. Michael V. Sheridan. Russian and U.S. members of the party form the back row. This group includes, from the left, Frank Thomson (of the Central Pennsylvania Railroad), Dr. Vladimir Koudrin, Lt. Col. George Forsyth, Count Alexander Olsenfieff, Dr. Morris Asch (in uniform), Bvt. Brig. Gen. Nelson Sweitzer, and Russian Lt. Karl Tudeer (in civilian dress). Moving this group westward to their departure point at Fort McPherson, thence to Denver, and back to St. Louis involved complex coordination with Union Pacific and other carriers.

A second cabinet-sized image was taken of Sheridan and his U.S. Army contingent without the Russian dignitaries.[2] And two other images apparently were taken during the sitting: the first, of the imperial party, including Frank Thomson; the second, a full-length portrait of the grand duke in civilian attire.[3]

Scholten St. Louis Images

While the party was in St. Louis, James A. Scholten took another series of photographs of Custer and Grand Duke Alexis. Scholten entered the photography business in St. Louis in 1857, continuing the business until his death in 1886. A fire at his studio in December 1878 destroyed more than thirty thousand of his original negatives.[4] There are four known Scholten bust photographs of Custer in civilian dress with his fur-collared overcoat taken during the St. Louis visit. Three full-length Scholten images also portray Custer. In the first, Custer poses in his buckskin outfit with his Model 1866 Springfield sporting rifle. In the second, Custer reclines on the ground and the grand duke sits on a prop stump. In the third, Custer poses in his buckskin outfit and with his Officers sporting rifle, and the grand duke, in his hunting outfit, holds a puppy in his left hand and a revolver, likely his Smith & Wesson, in his right. Draped over a bentwood arbor in the background is buffalo-tail trophy. More famous

Figure 30. George Custer and Grand Duke Alexis posed with their hunting weapons, field dress, and buffalo-tail trophies of their hunts in Nebraska and Colorado. Courtesy Little Bighorn Battlefield National Monument.

among the Scholten images is the portrait of the grand duke seated on a prop stump and Custer standing on the left. The grand duke appears in his hunting outfit complete with leather belt from which a revolver and hunting sword are suspended. Custer stands with his sporting rifle in his left hand and a buffalo-tail trophy in his right. One buffalo tail is draped over a bentwood arbor, and four more are seen to the right of the grand duke.[5]

The Knight and Scholten images show clearly the facial features of main members of the hunt party and details of the grand duke's and Custer's hunting outfits. The images materially aid in the identification of several members of the party in photographs taken by Edric Eaton at Camp Alexis.

Eaton of Omaha Images

Accounts of the hunt appearing in the *Nebraska Intelligencer* on January 16, 1872, mention that Omaha photographer Edric L. Eaton took photographic views of Camp Alexis and the party. William Warren Tucker's compilation of the grand duke's travels in the United States simply notes a photographer was active in the camp: "An enterprising photographer, who had arrived in camp, took a picture of it as it stood with the grand duke, General Sheridan, and General Custer at the head, followed by the remainder of the Imperial suite, the officers and soldiers, and the great Indian Chief Spotted Tail and his band of experienced warriors."[6] Tucker's newspaper compilation mentions several specific views that were recorded, including a view of the party at breakfast, camp views, and photographs of Buffalo Bill and George Custer: "Before leaving the camp several photographs were taken by the enterprising artist. They will be interesting souvenirs, especially to the Imperial members of the party who participated in the hunting expedition with General Sheridan and His Imperial Highness. One large view was taken of the party as they sat a breakfast. Pictures were also made of the camp itself, and among the others which were taken by request of the Grand Duke were those of Buffalo Bill and General Custer in his buckskin hunting dress."

Until the mid-1990s Custer researchers thought that none of Eaton's photographs of the buffalo hunt had survived. None were known to have been published, and none had been found in archives. Since then, historical-image collectors Jim Crain and Larry Ness have found that the Smithsonian Institution and the New York City Public Library have between them copies of five stereographic images of the camp, images they kindly shared with us. In addition, at least four variations of a studio image of Buffalo Bill Cody were rediscovered. And we identified a published image of an Indian camp purported to be that of Lakota Chief Spotted Tail adjacent to the hunting party camp.

Today Edric L. Eaton is largely unknown beyond a small group of western-photograph aficionados, but in 1872 he was among the foremost photographers in Omaha. Edric was born in Franklin County, Vermont, on May 31, 1835. The 1850 U.S. Census shows Edric (spelled "Edrick") as residing in Enosburg, Franklin County, Vermont, with his family. His father, Man Eaton, is listed as a forty-four-year-old

Figure 31. Edric L. Eaton, self-portrait ca. 1870. From Edmunds, *Pen Sketches of Nebraskans*, 1871.

cabinetmaker; his mother, Mary, as a forty-one-year-old housewife. Also listed were an older sister, Sarah, age seventeen, and a younger brother, eleven-year-old Forrester.

By age fifteen, Edric had learned the profession of photography, and in 1857 he moved to Omaha, where he opened a photographic gallery.[7] Eaton is credited with being one of the first photographers in Omaha and with taking some of the earliest surviving images of the growing town. In 1859 he spent about six months photographing Mormon immigrants in and near Florence.[8] The *Nebraska Enquirer* of February 14, 1861, noted that he had opened "Daguerrean Rooms" in Omaha's Pioneer block (modern 1100 block of Farnam Street), where he would "secure the shadow ere the substance fades." Eaton's studio was over Rogers' Tin Store.[9] He remained in Omaha until the outbreak of the Civil War when he became a traveling photographer, apparently accompanying the Army of the Southwest.[10] Others record that he spent the war with the First Nebraska Volunteers.[11] If so he would have been in the Department of the Missouri and spent his time in Missouri, Arkansas, and Tennessee from 1861 to 1863, after which the First Nebraska Volunteer Infantry was reorganized as the First Nebraska Volunteer Cavalry and sent to guard the overland trail through Nebraska, Colorado, and Wyoming.[12]

In 1866, after returning to Omaha, Edric opened Eaton's Gallery of Art. In that same year he married Emma L. Salveter, a German immigrant from St. Louis, Missouri.[13] According to the 1910 U.S. Census records, they had four children, of whom two daughters, Fannie and Mabel, survived to adulthood. In 1867, Eaton's studio was at 15th and Douglas Streets, and he was in partnership with a man named Mueller. Apparently Eaton bought out the partner in early 1867, whereupon he remodeled the studio and was prepared to take "all kinds of pictures from gem photographs on a finger ring to a life-size portrait."[14]

Noted frontier photographer William Henry Jackson arrived in Omaha in 1867 and attempted to find employment with Eaton but was turned down.[15] Jackson found employment with rival photographer James Hamilton and, with his brother, bought Hamilton's studio in 1868 and Eaton's studio at 15th and Douglas Streets in 1869. Eaton apparently maintained another studio, at 234 Farnam, and continued to operate his business there: *Wolfe's Omaha City Directory 1870–1871* lists him as a photographer at that address. The 1870 U.S. Census lists Edric, Emma, and Fannie, as well as a twenty-year-old cook, Mary McCrea, a twelve-year-old servant, Annie Neidemier, a thirty-five-year-old laborer, Thomas Jeffris, and a twenty-two-year-old art-gallery employee, Lorenzo Burnhard (or Burnal), as residing with Eaton. In 1870 and 1871 Eaton provided thousands of photographic prints to be pasted into *Pen Sketches of Nebraska* (1871), essentially a compilation of biographies of prominent Omaha citizens.[16] Those acknowledged for having helped produce the book include Eaton, his assistant D. W. [should be "D. R."] Powers, and printers Frank Barlange, Henry Holt, William Griffin, N. Sheridan, D. Hays, Miss Lou Davis, and Miss Kate Metsker. The fact that none of the 1870 U.S. Census employees are listed in the 1871 book acknowledgments suggests a significant turnover rate in Eaton's studio employees. It is noteworthy that Eaton's operator, D. R. Powers, who is listed in the 1871 book and on the back of many of his 1870s stereographs, including those of the hunt camp, is not listed in the 1870 or 1880 Nebraska or Iowa U.S. Censuses, or at least cannot be reliably identified.

Sometime during the 234 Farnam sojourn, likely around the time of Eaton's documentation of the royal buffalo hunt, a young Swedish immigrant, Sophia Holt Nelson, found work with Eaton. At about the same time a young man, N. J. Anderson, found employment there. A romance blossomed, marriage ensued, and they became pioneer photographers in eastern Nebraska. In her later years, Sophia recalled that during her time in Eaton's employment she met William F. Cody, who was a frequent visitor to Eaton's studio.[17] She reported that Cody had Eaton take numerous images of him and was friendly enough with him to bring buffalo meat to the family and even a turkey on one Thanksgiving. She also recalled that Emma Eaton was a skilled crayon worker. At the time of the 1927 interview, Mrs. Anderson still retained a number of Emma's pieces, as well as photographs by Edric.

Eaton stayed busy in the photography business in the 1870s, taking photographs not only of people but also of Omaha's buildings and streets and of the Union Pacific Railroad. He advertised his images of Omaha views and of Indians for sale but made no mention of his photographs of the recent buffalo hunt.[18]

Eaton appears to have relocated to Chicago about 1892 to document the World's Fair photographically.[19] He died in Chicago on April 1, 1909, and is buried in the J2 Division, Plot 180 of Oakwood Cemetery.[20] His wife and children are also buried in the family plot. Apparently they died with no direct descendants.

Eaton's images of Camp Alexis are not particularly artistic, but they do document the dignitaries who occupied the camp on January 14–15, 1872. They are quite remarkable in that they were taken outdoors during the winter, and they document the camp as well as its distinguished occupants. Outdoor photography was not new in 1872, but the demands of the photographic process at that time make these images a testimony to the skill of the artist.

Eaton's camp stereographs were taken using the wet-plate process. This process required that a glass plate be coated with collodion, a mixture of nitrocellulose, alcohol, and ether at a temperature above 50°F and then, before it dried, that it be sensitized with silver nitrate, placed in a negative carrier, exposed in the camera for about one-fifteenth of a second, and processed before the plate could dry completely. Processing the negative required that it be fixed in pyrogallic acid and then stabilized in a hyposulfate of soda solution. Once fixed and dried, the negative was crisp, sharp, and stable, and many prints could be made from it.[21] Eaton likely had a portable darkroom, such as a tent or a wagon. Each photograph Eaton took required that he make a wet plate, take the photograph before the plate dried, and process the negative before he took the next shot.

Preparing an image might have taken as long as a half-hour from wet plate to finished negative. Even though the temperature might have been moderate for western Nebraska in January 1872, the party members in the photographs are bundled up for warmth, and the fact that the guidons are blurred in the images makes clear that the wind was blowing. Keeping the temperature in the darkroom above the required 50-degree minimum, probably by means of a stove, makes the fact Eaton that obtained the images a real achievement.

The Valley Camp Image

The first image we rediscovered, a purported view of Spotted Tail's camp on Red Willow Creek, had been published in 1894. Using his Buffalo Bill stage name, William Cody published an illustrated article in *The Cosmopolitan* entitled "Famous Hunting Parties of the Plains." With the caption "Camp of Indian Braves, Arranged for the Grand Duke Alexis," the reproduction is small, and the quality of the image is poor. As a consequence, details to be gleaned from it are limited.

Figure 32. An American Indian camp, purported to be Spotted Tail's, in the Red Willow Creek valley. "Buffalo Bill," *The Cosmopolitan*, December, 1894.

The scene depicts rising land or ridge lines in the background and an open, flat valley with scattered tepees. In the foreground is indistinct vegetation. What can be seen with certainty are at least twenty-three tepees or lodges in the foreground and middle ground. The tepees seem to be clustered in groups, a near group with five tepees clearly visible, a second with seven, a third in the far distance with at least six tepees, and several scattered as single or paired lodges. The clustering could indicate different band or family-group camping circles. One or more meat-drying racks can be seen between two lodges in the foreground. In front of the racks are a few linear objects, likely long wooden poles. In the middle ground is a group of dark objects, perhaps horses grazing between camp circles.

The general lay of the land in the photograph, with rising hills in the background, is similar to that of the Red Willow Creek drainage valley. And the fact that the lodges are in a valley is consistent with the historical description of the Spotted Tail camp location. Attempts to superimpose the image on the current terrain, however, have proven unsuccessful. The valley expanse might have changed as silt built up during floods, or as erosion dissected the valley floor or the hillsides. It seems unlikely, though, that the ridge profile changed enough to make superimposition impossible. Because this image is not attributed to Eaton, and no attributed Eaton image or stereograph card of the camp has been located, and because the only evidence that this is Spotted Tail's camp is the photo legend in the Cody article, it seems prudent to note that Cody's assertion cannot be confirmed by historic documents, photographs, archaeological materials, or photographic superimpositions. Regardless of Cody's attribution, however, the image is important in its own right as an early photograph of an American Indian village sometime prior to its 1894 publication.

Eaton Stereograph Number 1: "The start of the Grand Hunt. Grand Duke, Gen. Sheridan, Gen. Custar [sic], Gen. Forsyth, Gen. Ord, Buffalo Bill, and the Russian Officers."

Three copies of this stereograph are known to exist. Two are in private collections, and one is in the New York Public Library.[22] As described by the photographer, this image presents the royal party as it was about to depart for a day of hunting. We cannot be sure on which of the two days of the hunt the photograph was taken, but

Figure 33. Eaton Number 1. The mounted party ready to depart for the hunt. Jim Crain collection.

Figure 34. Those of the mounted party who can be identified: (1) Gen. Edward O. C. Ord, (2) Adm. Constantine N. Possiet, (3) Count Alexander Olsenfieff, (4) Dr. Vladimir Koudrin, (5) Grand Duke Alexis, (6) Lt. Gen. Philip Sheridan, (7) Lt. Col. George A. Custer, (8) Lt. Col. James Forsyth, (9) Lt. Paul Shouvalov, (10) Consul Gen. Waldemar Bodisco. Jim Crain collection.

because it shows the camp well pitched, and because no Brulé Sioux are present, it likely was taken on the morning of January 14, before Spotted Tail and his group arrived. The party is posed in an open area behind a group of tents. Estimating the size of the area where the party posed is difficult because there are few obvious boundaries. Based on estimates of the average horse size, however, the front row of riders covered a width of at least sixty feet.

The apparent leaders of the hunting party, the front row of riders, consist of four mounted men. A number of less well organized riders are arrayed around and behind them, and seven standing figures are visible. Details are less than perfect, but based on clothing and carriage, the hunt leaders' identities can be suggested if not completely confirmed.

Grand Duke Alexis is mounted on a dark horse at the center of the first row. He appears to be wearing a Cossack-style astrakhan-fur hat and a bulky, belted overcoat. Three riders are to the grand duke's right. The closest, on what seems to have been a fidgety steed, is General Sheridan, wearing a bulky overcoat. Beyond General Sheridan, George Custer is strikingly posed on what might have been a gray horse. He is wearing his distinctive astrakhan hat and buckskin jacket.

To Custer's right, at a slightly different angle, is a rider slightly separated from others in the row. It might be Lt. Col. James Forsyth but cannot be positively identified. The separation might suggest that he was not one of the hunt leaders but one of the group behind them. Because that group was not arranged precisely, its members cannot be identified or even clearly counted, but they are close enough to the leaders to have been a part of the main party. There also seems to have been a space between them and a third, larger, group of riders. All appear ready to cry "tally ho" and be on their way. The evidence of this image suggests that the hunting party was both carefully structured and quite large.

The large mounted figure to the far left of the grand duke might be Gen. E. O. C. Ord, commander of the Department of the Platte. The figures between Ord and the grand duke are out of focus and cannot be identified. The one in light-colored clothing might be William Cody, but this is by no means certain. To the right of the hunt leaders are three men standing beside one of the tents that formed the side of the open area of the camp. Their similarities to figures identified in the formal photograph of the hunting party taken in Topeka at the end of the hunt enable us to give them tentative identifications. The man nearest the riders, with his hands in his pockets, seems to be Lieutenant Shouvalov. Beyond him, wearing a felt hat and a long coat unsuitable for a hunting trip on horseback, is Consul Bodisco. That he appears to have only one hand in a pocket suggests he might have been smoking. The third figure cannot be identified. Standing apart from one another without apparent clustering, they seem to be on the margins of the action.

By contrast, the four men standing to the left of the grand duke seem to be more prominently placed and posed. It is not certain that they were ready to join the hunt, but some of them might be set up for more than a day in camp. Most of them wear short-billed caps, but one wears a Hesse Homburg dress hat. All have short coats that could have been worn while sitting a horse. The man nearest the grand duke looks directly at the camera and appears to hold a cigar in his left hand. He cannot be identified with certainty but might be Dr. Koudrin. Next to him is Count Olsenfieff. Admiral Possiet is wearing a felt hat and perhaps no more than a suit coat and vest. He seems the least ready to take part in a day of hunting. The fourth man, wearing a short coat, cannot be identified.

Clearly the hunters were the central focus of this image, but tents visible beyond the departing hunters present information on the organization and appearance of the camp. The largest tent in the picture, at the far right, appears to be a pair of 11-foot-high hospital tents pitched end to end. The end of the tent is not visible, but it seems to match the tent arrangement described as the main mess tent. Each tent section is equipped with a stove, indicated by a stovepipe passing through the tent roof. The pipes come out of different sides of the roofs, however. The pipe at the end of the tent nearer the hunting party is on the left side. On the farther section of the tent, the pipe is on the right side. The arrangement is the same on the tent that was the backdrop for the photograph of Spotted Tail and Custer.

Opposite the narrow end of the paired hospital tents, the image shows what appears to be the rear of a row of three tents with a ridge height of some seven feet. These probably are comparable to common wall tents, but because the photo does not show that they have side walls, they might be "A" or wedge tents.[23] Whatever their style, they were not equipped with stoves. Pitched in a row that faces and is perpendicular to the long axis of the hospital tents, they appear to open toward the hospital tents and to be no more than ten feet from their entry.

Eaton Stereograph Number 2: "The Grand Duke, Admiral and Russian Officers, with Spotted Tail and Eight Chiefs."

This second stereo view of the camp depicts a mixed group of whites and American Indians standing in front of several tents on flat ground. The group, clearly bundled in winter garb, appears to number about thirty individuals arranged in a slight semicircle. Most are in focus; those who are not probably moved during the exposure process. The Indians are on the left; the whites, on the right. Some individuals can be identified: Admiral Possiet, possibly Dr. Koudrin; Count Olsenfieff; Spotted Tail's daughter; Spotted Tail; Grand Duke Alexis; Lt. Col. George Custer; Maj. Nelson B. Sweitzer; Lieutenant

Figure 35. Eaton Number 2. A group of standing members of the camp. Jim Crain collection.

Figure 36. Those of the standing party who can be identified: (1) Adm. Constantine N. Possiet, (2) possibly Count Alexander Olsenfieff, (3) possibly Dr. Vladimir Koudrin, (4) Spotted Tail's daughter, (5) Spotted Tail, (6) Grand Duke Alexis, (7) Lt. Col. George A. Custer, (8) Maj. Nelson B. Sweitzer, (9) Lt. Paul Shouvalov, (10) Lt. Col. George Forsyth, (11) blurred figure, might be William F. "Buffalo Bill" Cody, (12) Consul Gen. Waldemar Bodisco. Jim Crain collection.

Shouvalov; Lt. Col. George Forsyth; a blurred figure who appears to be attired in buckskin outfit, possibly William Cody; and Consul Bodisco.

Immediately behind the people are canvas tents. One is to the extreme left; then after a gap, at least two additional tents tops are seen behind the center part of the group. A swallow-tailed cavalry guidon is clearly seen flapping in the breeze to the immediate right of the left tent. The left tent is large and is at an angle to the photographer, with part of the side and the end visible. The guidon pole being nine feet tall, the tent to the left is likely the end of a hospital tent. A top to another large tent, possibly a wall tent, with a stovepipe protruding from it is visible behind the middle of the assembled group. Additional stovepipes and part of a tent apex are visible to the right of the middle of the group. There might be a total of five stovepipes, and these likely represent tents arranged in a row and viewed at an angle slightly oblique to their long axis. They appear to be separate from the hospital-tent line. The background of the image shows rising ground and a ridgetop with snow drifts scattered across the ridge face. Shadows fall to the right of the figures, suggesting that the image was taken in the early morning hours and roughly from the southeast. The fact that Spotted Tail and some of his band are present and that the image was likely taken during the morning hours suggests that this image was taken on the morning of January 15 or 16. Spotted Tail and his entourage did not arrive on Red Willow Creek until the evening of the 14th, and they departed during the day on the 16th. The fact that Sheridan and the imperial party departed around nine o'clock on the 16th, limits the time when the image was taken to the morning hours of those two days.

Two copies of this image are known to exist. One is held by the New York Public Library; the second is in a private collection.[24]

Eaton Stereograph Number 3: "Private Tent of the Grand Duke."

The discovery of the stereoview of the grand duke's tent, with a view of its interior, was one of the more exciting elements of the research. Two copies of the image are known to exist, both in private collections. A third might exist in a public collection, but this has not been confirmed. The image depicts an end-on view of the grand duke's private accommodations with two men flanking the opening and what appears to be a U.S. guidon on a pole just to the right of the tent front quarter. To the viewer's right of the tent pole, a third individual, Spotted Tail, is seated on a wooden chair, possibly the same chair seen in view 6, with a buffalo robe draped from it. Spotted Tail wears a fur hat and has a Spencer carbine cradled in his arms. The

Figure 37. Eaton Number 3. The tent of the grand duke. The individuals depicted in the photograph are, L. to R., possibly Dr. Vladimir Koudrin, Chief Spotted Tail, and Lt. Paul Shouvalov. Douglas Scott collection.

man to the right of the noted Lakota chief wears a long overcoat and a small billed cap similar to the modern captain or Greek fisherman's cap. The individual to the left, with a partially open overcoat and a brimmed homburg-style hat, might be Dr. Vladimir Koudrin.

The foreground is relatively flat and appears devoid of snow. In the background, patches of snow lie on terrain that rises toward a ridgeline. Along the left side of the image, near a snow patch in the middle background, is a series of at least five small "A" or shelter tents. Because they are seen from the side and at a slightly oblique angle, parts of their ends can also be seen. They are arranged in a line running perpendicular to the long axis of the grand duke's tent. Just beyond the small tents is a group of dark, nearly indistinguishable objects. These might be horses on a picket line.

The near middle ground behind the grand duke's tent shows three more tents seen end on. Clearly seen to the left of the grand duke's tent is a tent with a portion of its door flap visible. The rear quarter of a second tent is seen to the right edge of the image, and the peak of a third, with a stovepipe protruding from it is behind and slightly to the right of the grand duke's tent.

A regulation wall tent was 8 feet 6 inches high, 9 feet long, and 8 feet 11 ½ inches wide. The walls were 3 feet 9 inches high. Judging from the guidon pole, which was 9 feet in length, the grand duke's tent and the one to its right are wall tents, and the one to the left might be a common tent or "A" tent, which was only 6 feet 10 inches tall. The tent behind the grand duke's is likely a wall tent as well.

The grand duke's tent is supported by guy or eave ropes, three of which, with their wooden stakes or pins, can be seen on the left side of the tent. Two similar stakes are visible on the right side, and part of a third guy rope is evident. On the left side of the image another set of guy ropes slopes downward to the right. These undoubtedly lead to another tent pitched to the left of the grand duke's.

A vertical tent pole is visible at the grand duke's tent entrance. Regulations called for the poles to be 10 feet 2 inches long with a 4-inch iron spindle at the top to fit through the ridgepole. Given the height of the tent, the pole was set into the ground about eighteen inches. Leaning against the upright entrance tent pole is a military-style, three-band infantry rifle. The photographic details are not clear enough to identify the weapon, but it is likely a Springfield Model 1866, 1868, or 1870 .50–70-caliber rifle. Possibly the rifle is William Cody's famed Springfield Model 1866 that he was renowned for using during his buffalo-hunting days. Buffalo Bill is known to have loaned his rifle, which he named Lucretia Borgia, to the grand duke during some of the hunt. If the image was taken while the hunt party was away, the rifle might be a just a rifle that was around camp and employed as a convenient prop. The *Lincoln (Nebraska) Daily State Journal*, January 23, 1872, reported, "Three wall tents are floored, and the duke's is carpeted." The tent has a wood floor, but no carpet is visible.

Wooden floors for camp tents are nothing new. Little is written on the subject, but the army often employed wooden floors in long-term camps and hospitals during the Civil War. When men and officers floored their tents, they did so at their own expense. A Delaware officer describing his effort to deal with chilling winds and rain in his camp near Alexandria, Virginia, in December 1863, wrote, "I first only put a board floor in my tent."[25]

In the summer of 1867, when General and Mrs. Custer abandoned their tent following its near-collapse during a severe rainstorm at Fort Hays, Mrs. Custer noted: "The voices of officers in an adjoining tent called out to come over to them and said there was yet room for more in his place, and, besides it had a floor. It was a Sibley tent, which having no corners with which those Kansas breezes can toy is much more secure. The officer owning the tent had taken the precaution, while at Leavenworth, to have a floor made in sections, so that it could be easily stowed away in the bottom of a prairie-schooner in marching."[26]

The grand duke's tent furniture includes a small, four-leg parlor or box stove in the left front, with the stovepipe running out the left side of the roof. The stovepipe protrudes well above the roof line and well above the height of the guidon pole seen to the right of the tent. This suggests that the total height of stove and stovepipe is about ten feet. A wooden bucket sits to the side of the stove but toward the front of the tent. There appears to be a small crate or box near the left side of the tent behind the stove. Near the center rear of the tent are two large crates set on their ends next to one another. The rough, broken edges on the bottoms of the crates suggest that they are storage crates pressed into expedient service. Small objects, possibly cloth covers and towels and a shaving mug and brush, rest on the top surface of the crates. Spotted Tail's position obscures the contents on the right side of the tent.

The upright pole and the rifle cast shadows nearly straight back into the tent, falling just to the left of the upright. The figures, tent pegs, and guy lines all cast shadows nearly aligned with the long axis of the tent. The position of the shadows suggests that the image was taken near the time of the sun's zenith on January 14 or 15, 1872, probably while the majority of the party was out hunting and certainly after Spotted Tail's arrival on the 14th. Given the angle of the sun in winter, the tent likely faces to the south.

A single, narrow shadow extends from near the bottom right of the image well past the right side of the tent. The width of the shadow and its relative length suggest a sizable lone pole, perhaps the flagstaff. If so the flagstaff was positioned to the left front and at least ten feet away.

Eaton Stereograph Number 4: "Spotted Tail Head Quarters, with Favorite Squaw and Daughter."

Unlike other photos Eaton took during the buffalo hunt, this image shows only native participants. In that regard it emphasizes Indian participation in the hunt and documents the "wild" nature of the affair. Placing the image within the context of the campsite, however, is difficult. Three copies of the image are known to exist. One is in a private collection. One is in the National Anthropological Archives of the Smithsonian Institution.[27] The third is in the New York Public Library.[28]

The photograph is well composed. Its center is a roughly pitched conical tent set near the edge of a flat surface that, on the right side, falls away into a wooded valley. The tent was far enough from the valley edge on the left side of the image to accommodate a parked wagon. Two women are seated in the tent entrance. Beyond the wooded valley the horizon is formed by high ground and some rather sharp cut banks. Relatively little snow is visible, but the photograph conveys a cold, wintry feel.

Eaton identified the women as Spotted Tail's "favorite squaw and daughter." Both women wrap themselves in blankets and look in the general direction of the camera. They are seated on the ground in front of the tent entrance behind what appears to be a small pile of firewood. The woman in the tent entrance appears younger. She has her hair combed back and behind her ears. The other woman, seated to the right and slightly farther from the entrance, appears to be older. She wears her hair down.

The caption describes this tent as Spotted Tail's "headquarters," but it seems to be an almost expedient structure. It follows the general model of a conical plains tepee but is constructed of improvised materials. The frame, composed of irregular small logs and branches of varying length, is atypical of formal plains tepees. These "poles" are so variably shaped and poorly trimmed that they cannot be counted, but there must be at least ten arranged in a circle. Normal practice in tepee construction is to tie the poles together, but these seem simply to rest on a single crotch and a nest of interconnections. This frame is covered by what appears to be a canvas tarp. The corners of the tarp meet above the entrance, which is directly opposite the wagon. They are gathered in a tight point, but below that the cover hangs loose and is amply bunched on the ground.

EDRIC EATON AND THE HUNT PARTY PHOTOGRAPHS 97

Figure 38. Eaton Number 4. Spotted Tail's lodge with his wife and daughter seated at the entrance. Jim Crain collection.

A large portion of the tent frame is left open to the sky. All this suggests that the tarp was a simple rectangle rather than the fitted semicircular "tent cover" of the formal plains tepee.

The proximity of wagon to the rear of the tent seems significant. The wagon is uncovered, but three cover frames or bows are in place. Likely the tent frame was set up so that the wagon would provide a windbreak and so that the wagon cover could conveniently be pulled onto the pole frame. The wagon, lightly built and with few iron strap reinforcements, does not appear to be army issue. The army wagon had several iron straps along each side. The wagon in the photograph has a simple, straight-sided box without sideboards. Whereas army wagons typically were painted army blue with a prominent block "US" in black on each side, this wagon is painted with lined details.[29] The spring seat and fourteen-spoke rear wheels are consistent with those of the common nineteenth-century farm wagon, and the fine-lined paint scheme is similar to that on wagons being produced both by the famed Studebaker Company of South Bend, Indiana, and the Peter Shuttler Company of Chicago. No horses are visible in the photo; presumably they were pastured or picketed elsewhere.

No fire is visible in the photo, but the woodpile near the entrance suggests that one was maintained in the tent. The base of the tent appears to be ringed by buffalo hides. These cover most of the visible side of the tent, and the presence of a dark mass behind the seated women suggests that the hides continued all the way around the structure. Piled this way, the hides would have added bulk and insulation to the tent, functioning like a windbreak. More formal windbreaks were commonly found around tepees of the plains tribes during the nineteenth century.[30] The hides shown in the image appear to be unprocessed. That both wooly and smooth sides of the hides are visible suggests that they were piled rather than folded. The number of hides shown in the photo is not clear, but there easily could be fifteen or twenty in the visible pile. This seems to be where the party's buffalo hides were gathered, and the number suggests that the photo was taken late in the hunt.

Because no other identifiable feature or structure is visible in this photo, it is hard to know how Spotted Tail's "headquarters" related to the rest of the hunting camp. The image does, however, present information suggesting that it that was located well away from the rest of the action. The large wooded drainage immediately behind the tepee is not apparent in any other camp photo. With clearly visible cut banks, the horizon of this scene also differs from any other that Eaton recorded. Furthermore, whereas in virtually all of Eaton's other images, the shadows fall to the left, in this scene the shadows fall to the right. Assuming that Eaton framed his pictures so that the sun was "over his shoulder" to illuminate the scene he was recording, the shadows in this picture indicate that it probably was taken from west to east in the afternoon. In other words, Spotted Tail and his party seem to have occupied a separate area of the campground.

Eaton Stereograph Number 5: "Buffalo Bill Mounted."

No actual image of this title is known to exist. Images with this title on Eaton imprint stock are known, but the image is of Buffalo Bill either standing alone or seated alone. In a third variation, labeled Number 7, Buffalo Bill is standing with Professor Henry A. Ward.[31] One online attribution of this variation has Ward erroneously identified as Allan Pinkerton. In a fourth variation, Ward stands holding a Winchester Model 1866 rifle, and Cody, standing at his side, holds a Remington Rolling Block rifle, likely a Model 1867.[32] Unlike other Camp Alexis images, all the variations of Number 5 were taken in a studio setting. Cody is attired in what appears to be a fur-trimmed, fringed buckskin suit. He wears a low-crowned, wide-brimmed hat (known today as a "sugarloaf hat") cocked to one side on his head. In the image in which Cody is seated, he cradles a Remington Rolling Block rifle in his arms. The background appears to be a plain wall, possibly plastered, with a wide baseboard. The floor is covered with a patterned carpet. In the images in which Cody is standing, a photographer's posing stand can be seen behind each figure.

Knowing that Ward did not meet Cody until shortly after the buffalo hunt, we think it unlikely that the images were taken in the field.[33] Indeed, an Eaton image of George O'Brien (Brevet Brigadier General Seventh Iowa Volunteer Cavalry) known to have been taken in 1870 or 1871 has this same studio background.[34] The posing stand seen in the O'Brien image is identical to the one behind Cody in the Cody-Ward image. It appears that both the Cody image and the Cody-Ward image were taken in Omaha after the hunt. As Ward's son noted, Ward did not participate in the hunt but met the party on their return to North Platte. His purpose was to pick up the grand duke's trophies for mounting. It is also possible that Ward met the grand duke's party in New York sometime earlier and ran into Cody only when he picked up the buffalo trophies. Cody's autobiography states that, immediately after the hunt, he returned to Fort McPherson with General Ord and then, intending to become a showman, left western Nebraska by early February 1872 and made his way eastward.[35] Perhaps Cody accompanied Ward back to Omaha when Ward took possession of the grand duke's trophies for taxidermy and mounting in late January or early February. Cody and Ward did travel to Chicago together, and Ward was traveling eastward by February 8.[36]

The Eaton Number 2 image of the party standing in the camp shows an individual who might be Cody. He appears to be wearing the fur-trimmed buckskin outfit seen in the standing and seated images. The image is consistent with the description of Cody as he appeared on horseback to guide the hunting party from North Platte Station to the camp on Red Willow Creek.[37]

In his *Ten Days on the Plains*, Henry E. Davies described Cody as wearing an outfit similar to the one he wore during the "millionaires' hunt" of the preceding September and October. Davies described the outfit as a "light buckskin, trimmed along the seams with fringes of the same leather, his costume lightened by the crimson shirt worn under his open coat, a broad sombrero on his head." If this is Cody,

Figure 39. Eaton Number 5. William F. "Buffalo Bill" Cody seated in Eaton's Omaha Studio. Jim Crain collection.

Figure 40. A variation of Eaton Number 5. Professor Henry Ward and William F. "Buffalo Bill" Cody at Eaton's Omaha Studio, probably shortly after the hunt. University of Rochester.

the buckskin suit corresponds to the one depicted in Eaton's indoor scenes. This embellished buckskin jacket or one nearly like it is pictured in later Cody photographs.[38] By the time of the later images, beadwork or quillwork had been added at the shoulders and along the back of each sleeve, and metal, probably brass military buttons, also had been added. But the cut of the garment and the cut of the fur trim on the sleeves, around the collar, along the bottom, and up the front opening clearly show that this is the coat featured in the earlier images, or a close copy. A profile photograph of Custer seated in a chair is held by the Kansas State Historical Society. In it he is wearing civilian clothes and his astrakhan-fur hat.[39] The image is purported to have been taken in Omaha in January 1872. The background, while indistinct, is similar to the background seen in the Cody and Cody-Ward images. The images are unattributed, but the background and context suggest that the photographer was Eaton.

Variations of the Buffalo Bill image are known to exist in several private collections as well as in public collections. Number 5, Buffalo Bill seated alone, is in the New York Public Library.[40] The Ward-Cody image is in the archival collection of the Rhees Library at the University of Rochester, New York.[41]

Eaton Stereograph Number 6: "Gen. Custar [sic] and Spotted Tail at the Grand Duke's Mess Tent."

The second image "discovered" during the initial research is a stereographic view of George Custer and Spotted Tail posed in front of an army hospital tent. Two copies of this image are known to exist, both in private collections. Spotted Tail stands at the tent entrance with Custer to his left. Seated on a wooden chair, Custer holds the barrel of an officer's customized sporting rifle, its butt on the ground at his side. He is dressed in a fringed buckskin coat and dark astrakhan hat, almost certainly the buckskins and fur cap he wore in the photograph taken with the grand duke in St Louis at the end of their hunting trip.

After studying Custer's personal firearms for many years, C. Vance Haynes, Jr., published a treatise on the subject.[42] One section deals at length with Custer's Springfield .50-caliber sporting rifle, which is easily recognizable. Among the most significant specific insights to be derived from this image is confirmation that Custer did indeed wear his buckskin suit in the field, not just in the photographer's

Figure 41. Eaton Number 6, Lt. Col. George A. Custer and Spotted Tail seated in front of the hunt-party dining tent. Larry Ness collection.

studio. Douglas McChristian's insightful study of Custer's buckskins supports the conclusion that this is the first buckskin suit the company tailor, Pvt. William Frank, made for Custer.[43] Custer had company tailors make three buckskin suits for him. Two survive today; he wore the third (pictured at Camp Alexis) at the Little Bighorn.

In Number 6 Custer seems well bundled and stiff. His legs are crossed, and he looks to the photographer's left. Custer's chair appears to have four turned legs with a separate back that was drilled into the top of the seat. The type cannot be identified, but it is consistent with early Indian War period barrack chairs. Chief Spotted Tail appears to have moved during the exposure: details of his dress and appearance are unclear. He appears not to be wearing a hat, but he has a robe wrapped around his shoulders and a long narrow object (perhaps a rifle) cradled in his arms. He looks directly at the photographer.

The scene beyond these two famous figures seems to have been selected primarily as a backdrop. It is not embellished or elaborately prepared, but it does present details about the equipment, construction, and organization of the camp.

The central feature of the image is the end of a large white tent. The photographer composed the image on the end of tent so that its sides are not visible, but based on apparent size and shape, it can be identified as a variant of the U.S. Army Hospital Tent. The pictured tent is about twice the height of Spotted Tail, which would make it similar to the regulation height of a hospital tent, which was 11 feet.[44] The regulation width, 14 feet 6 inches, likewise seems consistent with the scale of the two figures standing in front of it. There appear to be some differences between this tent and the official design authorized in the later Indian War period. The Camp Alexis tent has three tie closures rather than four on the door, and it has no peak ventilator. In spite of these minor variations, the tent seems to be regular Army equipment.

The tent does not appear to be well pitched. Regulation upright poles measured 12 feet long with 6-inch iron tips to fit into the ridgepole. Because the upright poles passed through the 3-inch ridgepole and supported the 11-foot height of the tent, their bases had to be buried some 15 inches in the ground for the doorway to rest on the ground. The pictured tent has a noticeable drape from the ridgepole, and the bottom of the door does not rest on the ground. A strip of "ground cloth" might have covered the gap, but the picture suggests that the tent was a drafty dining area.

Behind Custer, at the front corner of the tent, the picture shows what appears to be a piece of rustic furniture. Resting on the ground, its base is a square section of board. Attached to that board (presumably with nails) is a branching section of a small tree. The trunk was cut off just below a crotch, and the top was formed by a horizontal cut through five branches. Comparing it with the height of the side of the hospital tent, which by regulation was 4 feet 6 inches, suggests that it was slightly more than 3 feet high. The function of this object is not clear, but it might have served as an expedient rack.

In addition to the postholes at the center of the front and the back walls, this tent would have had seven tent "pins" at the base of both walls. Regulation "small pins" for a hospital tent were 20 inches long, suggesting that they would reach at least 12 to 14 inches into the ground. The pictured tent does not have a fly. Its roof edges would have been pulled taut by at second set of seven small pins driven three feet from the side wall to hold rope lines or guys. These pins made small but potentially visible subsurface irregularities that might survive archaeologically.

Because the interior of the tent is not visible, its floor and fixtures cannot be seen, but the exposed area below the door suggests a ground cloth, possibly overlying a wood floor. The photograph shows three stovepipes immediately behind the tent front. The largest, on the left side of the tent, seems to reach the height of the ridgepole. The other pipes are on the right side. Probably there are two tents, pitched end to end, with a stove in each. The rearmost stovepipe, which appears to be smaller in diameter than the other, is some distance behind the dining tent.

The photograph reveals that another tent was set up to the left of the dining tent. The visible portion shows that it probably was a wall tent, which had side walls 3 feet 9 inches high.[45] These tents seem rather close, but because both were supported by side pins, they must be roughly 5 feet apart. Nothing is visible beyond the smaller tent.

The shadows visible in this image deserve some discussion. Shadows cast by Spotted Tail, Custer, and the rustic "rack" are all clear. They indicate that the picture was taken when the sun was rather low and generally over the photographer's right shoulder. More problematical is what might be a larger geometric shadow cast over the tent's lower left corner. This shadow, which appears clearly on both images, might have been produced by the corner and ridge of another tent, where its flat ridge and sloping roof met. If so, the shadow would indicate that another tent was set up directly across from where Custer and Spotted Tail were posed. Combined with the possibility that the stovepipes are evidence of other tents arranged directly to the rear, the shadow makes it appear that the "Duke's Mess Tent" was in the midst of a series of tents that faced the same direction.

The small area to the right of the mess tent provides no evidence of a tent on that side. Behind the tent, however, a couple of features are visible. In the middle background, well behind the tents, are some white objects initially thought to be canvas coverings, possibly for crates.[46] Magnification suggests, however, that they are small canvas tents seen from the side. At least three are visible. They appear to be aligned with one another and arranged in a line running perpendicular to the axis of the dining tent. These tents appear to be small shelter or wedge tents, also called "A" tents, likely occupied by the soldier escort. Some dark objects near the tents could be human figures. In the far background, below the ridges, are other white objects. Using electronic filters and enhancers in Adobe Photoshop, we determined them to be canvas covers on wagons. They depict a part of the wagon park at the camp. Some indistinct dark objects appearing with the wagons might be horses hitched to the wagons.

The story of the dining parties within the tent conjures up many images of a banquetlike atmosphere in which toasts with wine and champagne must have been frequent. The historical accounts refer to Eaton's having taken an image of the hunt party at breakfast, but of course the absence of adequate light would have prohibited him from photographing the dining parties. Unfortunately the breakfast image, if it was taken, is not known to survive. However, a sketch of an earlier hunting-party dinner associated with an 1867 buffalo hunt in Kansas might be similar to the tent arrangement and interior organization at Camp Alexis. The hunt, a "match" or competitive hunt, is recalled by Elizabeth Custer in *Tenting on the Plains:* "The officers regretted our absence at their great 'feed' as they termed it, and it must, indeed, have been a great treat to have for once, in that starving summer, something palatable.[47] Two wall-tents were put together so that the table, made of rough boards, stretching through both, was large enough for all. Victors and vanquished toasted each other in champagne, and though the scene was the plainest order of banquet, lighted by tallow candles set in rude brackets sawed out of cracker-box boards and fastened to the tent-poles, and the only draping a few cavalry guidons, the evening brightened up many a dreary day that followed."

A sketch of the dinner party accompanies Mrs. Custer's description.[48] Signed in the lower right corner by Albert Berghaus, it depicts the scene just described. Berghaus, an artist with *Leslie's Weekly*, signed all the sketches accompanying the book. They are not period pieces but were drawn to illustrate Mrs. Custer's prose. The publisher probably hired Berghaus to illustrate Mrs. Custer's book.[49]

The image of the interior of the dining tent depicts a rectangular table around which are gathered military officers in their dress uniforms. The officers are seated on folding camp chairs or on wooden crates with nails clearly evident. General Custer stands at the near end of the table on the side opposite the viewer. He is speaking or offering a toast. The table is devoid of plates or food, but wine bottles

Figure 42. A Berghaus sketch of the 1867 buffalo-hunt dinner, which might be similar to the dinners of the royal buffalo hunt, in 1872. Elizabeth Custer, *Tenting on the Plains*, 1893.

and stemmed wine glasses are evident. Cavalry guidons and a regimental U.S. flag decorate the tent. In the left foreground is a small, rude, rectangular table on which are several wine or champagne bottles and a tureen. On the near side of the small table and beneath it are open crates of wine or champagne, and three bottles are sitting on the ground. The ground is depicted as grass. Lettering appears on the boxes, but is backward, possibly the result of the printing or etching process. Even though this sketch likely was done simply as an illustration for *Tenting on the Plains*, it does reveal what the dining-tent layout might have looked like. Additions to the tent would have been good-quality china dinnerware and perhaps a serving service. Decorations might have included imperial Russian flags or bunting to honor the grand duke. The sketch certainly evokes the camaraderie that usually resulted from the free flow of wine throughout the evening.

What the Photographs Mean

Photographs like those presented here are of real value to students of the West because they provide visual evidence than can be used to judge the veracity and quality of the written records. These photographs are consistent with some published descriptions of Camp Alexis but are in marked conflict with other parts of the written record. The stereographic photographs confirm, for example, that most of the hunting party, including the grand duke, and their escorts lived in army wall tents. The view of the interior of the grand duke's tent suggests that, in general, the tents were simply furnished. The grand duke's tent was supplied with crates for storage and for his toilette articles. Stovepipes in the images reveal that the tents generally had heating stoves, and the grand duke's was no exception. His tent was floored, but, contrary to some reports, no carpet is evident. The dining tent, two hospital tents set end to end, appears to have been warmed by a couple of stoves.

The photographs show that the camp had an orderly arrangement, which appears to be four rows of wall tents oriented roughly east to west. The southern row appears to have had at least three tents. In the next row the dining tent is on the east side and a wall tent and at least one other tent are on the west side. The next row to the north has at least five wall and wedge tents, all with stoves. And the northernmost row has at least three "A" tents, the center one having a stove. Running perpendicular to the main line of large tents are two parallel rows of "A" tents set at some distance from the main cluster. A minimum of three tents is seen in the eastern row and perhaps four or five in the western row.

Thus there are at least two hospital tents, used for dining, and thirteen "A" tents arranged in four rows. This is consistent with the majority of observations that the officers and the dignitaries lived in ten or twelve "A" tents. The smaller "A" tents in the far background appear to run in a line perpendicular to that of the wall tents. The two rows appear to be aligned north to south and facing each other on opposite sides of the larger tents. The smaller tents are likely for the two cavalry companies and the band that provided logistical support and entertainment for the hunt party. If there were four enlisted men to a tent, then about thirty-one tents would be needed to accommodate the approximately 125 men who made up the two cavalry companies and band. If each tent slept six men, about twenty-one tents would be required. Either way is consistent with the total of thirty to forty other tents noted in the credible historic accounts. The tent arrangement—officers on one end pitched tents in parallel lines running perpendicular to the officers' line—and the parking of wagons well off to the north indicate that the camp followed standard military protocol for a camp arrangement, and they are consistent with General Sheridan's penchant for organizing camps according to regulation.

6

THE ARCHAEOLOGY OF CAMP ALEXIS

The buffalo hunt required logistical support in the form of a field camp. Because military personnel supervised its construction, we can assume that Camp Alexis was well organized and carefully policed. Still, because much of what was brought there was intended for consumption, the camp passed quickly. Everyone there, nonmilitary as well as military residents, worked with chilled fingers that fumbled with gloves and extra buttons. These are conditions that create an archaeological record. Litter and loss would have been unavoidable. This chapter presents the archaeological record of Camp Alexis. The goal is to use the things left or lost at the site as a new source of information about the grand duke's western adventure. To do so, we shall explain how artifacts were recovered and describe those artifacts as residue of camp activities and human behavior.

The tools of modern archaeology run the gamut from traditional to modern. As the need to find, assess, and recover cultural resources with minimal time and resource expenditure becomes more pronounced, archaeology is constantly expanding its toolkit with techniques that save both time and money. Many geophysical and remote-sensing techniques have been applied to archaeology, and although these techniques can yield outstanding results, they also require significant investments of money and time for both equipment and personnel. Metal detectors, for example, can identify sites quickly and accurately. After much discussion and some debate, procedures for the application of metal detectors to archaeological sites have become standardized. Metal detection is the method we employed in looking for and defining Camp Alexis.[1]

Surveying Camp Alexis

Local tradition has long placed the campsite on a low plateau just north of Red Willow Creek where it joins a tributary that has formed a ravine along the eastern boundary of the site. This area has several distinct landscape features. The first to be considered is the floodplain of Red Willow Creek. According to the Natural Resources Conservation Service, the floodplain, which consists almost entirely of fluvaquental silt loam (a young, gray, unlayered sediment resulting from flooding), is frequently flooded and likely is aggrading. Oral histories of the region confirm that there have been floods. The soil shows signs of possible cultivation. It is not now under cultivation, but because it is heavily vegetated, reconnaissance efforts are difficult.

The second landscape feature is the lower plateau directly north of the junction, the site of the monument to the royal buffalo hunt. This plateau, which consists mostly of sulco silt loam (a very fine sandy loam), has three sides. Two have moderately steep slopes that drop down onto the floodplain; the third slopes up onto a higher plateau. The third feature is the southern portion of the higher plateau. This plateau, composed of sulco and sulco-ulysses silt loam (fine sandy loam found on well-drained areas), is much larger than its lower counterpart. It is bounded on the east by the previously mentioned ravine and on the west by a high ridge that drops abruptly into Red Willow Creek. To the south the terrace slopes down to the small plateau on which the buffalo-hunt monument is located. The ravine forms a boundary between this area and the fourth feature, the northern part of the plateau. This feature, whose soil is similar to that in the southern part of the plateau, includes the ravine or erosional cut that divides the two areas.

During 2008 and 2009 the University of Nebraska Summer Field School in Archaeology performed two-day archaeological investigations of Camp Alexis. The fieldwork was intended both to determine the presence or absence of physical evidence that would corroborate the historical record and oral histories and to determine if Camp

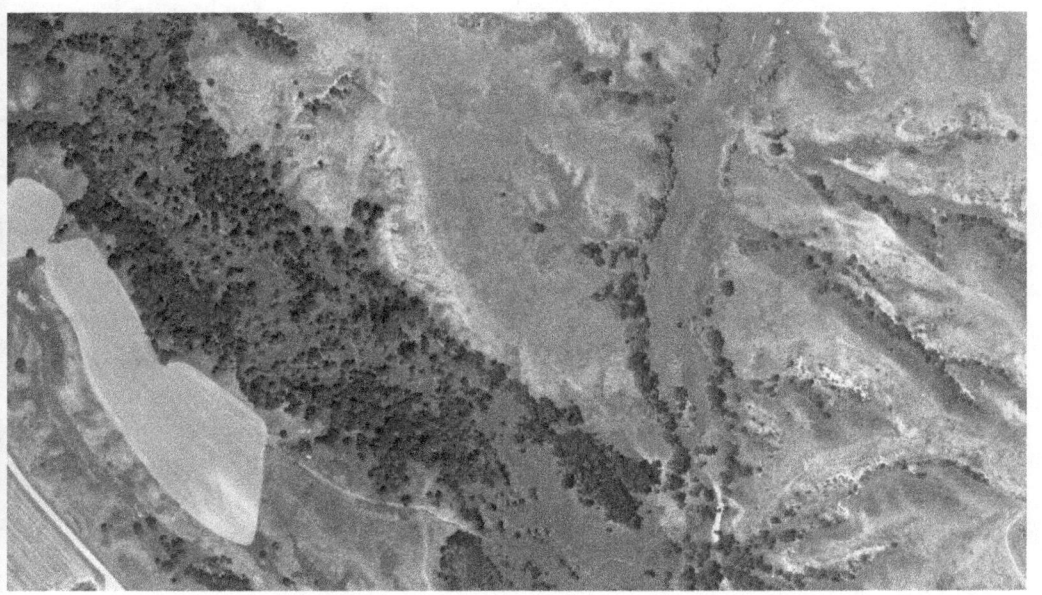

Figure 43. The traditional Camp Alexis site is in the lower part of the triangular upland at the juncture of Red Willow Creek on the left and an unnamed tributary on the right. Photograph by Douglas Scott.

Figure 44. The monument on the lower terrace of the site commemorating the royal buffalo hunt. Photograph by Douglas Scott.

Alexis was located on the traditional site. The survey was divided according to the four landscape features. The northern floodplain of Red Willow Creek yielded no metal-detector hits other than modern debris. This absence is likely caused by the aggrading nature of the Red Willow Creek floodplain. If any early materials are present, they likely are buried well beyond the reach of metal detectors.

The lower plateau—home to the buffalo-hunt monument—was surveyed next. Metal materials from later periods were recovered en masse, most notably bottle caps, cone-top beverage containers, and wire. An early- to mid-nineteenth-century iron awl and an iron scraper also were recovered.

The third area, the southern part of the higher plateau, was bounded on the south by a large bundle of chicken wire and on the north by a ravine. The chicken wire is likely the remains of the baseball backstop in use on the site during the 1930s. High-resolution aerial photography reveals the outline of the baseball diamond. This survey zone revealed the majority of recovered artifacts and the highest concentration of hunt-camp materials.

The northern part of the plateau, defined by a ravine cut into the terrain, was the last surveyed. It is a large area but, beyond some scattered 1870s-period materials, yielded few artifacts.

Starting on the floodplain of Red Willow Creek, metal-detection sweeps were performed using the transect method.[2] There were no artifacts. Next the plateau immediately surrounding the monument was searched. With two notable exceptions—one iron awl and a small iron scraper blade—only modern debris was recovered. The modern debris was not recorded. Moving up the slope to the north, researchers surveyed the plateau above. The southern portion yielded mostly modern debris, including the chicken wire that most likely was a baseball-field backstop. Farther onto the plateau, however, bona-fide nineteenth-century artifacts emerged. Machine-cut nails were the most common. Recovery efforts also found nonmetal artifacts such as ceramics, charcoal, and glass. Initially these were recorded under the field-specimen number assigned to the nearest metal artifact the detector had located, but when we realized that further recovery efforts might compromise data the metal detectors were unable to locate as well as their context with other artifacts, we halted the reconnaissance. It became clear that the distribution of nonmetallic artifacts was extensive and not directly linked to artifacts being located with metal detectors. The campsite certainly

Figure 45. Members of the 2008 University of Nebraska Summer Field School in Archaeology working in a cluster of metal finds at the campsite. Photograph by Douglas Scott.

holds many more artifacts and has more information to offer, but traditional archaeological techniques are better suited to the recovery of that information.

The 2009 effort focused on the upper terrace. In searching for evidence of the camp, we crossed this part of the campsite with 3-meter-wide transects oriented east to west. Starting at the edge of the upper terrace near the large deposit of woven wire, transects moved northward as far as the base of the large rise or hill. Next the transects swept up the slopes of the westerly rise to its crest. Then a set of north-south transects, run on the west side of a pasture fence from the base of the rise to the edge of the upper terrace, completed the 2009 field investigations. Artifact recovery in 2009 was similar in type and quantity to that in 2008. During the 2009 metal-detector survey of this area, the distribution of modern material was recorded, but the items were not collected. The distribution of modern and late historic artifacts was plotted in an effort both to document the range and distribution of the modern debris and to determine how they impacted the buffalo-hunt campsite.

Archaeological Results

Tradition holds that the buffalo-hunt camp was on a small plateau north of the Red Willow Creek, and in 1931 a monument was erected on that plateau at the purported site of the grand duke's tent.[3] A contemporary account of Camp Alexis describes the site: "This Camp Alexis embraces about four acres of ground, and is situated on a low grassy plateau ... at the junction of the Red Willow [Creek] with one of its small but now frozen tributaries.... The camp faces south, and looks out on Red Willow Creek."[4]

The greatest concentration of 1870s-era artifacts came not from this lower terrace but from the upper plateau. The upper area also had a significant concentration of post-1872 material, ranging from wire nails and woven wire-fence fragments to tinfoil soda-bottle liners, cigarette-package liners, and plain tinfoil. Some recovered artifacts could not be dated accurately. They might be from any period of use at the site. As the detectors moved farther to the north, the artifact concentration dropped off markedly. The southern edge was bounded by the chicken wire. The eastern edge was bounded by a ravine that, when surveyed with metal detectors, yielded no significant results. Where the ravine jutted into the plateau, dividing the area into two parts, several tin cans and suspender buttons were recovered. Possibly it was a trash dump for the camp. Defining the western edge were a high ridge, upon which no artifacts were found, and a fence that demarked the property line. The northern edge, which is the least defined, produced a gradually declining concentration of ferrous materials, period and otherwise.

The Artifact Assemblage

A metal-detection survey of the campsite vicinity exposed an array of objects. The numerous wire nails, fence staples, aluminum-can fragments, and crown bottle caps could be identified easily as postdating the hunt. These items had not been developed when the grand duke came to America. By contrast, the assemblage of arti-

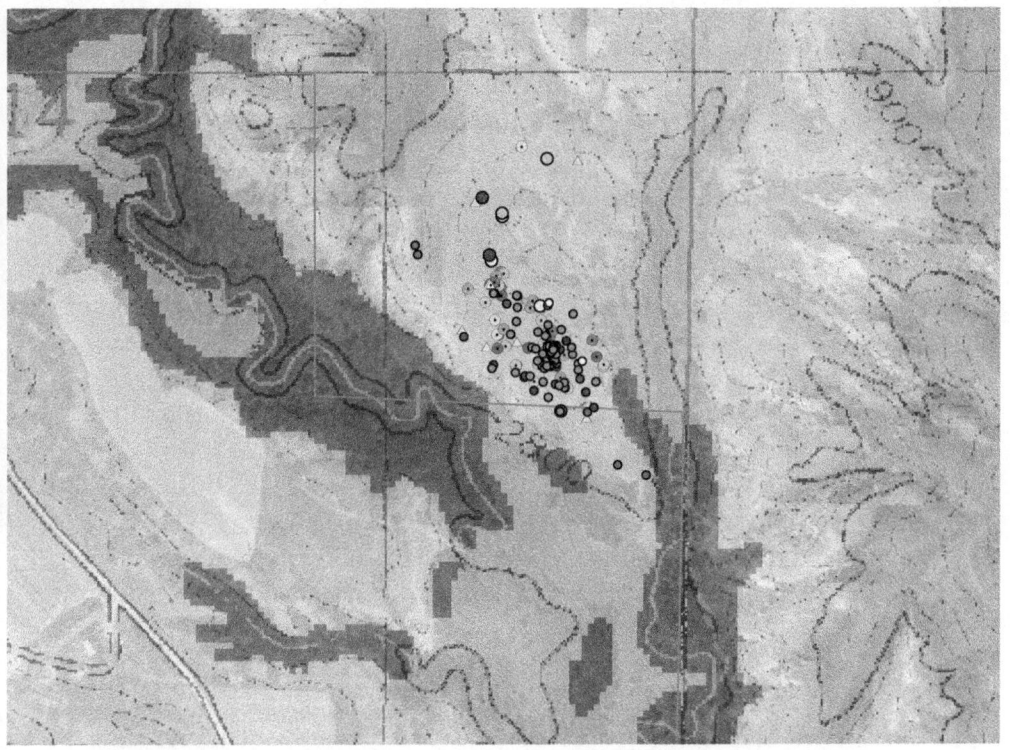

Figure 46. The circles on this topographic map of the site reveal where metal artifacts were recovered during field investigations by the University of Nebraska Summer Field School in Archaeology. Graphics by Douglas Scott.

facts dating from the 1870s—the archaeological record of the grand duke's American sojourn—is quite modest.

The American Indian Assemblage

The landowners do not recall finding stone artifacts on the Camp Alexis site, but the number of precontact sites nearby and in the Red Willow valley confirms that American Indians visited the site. Our survey techniques are unlikely to have identified stone tools, pottery, or other nonmetal objects, but in the course of exposing a "target" identified by a metal detector on the upper terrace, we did find a single stone flake (FS4) that appears to be a piece of lithic debris created during tool production. We cannot guess what kind of tool was being made or when the stone working took place, but it certainly predates Spotted Tail's visit in 1872. By that time, stone tools were obsolete. The waste flake reminds us, however, that the familiarity Spotted Tail's community brought to their guiding duties in 1872 drew on a deep past.

Two American Indian metal artifacts form the major discoveries from the lower terrace of the campsite. We began our metal-detection survey here because it is near the campsite marker. We crossed it systematically but found very little pre-twentieth-century material. The major discoveries were an iron awl (FS1) and an iron scraper blade (FS2). The awl is a very nice one and rather large, 182 mm (7⅜ inches) long. It is pointed at both ends and has a spiral twist in the midsection. Bipointed awls were a primary part of a Plains Indian woman's sewing kit. The scraper blade (FS2) is flat bit of steel plate about 35 mm (1⅜ inches) long and 31 mm (1⅖ inch) wide with one end slightly curved in a convex form. It is less than 4 mm (5/32 inch) thick. Women of the plains tribes used scrapers like this, bound to the curved end of elk-antler handles, to clean buffalo hides. Neither of these pieces would have been especially valuable, but each was an important domestic tool that appears to be in a usable state. This makes it probable that they were lost rather than discarded. Hides generated by the hunt party would have required a great deal of skin cleaning and sewing. Hence the awl and the scraper blade could date from the grand duke's visit. Still the fact that the area where they were found contained few other nineteenth-century artifacts suggests that the lower terrace was not heavily occupied at that time. The awl and the scraper blade might also be the residue of earlier postcontact Indian visits to the site. They offer further evidence that native people used the site that was selected for the grand duke's visit.

The fourth American Indian item (FS185) seems to have been associated with the grand duke's visit. A trapezoidal sheet of silver, it measures 35 mm (1⅖ inches) by 13 mm (½ inch) by 25mm (1 inch). The narrow edge seems to have been the top: a 3 mm (⅛-inch) hole was punched near its center about 3 mm (⅛ inch) from the edge. The punch left a burr that was filed flat: the file marks are still clear on the surface. The wide edge is slightly rounded and has six small, irregularly spaced notches filed into one side to create a decorative effect. The piece seems to have been entirely hand made; possibly it was recycled from a larger object. It would have been a handsome

Figure 47. American Indian tools. An iron scraper blade and an awl found during the fieldwork. Graphics by Douglas Scott.

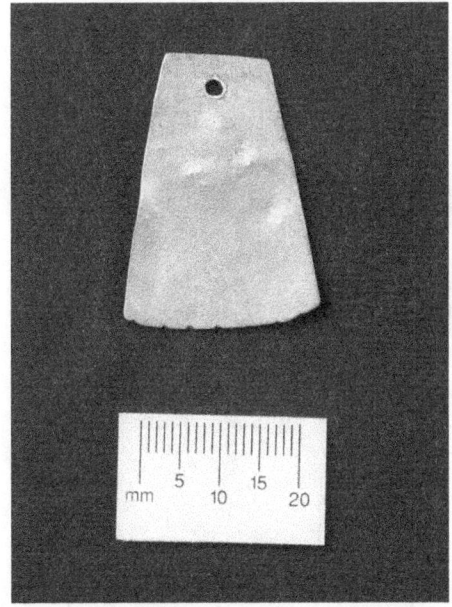

Figure 48. American Indian German silver dangle, likely from an earring. Graphics by Douglas Scott.

dangle or earring drop. It was found near the photographically identified site of Spotted Tail's tepee. Similar drops can be seen on earrings worn by Black Elk, a Lakota, in a late-nineteenth-century photograph. And in an 1833 Karl Bodmer painting a Blackfoot warrior's war shirt is decorated with silver ornaments, several of which resemble the specimen recovered at Camp Alexis.[5] In a photograph

Figure 49. Photograph of Spotted Tail taken by Alexander Gardner at the 1868 Fort Laramie Treaty. (The hoop earring in the inset has a dangle resembling that found at Camp Alexis.) Nebraska State Historical Society.

taken by famed Civil War photographer Alexander Gardner during the 1868 Fort Laramie Treaty negotiations, Spotted Tail himself wore hoop earrings with a similar drop.

Personal Items

As we surveyed the campsite and began discovering artifacts from the right era, surveyors joked about finding a "double-headed eagle" button. Photographic evidence indicated that the grand duke did not wear clothing that fastened with fancy metallic buttons. Nor did we recover anything like that. In fact the only personal artifacts recovered from Camp Alexis appear to have been lost by soldiers. Four army buttons were found. Two are U.S. Army general-service blouse buttons, both with eagles on them. One (FS92) is an enlisted general-service button.[6] The other (FS10) has a "C" for Cavalry on the center of the eagle, and the back is marked "Waterbury Button Company." Both are consistent with 1854-pattern cavalry-service buttons and could have been worn on an enlisted man's blouse coat, woolen greatcoat, or forage cap. The other two buttons (FS93 and 96) are iron, slightly concave, undecorated, four-hole buttons. They are consistent with suspender or fly buttons used on military trousers throughout the Civil War and the Indian War.[7] The other personal item is a brass stud (FS48) 13 mm (½ inch) long and 19 mm (¾ inch) in diameter across the head. This item could be associated with leather harness but is more consistent in size and shape with the studs used on Civil War-era straps for the cavalry saber belt.[8] We have no evidence that the cavalrymen who served the grand duke carried sabers, but they certainly seem to have worn sword belts.

Figure 50. Iron trouser buttons (top row) and two army general-service buttons and a saber-belt stud (bottom row) from the camp area. Graphics by Douglas Scott.

Construction Materials

Camp Alexis was a community of tents, and artifacts recovered from the site indicate where those tents were located and that some tents were equipped with constructed elements, such as racks and wooden floors.

Machine-cut nails or "square" nails, so called because of their tapered square shafts, form the bulk of the collection from Camp Alexis. These nails replaced hand-forged nails early in the nineteenth century, and they were superseded by "wire" nails, which have round shafts.[9] Mass-produced throughout the later nineteenth century, machine-cut nails are a mainstay of frontier archaeology. Wire nails were introduced in 1886, but machine-cut nails dominated the market for some time after that. In 1872, at the time of the buffalo hunt, only machine-cut nails were available to the troops charged with setting up the camp. The great majority of the nails were found on the eastern side of the upper terrace, indicating that this is where the majority of the floored tents were set up.

Nail sizes are given using the traditional pennyweight (d) system. Many sizes were available to the men who set up and maintained Camp Alexis, but the nails found were 10d or smaller (see Table 1). Small nails (2d and 3d) constitute 16 percent of the assemblage. They were suitable for light work, such as holding the sides of boxes and crates. Medium nails (4d to 8d) could be used to join one 25 mm (1-inch) board to another but would not reach through a 50 mm (2-inch) thickness. Thus they were suitable for making a flat board surface, such as a tabletop or a tent floor. This size constituted 66 percent of nails recovered from the campsite. The largest, 10d, nails were substantial connectors. They could join a pair of 25 mm (1-inch) boards with enough left over to "clinch." These nails represent only 18 percent of the assemblage. The nails found at Camp Alexis are clear evidence that the camp builders worked with light lumber. They may have opened light boxes and crates made of boards less than 13 mm (½ inch) thick. And they might have had boards up to 25 mm (1 inch) thick. But few if any boards were 50 mm (2 inches) thick. This is significant because it suggests that the officers' wall tents were not set up with board frames that could add strength to the ridgepole and the upright poles. Framed wall tents can be quite solid, but the archaeological evidence indicates that Camp Alexis had lots of loose canvas.

THE ARCHAEOLOGY OF CAMP ALEXIS

Figure 51. Small and medium-sized cut nails found at the campsite. Graphics by Douglas Scott.

The condition of nails—how they were bent and broken—reveals how they were used. Straight nails are easily measured and described, but nineteenth-century woodworkers commonly bent, broke, or "clinched" nails. Clinching occurred when, after a nail was driven in, its point was hammered over at a roughly 90-degree angle. This was done to strengthen the connection.[10] There are few clinched nails from the camp, and essentially all are medium-sized nails that could have been used only to attach pairs of boards each less than 25 mm (1 inch) thick. That is the kind of work involved in making the flat floor for a tent.

Well-struck cut nails do not bend easily when they are being driven, but bending and breaking occur regularly when nails are "pulled" from wood with either a pry bar or a hammer claw. About one-quarter of the nails from the camps are broken or bent. Most head fragments are from 6d or larger nails, suggesting that they broke during an attempt to pull them from lumber. The bent and broken nails might reflect the demolition of camp structures by troops who stayed behind to police the site after the grand duke and his hosts had left to return to their train. This would have been cold work, and because there was no plan to reuse the camp, the demolition might not have been carried out with care.

The work construction certainly involved saws, hammers, and other tools. The crew might have included a contract civilian carpenter from Fort McPherson, but this kind of construction was within the capability of a cavalry unit on detached service. Army wagons carried tools kits for expedient repairs. At this time the army was also developing standardized toolboxes and tool kits so that the noncommissioned officers who oversaw such activities could easily assure that all major tools were returned and properly stored.[11] The only construction tool we found on the campsite was a "gimlet." Gimlets were small drills that might be overlooked.[12] They were well suited for expedient work, but they were not a craftsman's tool. The holes they augered through a board were rough but were adequate for affixing a guy line, setting up a small rack, or helping to drive a nail into a very hard board. The gimlet shaft we found (FS95) was somewhat removed from the main concentration of nails, which suggests it was a tool of the troops, not the hunters. It is complete except for the handle. It is 92 mm (3⅗ inches) long and 4 mm (5/32 inch) in diameter.

Most men who camped at Camp Alexis slept in shelter tents made of two "halves." Together with a set of guy lines, two poles, and a set of turned wooden pins, shelter halves were part of an individual trooper's kit. Two iron stakes (FS34 and FS 76) were found toward the northern edge of the upper terrace. These appear to be expedient tent pins. Because one (FS 76) is broken, its original length cannot be known. The square bar is 94 mm (3 7/10 inches) long, 18 mm (7/10 inch) wide, and 10 mm (⅖ inch) thick. It has a roughly formed hook at what appears to be its head end. The intact stake is 270 mm (10⅗ inches) long, 15 mm (⅗ inch) wide, and 8 mm (5/16 inch) thick. It is pointed at one end and has a U-shaped bend on the other, and it is flat on one side and rounded on the other. Neither of these was a manufactured or regulation item, but both are similar in design to expedient tent stakes recovered from campsites associated with the Seventh Cavalry's 1874 Black Hills Expedition and with a Buffalo Soldier campsite in Texas. They might have helped cavalrymen secure their shelter tents against wintry winds.[13]

The only other artifacts that might be a record of the work that went into building Camp Alexis are two small wood screws—one complete wood screw (FS29) 20 mm (¾ inch) long and one

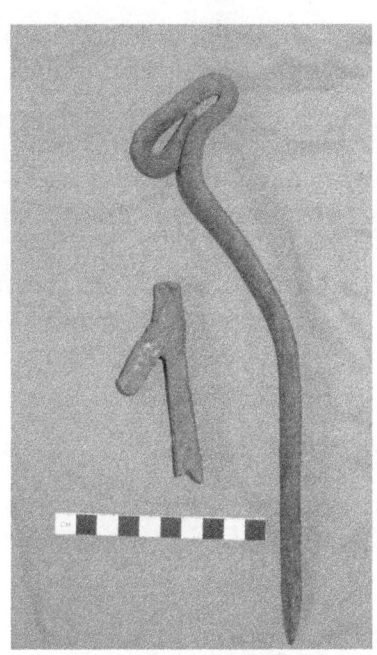

Figure 52. Expedient iron tent stakes recovered by metal detecting. Graphics by Douglas Scott.

Figure 53. Miscellaneous artifacts: a small buckle, possibly from chaps; a center-bar army-style harness buckle; a finger loop from scissors; a fastener for a carriage cover or top; a bucket or bale and a bale-ear fragment; and a gimlet or boring tool. Graphics by Douglas Scott.

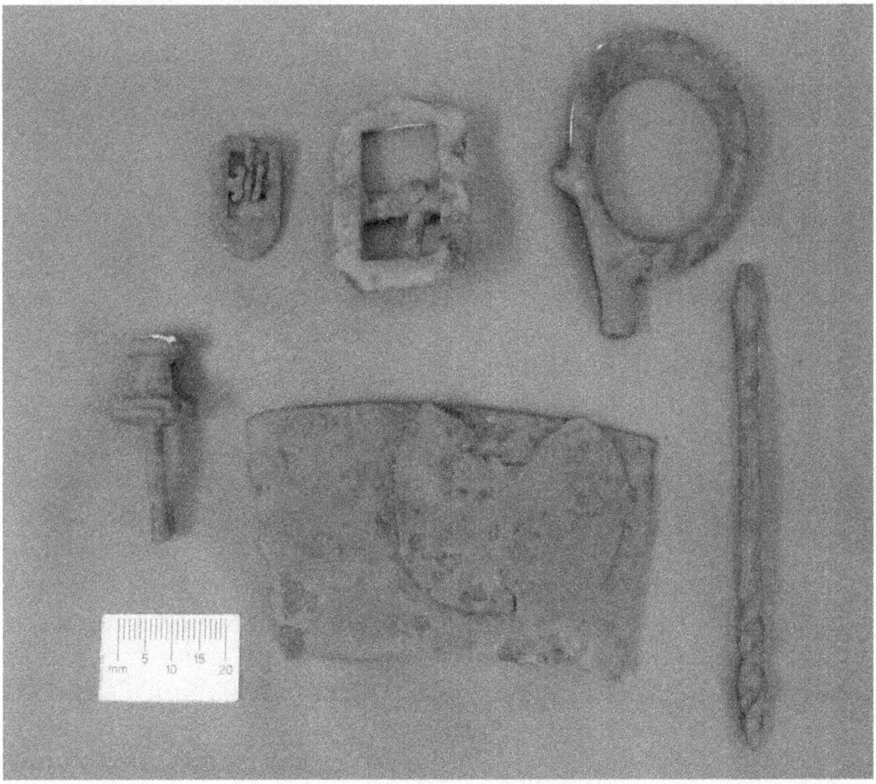

wood-screw shaft fragment (FS78)—recovered on the upper terrace. It seems unlikely that they were used in construction. They might have been removed while opening a crate or box, or, because they are common types, they might postdate the hunt. The same can be said about the finger-loop portion of a heavy iron scissors (FS131) found on the western side of the upper terrace. A nineteenth-century type, it might have broken while being used at the camp, but it could also reflect a later activity.

TABLE 1
The Camp Alexis Machine-cut Nail Assemblage

2d: 7 specimens (FS6, 44, 69, 79, 90, 182, and 193)
3d: 7 specimens (FS7, 57, 84, 87, 125.1, 125.2, and 169)
4d: 12 specimens (FS5, 20, 22, 30, 33, 36, 41, 67, 86, 89, 177, and 198)
6d: 25 specimens (FS13, 15, 18, 25, 26, 28, 40, 39, 51, 52, 68, 75, 134, 136, 145.1, 149, 153, 154, 156, 160, 161, 162, 164, 175, and 194)
8d: 21 specimens (FS19, 21, 38, 42, 61, 64, 69, 128, 129, 130, 140, 144, 147, 150, 171, 173, 176, 191, 195, 199, and 204)
10d: 16 specimens (FS39, 56, 60, 63, 77, 81, 142, 146, 148, 163, 170, 174, 186, 188, 189, and 201)
Unknown (broken, head, shaft, and tips): 32 specimens total; 19 shaft and tip fragments (FS23, 43, 45, 50, 53, 54, 58, 62, 73, 74, 82, 88, 91, 126, 127, 143, 145.2, 151, 155, 158, and 187), 11 head fragments (FS12, 17, 27, 35, 46, 47, 55, 59, 132, 137, and 197), and 1 shaft fragment (FS74)

Horse and Transportation Equipment

Horses were a major part of Camp Alexis. They were involved in getting the party, their gear, the American Indian visitors, and the army support staff to the camp. And while the hunters pursued buffalo—on horseback—the other horses and the mules were tethered across a major part of the campsite. Caring for them would have been an ongoing activity, so it is not surprising that they are reflected in the archaeological record.

The horses at Camp Alexis would have been secured to sturdy, wrought-iron individual picket pins or tied along picket lines. A figure-eight-shaped loop (FS32) recovered on the upper terrace is consistent with the Model 1859 picket-pin loop. Once the pin had been driven into the ground, a horse was attached to this free rotating loop by a snap hook. Clearly it could have received a serious tug. The tug this pin received seems to have been enough to deform the loop.

Two 13 mm (½-inch) iron harness buckles (FS80, 83) were recovered on the upper terrace. One is more robust than the other, but both are consistent with harness and bridle buckles used by the post-Civil War army. A small, decorated iron buckle (FS183) was also found on the upper terrace. It was meant for a 6 mm (¼-inch)-wide strap. It is 25 mm (1 inch) long and 13.5 mm (½ inch) wide with bossed decorations on the stamped iron buckle. The buckle could have been used in Camp Alexis, but it is also the sort of buckle that was used to fasten chaps or for similar light-duty work and might be late-nineteenth or twentieth century in origin. A small copper rivet (FS11) about 13 mm (½-inch) long was also found on the upper terrace. This rivet was bent steeply from the head and broken off down the shaft. Rivets like this were common in both army and civilian harnesses; it could have come from either the hunting camp or a later activity.

A carriage knob (FS190) was found on the western ridge of the campsite. Knobs of this type were used for fastening carriage covers. The style, a 63M is 22 mm (⅞ inch) long, had a long history of manufacture and use.[14] It might have fallen from a rig that accompanied the grand duke, but it might also date to a later use of the campsite.

Finally, some of the horses at Camp Alexis seem to have lost a shoe or to have required other services of a farrier. We found the head of a broken horseshoe nail (FS9) and three complete horseshoe nails (FS141, 172, and 191) on the upper terrace of the campsite. These nails might postdate the grand hunt, but they are not unexpected residue of the royal hunt campsite.

Food and Beverage Containers

Most container material found was tin cans or portions thereof, although glass bottle fragments also were recovered. Three caps from Hole-in-Cap tin-can lids (FS24, 31, and 97) were recovered. All three approximated the no. 2½ tin can. FS31 was found in association with a small rectangular—42 mm (1¹¹⁄₁₆ inches) by 27 mm (1 inch)—glass-panel bottle base with "BU" embossed on one side, likely part of a brand or manufacturer's logo. FS 24 had two small pieces of green wine- or champagne-bottle glass. A large piece of green bottle glass (FS72) was recovered. This piece was much more opaque than the two smaller pieces. Another fragment of dark-green bottle-glass body (FS138) was also recovered. Its shape and thickness is consistent with those of a fragment of the kickup base and body of a European wine bottle. A group of tin-can body fragments (FS100) was found near a lid from a Hole-in-Cap can (FS97). Two other tin-can body fragments were found with a bottom fragment, and all were assigned the same field-specimen number (FS181). Three other can bottom fragments (FS167, 168, and 179) and five other fragments of can tops or lids (FS135 [three fragments], 202, and 203) were also recovered. Two of the top or lid fragments (FS202 and 203) are likely from the same can top, which shows evidence of being cut with a knife or similar instrument in a roughly square manner to access the can's contents.

Two lead-foil items were recovered. One small piece (FS14) that was crumpled up and discarded is consistent with lead-foil seals from wine or champagne bottles. The second (FS165) consists of five pieces from the top and sides of a lead-foil bottle seal. It has no discernible lettering, but in one area is a cluster of grapes and grapevine tendrils in raised relief. This is undoubtedly a wine bottle seal and very likely associated with the hunt camp.

The only metallic vessel that might have been involved in food preparation at Camp Alexis is suggested by the broken section of a thin, cast-iron cooking pot (FS152). The section contains a bale ear that broke from the wall. The surviving fragment, which measures 40mm by 40mm (1½ inches by 1½ inches), seems to have come from a cylindrical or slightly flaring vessel. The size of the vessel cannot be determined, but it seems consistent with mid- to late-nineteenth-century cast-iron cooking pots.

Because our recovery techniques aimed at metal, we did not systematically recover glass or ceramic artifacts. In the course of searching for metal "targets," however, we did encounter some of these materials. A fragment of a soft-paste (ironstone) ceramic bowl rim (FS135.1) was found near the southern edge of the upper plateau. The rim is consistent with an octagonal bowl or tureen that could date to the hunt period and be suitable for a polite table service. Associated with that fragment was a clear glass base fragment from a round bottle (FS135.2). Given its clarity and style, the clear fragment likely dates to the twentieth century.

Figure 54. Containers, clockwise from top: a green glass fragment from the base of a wine or champagne bottle; the top of a hole-in-top tin can; and a fragment from a tin-can top with a rough-cut opening, probably to access the contents. Graphics by Douglas Scott.

Figure 55. Lead-foil seals from wine or champagne bottles: the left seal has tendrils and a cluster of grapes embossed on it; the right seal (from the Lyle Hutchens collection) has the partial words "P J De Tenet & Ed de Geo." and "Bordeaux" in the center. Graphics by Douglas Scott.

Firearms Artifacts

Camp Alexis was a hunting camp, and the archaeological record leaves no doubt that guns and shooting were part of camp life. Two unfired .44-caliber bullets (FS 8 and 85) were found at Camp Alexis. One, a solid-base lead bullet (FS8), 16.45 grams (254 grains) and 11 mm (⅖ inch) in diameter, has a recessed section around the lower

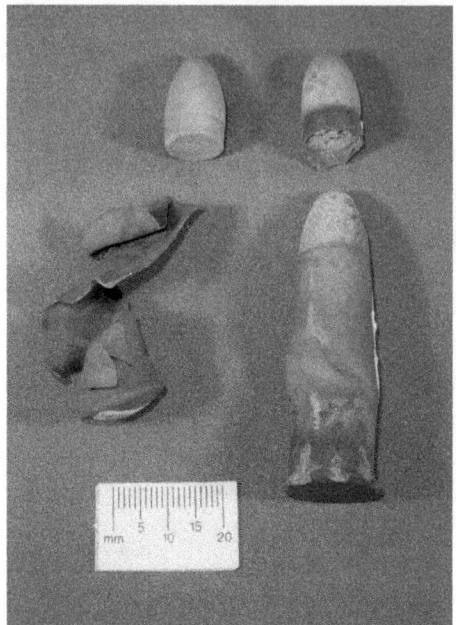

Figure 56. Bullets and cartridges: two unfired .44-caliber lead bullets, one with a partial cartridge case on the neck; one unfired but heat-exploded .50-70-caliber cartridge case; and an unfired but damaged .50-70-caliber cartridge. Graphics by Douglas Scott.

third. The second bullet (FS85), 14.75 grams (227.3 grains) and 11 mm (⅖ inch) in diameter, is identical to the first except that it is still seated in a portion of a Bloomfield Gilding Metal (copper) cartridge-case neck and body. The bullet is similar to the Civil War .44-caliber Colt bullet made by the U.S. government at its Frankford Arsenal for the black-powder muzzle-loading army revolver.[15] However, the presence of the copper cartridge-case neck fragment indicates that it was (and likely both were) seated in metallic cartridges.

The bullet does not match either the .44-caliber Remington conversion revolver-cartridge bullet or the Smith & Wesson Army Revolver metallic-cartridge bullet commonly carried by cavalrymen of the era. The Richards process converted percussion Colt revolvers into metallic center-fire cartridge revolvers. It does match the bullet used in the first Colt Army Model 1860 converted to fire metallic cartridges and likely represents cartridges for the converted Colts.[16]

In late 1871 the converted Colts were sent to various cavalry companies in the field for trials. Among those who received these pistols was Company E, Second Cavalry, which helped set up the royal-hunt camp and, according to a "Summary Statement for Miscellaneous Detachments" dated January 17, 1872, had seventy-five on hand just after their return from duty with the hunting party.[17] There are no reports regarding sidearms at that time for Company K, the other company on camp duty with the grand duke, but they might have been armed with the Colt Army Model 1860 revolver or the Remington 1858 New Model Army revolver, both percussion-fired pistols.

A single Benet-primed .50-70-caliber Bloomfield Gilding Metal (copper) center-fire cartridge case (FS70) was found in the camp. The cartridge case is unfired but severely ruptured and twisted, likely as a result of having exploded when exposed to a fire. One unfired .50-70-caliber Benet-primed round (FS133) was also recovered. The body is slightly crushed making it unusable, but whether the crushing occurred during the hunt or after its deposition cannot be determined reliably.

In their "Summary Statement of Ordnance and Ordnance Stores on Hand in the Cavalry Regiments of the United States" during the First Quarter of 1871, Companies E and K, Second Cavalry, reported that they had on hand .50-70-caliber Sharps metallic-cartridge conversion carbines. They reported seventy-nine and ninety Sharps carbines on hand respectively. The First Quarter 1872 ordnance statement lists Company K with eighty-five Sharps carbines on hand.[18] The 1872 First Quarter Statement also shows that Company E was field testing a series of trial carbines with twenty-seven Model 1870 Springfields, twenty-eight Remingtons, and twenty-seven Sharps carbines in the company.

Other Camp Alexis Collections

In addition to our systematic metal detection, collectors and local historians have searched the campsite for traces of the grand duke's visit. There are stories that the campsite once was littered with broken champagne bottles and other traces of high living, but if such items were found, they have not survived. Local landowner Scott Clifford, a descendent of William Clifford, one of the original homesteaders on the campsite, recalled that several years earlier he had found two glass bottles in the Red Willow Creek drainage about two hundred fifty meters below the site. He relocated one bottle and allowed it to be analyzed and photographed. The bottle is 241 mm (9½ inches) tall and 67 mm (2⅝ inches) in diameter at the base. It is of dark green glass with the body containing many small and large

Figure 57. A dark-green glass bottle for ale or stout, found by Scott Clifford below the campsite. Graphics by Douglas Scott.

air bubbles. The finish or lip, an applied-oil finish for a cork stopper, is 22 mm (⅞ inch) high. The body has side seams, and the base is cupped, a product of the cup-molding process of manufacture. There are no marks or lettering on the base, but the style is typical of an approximately 12-ounce stout bottle manufactured between 1865 and 1880.[19] The style is entirely consistent with beer, ale, and stout bottles that could have been used by the hunting party.

Artifacts carefully preserved in two private collections offer additional information regarding the hunt. Lyle Hutchens and David Chalfant, local residents, have had a long and avid interest in western history and sites related to the Seventh Cavalry. They metal-detected the Camp Alexis site on several occasions, and they generously allowed us to document their collections in the course of our research on the site.

The Hutchens and Chalfant collections contains one .38-caliber conical bullet with two cannelures (lubricating grooves). The bullet appears to have been fired in a Winchester rifled weapon, likely a .38-40 caliber, and therefore postdates the 1872 event.

Six spherical lead balls or bullets were noted in the Hutchens and Chalfant collections. All appear to be unfired. One is a .40-caliber ball, three are approximately .44-caliber, and three are approximately .50-caliber. If some soldiers were armed with the Colt Army Model or the Remington 1858 New Model Army revolvers, the .44-caliber spherical bullets could be rounds lost from cartridge boxes. The .40-caliber and .50-caliber spherical bullets are not military rounds but are likely associated with other nineteenth-century activities on the site. All three calibers are types used in nineteenth-century muzzle-loading firearms common both in hunting and in the Indian trade. All could be associated with weapons that might have been in the Spotted Tail camp or by American Indians who occupied the site earlier.

The Hutchens and Chalfant collections from Camp Alexis have four .44-caliber Colt-style bullets. Three are unfired. One was fired, probably from either a Colt Army Model 1860 or a Richards conversion. The barrel land-and-groove configuration is the same for both.

The collections also include eight .50-70 cartridge cases and two unfired cartridges. Two are Benet internally primed center-fire types, and the remainder are bar-primed types. The fired rounds were cast using Forensic Sil® casting compound and later viewed under magnification to determine the type of weapon in which each was fired. Six were fired in Sharps rifles or carbines, one and possibly two in Model 1868 or Model 1870s rifles or carbines. The cartridge cases were found on the west side of the site and on the edge of the upper terrace overlooking Red Willow Creek. These likely reflect the soldiers' guns, and the representation of both Springfield- and Sharps-made weapons is consistent with the firearms the cavalry support companies reported in their ordnance returns.

Two .50-caliber 450-grain army-style bullets were also noted in the collections. One is unfired, and the land-and-groove configuration in the other indicates that it was fired from a Sharps rifle or carbine. Two other large pieces of lead in the collections appear to be fragments of .50-caliber 450-grain bullets.

The unfired brass head of a coiled or foil 12-bore cartridge case was observed in the Chalfant collection. The brass cartridge-case head is headstamped "Eley Bros/London/No/12." This is not a 12-gauge shot-shell head, but a large-bore hunting-rifle round made by the famous English cartridge company between 1866 and 1874.[20]

The Chalfant collection also includes one lithic biface, two McClellan saddle-guard plates, three general-service army cuff-sized buttons, one coat-sized general-service button, two iron conchas, a piece of a trade-silver ornament, and a brass cone tinkler. Tinkling cones or tinklers were common ornamental items on American Indian dress throughout the eighteenth and nineteenth centuries. Some were manufactured for distribution; others were camp-made from tin cans or waste sheet metal. Both brass and iron are common finds.

Other items include three cut nails, a horseshoe nail, two fragments of green bottle glass, one fragment of brown bottle glass, a brass knapsack hook, two brass harness rivets, one small wood screw (about the size of those in McClellan saddletrees), one center-bar buckle for a bridle or similar harness, and a wadded-up piece of lead foil (likely part of a wine or champagne bottle foil seal).

Aside from its cartridges and bullets, the Hutchens collection includes a suspender buckle or brass suspender grip. The grip is a private-purchase style and could have been used by anyone during the period. The military did not have a standard-issue suspender during the Civil War and did not issue suspenders until 1883.[21] Another item is a lithic projectile point, likely late prehistoric in age. The collection also includes a brass projectile point or arrowhead. Metal arrowheads, primarily iron, were common trade items from the early seventeenth to the early twentieth century and had almost completely supplanted chipped-stone projectiles by the mid-nineteenth century.[22] The brass arrowhead, which appears to be hand made, is a stemmed or tanged point made from brass stock.

Other items are a nineteenth-century triangular file, an offset iron awl, an iron concha, a figure-8-shaped iron ring from a Civil War-era picket pin typical of those commonly issued to cavalry units during the Civil War and well into the 1870s,[23] a small iron, four-hole button (likely used as a suspender button on trousers), an overall button marked "Kelly & Ocherty" (probably twentieth century in origin), three army general-service cuff-sized buttons, and three coat-sized general-service buttons, one with an I for Infantry in the eagle's shield. These three military button types date to the Civil War era.[24] Also observed were a pocketknife (likely late nineteenth century in origin), a horseshoe fragment, and an incomplete lead-foil wine-bottle seal marked "P J De Tenet & Ed de Geo." around the edge and "Bordeaux" in the center.

Artifact Distribution

In addition to the artifact assemblage, our metal-detection survey produced distributional information reflecting the location of the campsite and its organization. The systematically recovered and recorded artifacts, together with the items found by Hutchens and Chalfant, reflect the story of the use of the confluence of Red Willow Creek and its ephemeral drainage. The artifacts and their distribution (which are discussed and fully interpreted in chapter 8) form the core of evidence regarding a three-day event in mid-January 1872.

7

Interpreting Camp Alexis

The Context of Military Camps and Camping in the West

The U.S. Army was no stranger to establishing and organizing field camps when General Sheridan called upon General Ord and Colonel Palmer to support the grand duke's buffalo hunt. Besides the personal experience of each officer and enlisted man who supported the hunt, the army had long issued guidance regarding the layout of camp facilities. Terrain and topography might dictate, to a degree, the arrangement of tents and general camp organization, but the regulations guided camp selection and organization. Reconnaissance normally preceded the selection and erection of a camp. A quartermaster, quartermaster sergeant, and other enlisted personnel usually were detailed to find a suitable site. Selecting and organizing Camp Alexis fell to Lieutenant Colonel Forsyth, Dr. Asch of Sheridan's staff, and Fifth Cavalry Regimental Quartermaster Lt. Edward Hayes, who were accompanied by enlisted personnel and guided by William Cody a few days before the hunt party dignitaries arrived.

Idealized Camp Layout

During the Civil War, the primary set of regulations for both the Union and the Confederate armies was the *Revised United States Army Regulations of 1861*.[1] The postwar federal army employed them as well. These regulations present the official manner in which

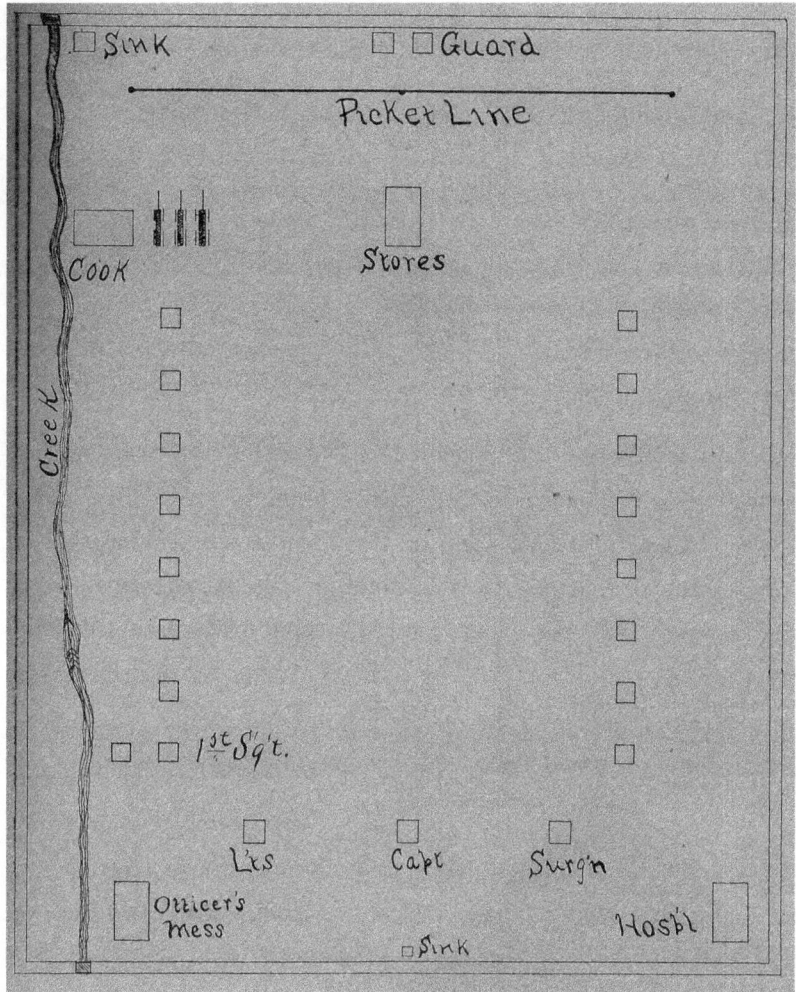

Figure 58. An idealized cavalry-camp layout showing the hierarchical arrangement of officers' and enlisted men's tents. Tutherly 1898:193.

campsites were to be selected and camps laid out. That the armies from both sides, and the postwar army, followed these regulations when laying out and maintaining campsites is demonstrated in the archaeological record.[2]

Guidelines in the regulations identified how different army branches were to organize their camps in spatial patterns that reflected rank and that met the functional and support needs of men and livestock. Generally company enlisted tents were organized in two files or lines along a company street. The individual tents were to be spaced two paces apart, and the company street was to be at least five paces wide. Enlisted tents were placed perpendicular to the color line, or the line of the officers' tents.[3]

The process that soldiers went through to set up their camps reflected the level of their training and discipline, the experience of the officers, tactical situations, orders, and, to a degree, health and sanitation. The relationship of camps to landscape allows some latitude in choice, orders, and strategy.

Military Camps, the Archaeological Record

Tangible evidence of soldiers' domiciles is routinely found archaeologically. The degree to which discipline, training, stress from campaigning, orders, topography, and other factors created variety both in camp layouts and in the distribution of different types of artifacts is addressed through examination of the archaeological record. By applying archaeological methodologies and anthropological theories to information obtained from these sites, researchers can answer questions regarding adherence to military doctrine, tactical positioning, group identity, ethnicity, foodways, vernacular architecture, landscape usage, and material culture. Camps often have detailed historic accounts written by participants. And they have archaeological remains whose features and distribution display distinct patterns that the reflect activities of the occupants. Joseph Balicki suggests that campsites reflect not only their military origin and organization but also, sometimes, the occupants' regional or other preferences regarding layout and organization.[4]

As an example, several different types of tents, including "A" (wall or wedge) tents and shelter tents, were available for soldiers. Archaeological evidence for tents, such as postholes, drainage features, platforms, and depressions, leave a physical expression that can be equated to known tent sizes and types and thereby can help determine a camp layout and functions.[5] Lost and discarded items—the material culture—systematically recovered during archaeological investigations of a campsite provide insights into military units using the camp, their armament, provisioning, decision-making, ethnicity, foodways, personal choice, and a host of other topics, such as a chronology of events, relevant to archaeologists. Kitchen ceramics, container glass, and faunal remains are common recoveries, but until recently analytical and comparative analyses of these materials have not been extensive. Balicki's preliminary comparison of material culture in field camps with that in permanent installations demonstrates that differences between types of camps can be established archaeologically using ceramics, glass, camp type, and access to urban centers.[6] These archaeological constructs are the bases upon which the Camp Alexis investigations were modeled.

To develop a model of what a western military camp might look like archaeologically, we reviewed literature of the archaeology of western U.S. Army camps and historical and archaeological information on campsites organized or occupied by Gen. Phillip Sheridan. Because General Sheridan was instrumental in organizing several hunts with prominent participants, it seems logical that the manner of camp organization and the associated material-culture remains in these hunting camps, and in Camp Alexis especially, would reflect his preferences in camp layout and organization.

The Fall 1871 Hunt and Camp on Medicine Creek

General Sheridan was no newcomer to hunting in western Nebraska when he took the Grand Duke Alexis to hunt buffalo. In fact, only three months earlier, Sheridan and a large hunting party, including William F. "Buffalo Bill" Cody, had been in the same region, where they reportedly killed six hundred buffalo. Sheridan was an avid sportsman, and when he could not join hunting parties in the West himself, he often smoothed the way for his friends and acquaintances by writing letters of introduction for them to commanding officers of army posts along their projected route. At these posts, many of those civilian parties availed themselves of food and equipage and even transport. A number of post commanders complained of the strain that supplying and escorting these parties placed on their usually understrength commands, but Sheridan had received the blessing of Secretary of War William W. Belknap to provide escorts and supplies for these parties when it was in the best interest—that is, politically advantageous—to the army.[7]

When his duties allowed and the political payback was potentially significant, Sheridan accompanied or hosted hunting parties. The September 22–October 3, 1871, hunt was composed of old friends, former comrades in arms, and powerful social and political figures. Following much the same route as the grand duke's party would follow three months later, Sheridan assembled the group in Chicago for a train trip to Council Bluffs and Omaha and on to North Platte or North Platte Station, near Fort McPherson, where they were equipped and escorted by a company of Fifth Cavalry, under the command of Capt. William Brown. The hunting party principals included Sheridan, guide and scout Cody, prominent New York lawyer Henry E. Davies, financial tycoon Lawrence R. Jerome, financial tycoon (later grandfather of Winston Churchill) Leonard W. Jerome, newspaperman James Gordon Bennett, Jr., New York Stock Exchange member Carroll Livingston, New York businessman John G. Heckscher, Bvt. Brig. Gen. Charles L. Fitzhugh, Philadelphia businessman M. Edward Rogers, wealthy New York sportsman John S. Crosby, Chicago businessman Samuel Johnson, Western Union Telegraph Central Division superintendent Anson Stager, Chicago newspaperman Charles L. Wilson, Col. David Rucker, Assistant Surgeon Dr. Morris Asch, Lt. Col. Michael Sheridan, and Col. William H. Emory.

The September 1871 Post Return, Record of Events section for Fort McPherson recorded, "Lieut General P. H. Sheridan and party arrived Sept. 22nd and left on Sept. 23rd, 1871 on a hunting expedition across the country to Fort Hayes [sic]. Company E, 5th Cav. With a detail from this post (aggregate 84 men) Capt. W. H. Brown, comdg, marched as escort to the above party, Sept. 23, 1871. Company G, 5th Cavly, Lieut A. B. Bache, comdg, left Post September 28 and marched to Killickenick (on the Red Willow) for the purpose of ascertaining whether any whiskey traffic was carried out there."[8] The escort party returned to their post on October 10, the Fifth Cavalry was transferred to the Department of Arizona in November, 1872, and the post was occupied by the Second Cavalry.

The millionaires' hunt party was fitted out with six wall tents for the main participants' sleeping accommodations, one hospital tent for use as a dining facility, a second hospital tent to serve as a kitchen and quarters for the servants, and tentage and equipage for the hundred-man escort. The train consisted of sixteen wagons carrying baggage, supplies, forage for the horses and mules, and ice. The party was also provided three four-horse ambulances to carry guns and the lighter baggage.[9] The number and types of tents for the millionaires' hunt and for the royal buffalo hunt were similar. The arrangements likely were similar, too, except that the grand duke had a wall tent to himself.

The camp arrangement is not clearly specified, but each wall tent was used as sleeping quarters for three men. Aside from a camp near Fort McPherson, the party camped four times in Nebraska before moving on to Fort Hays, Kansas, the end point of their foray. Davies recorded the dinner menu for the last camp in Nebraska, and it might be similar to the meals served during the grand duke's hunt. The menu consisted of buffalo-tail soup followed by broiled cisco and fried dace and the entrées: prairie-dog salami, stewed rabbit, and filet of buffalo with mushrooms. Also available were roasted elk, antelope, deer, and turkey, broiled duck, buffalo-calf steaks, and young wild turkey. The vegetables served were sweet potatoes, mashed potatoes, and green peas. The dessert was tapioca pudding. A variety of spirits, wines, and ales was served, including champagne frappé, champagne, claret, brandy, whiskey, and Bass Ale, followed by coffee.[10]

Sheridan's 1878 Canadian River, Indian Territory, Hunt and Camps

Sheridan's 1878 hunt party was composed of old friends and brother officers: Sheridan, Gen. George Crook, retired general and hunt chronicler William Strong, Asst. Adj. Gen. William Whipple, Col. Thomas Moore, Lt. Col. Frederick Grant (President Ulysses S. Grant's son), and noted southern plains scout and frontiersman Ben Clark. The hunt party began and ended at Wichita, Kansas. The party started for Fort Reno in Indian Territory on January 22 and returned on February 23. Like earlier hunts, this one was outfitted and escorted by the army. The escort consisted of a company of Fourth Cavalry under the command of Lt. Harry Sweeney.

The party hunted wild turkey, although other fowl and a deer were also taken. The turkey-hunt party, which was supplied at Fort Reno, included at least two six-mule army wagons with twenty days' forage, tents (including a tent with stove for cooking and wedge tents for sleeping), camp equipage, cooking utensils, a mess outfit, guns, ammunition, and private baggage. The party also had riding horses and two four-mule ambulances. Strong reported that a hospital tent served as the dining facility and headquarters. The hospital tent was equipped with camp chairs, a dining table that was assembled from sections, and General Sheridan's personal mess chest, which contained "the finest of table ware, crockery, napkins, etc., etc." Each tent was supplied with a stove, mattresses, and blankets.[11] Strong did not record the camp layout, but he does state that Sheridan was very particular about camp arrangements: "He likes everything in connection with it to conform as nearly as possible to the 'Regulations' . . . the escort camp near us; the wagons and ambulances are parked systematically every night; and the tents must be in line. A cavalry guidon flys in front of the General's tent."

Comparable Archaeological Research at Other Western Temporary Military Camps

Archaeological investigations of military camps, particularly as related to the American Revolution and the Civil War, are well known. The material culture found at various Civil War encampment sites often reflects the ethnic and political identities of the troops camped at those locations.[12] Likewise the idiosyncrasies of individual soldiers are regularly and clearly evident. Such activities as mess are often identified easily in the archaeological record, and individual activities, particularly leisure-time activities such as smoking and gaming, are often recovered archaeologically, giving rare insights into personal and interpersonal behavior among troops in camp. An artifact classification system has been developed for Civil War camp artifacts.[13] It divides the artifactual material into camp life and floor artifacts and then into seven general groups: kitchen, architecture, arms, clothing, personal, tobacco, and activities. Independently the artifact groupings are valid, but the mingling of functional and typological groups limits their application in archaeological analysis. Even so the work does provide a basis on which to identify and describe camp-related archaeological materials.

One large Civil War earthwork and long-term camp associated with General Sheridan has been tested and metal-detected by archaeologists. The Opequon site in Frederick County, Virginia, was occupied in November and December 1864 by units associated with Sheridan's VI, VIII, and XIX Army Corps and was known as Camp Russell. An elaborate site, Camp Russell featured earthworks and unit camps composed of mixed log cabins and tents with vertical log sides and chimneys. Intended as a winter camp, it was better developed than most. The area studied archaeologically revealed material culture related to one or two divisions of the XIX corps organized by unit.[14] The excavator concluded that the camps were well organized, that they were associated with specific earthworks for protection, and that areas within them were spatially discrete in a manner consistent with military requirements for camp organization and construction. The artifacts recovered during the testing and recording ranged from items associated with cooking and food to extracted bullets, likely pulled from muskets at the end of sentinel or picket duty. The recovered materials fall within the expected range of camp debris as suggested by other work.[15] The camp layout and organization as reflected in the surviving archaeological record suggest that, at least during the Civil War, Sheridan's command followed prevailing regulations and guidance.

Archaeological investigations of temporary camps west of the Mississippi, sporadic but ongoing for years, provide another basis for comparison with the archaeological record of Camp Alexis. The army established temporary camps for different purposes. Some were exceedingly transitory, occupied for only a night while commands were moving between specific assignments. Others had greater longevity, seeing use from a few days to months. One such trans-Mississippi Civil War camp is Camp Lincoln, near Van Buren, Missouri. The camp was occupied for approximately two weeks in January 1863. The historic record is nearly nonexistent for the units occupying the camp at that time, but archaeological research located an artillery emplacement, a possible forge locale, the quartermaster area, and shelter-tent platforms that had been ditched to drain water away from the tents. These physical features, together with artifact distributions, indicate a layout with discrete areas: officers' row on the east side of the main camp, enlisted men on the west, and the quartermaster and related functions on the north and south. The archaeological investigation also demonstrated that the camp layout followed general military prescriptions for an infantry camp.[16]

One camp established in Nebraska in 1867 was occupied briefly for the purpose of guarding Union Pacific Railroad construction near what is now North Platte. The archaeological record shows it was a tent camp occupied by about fifty men and officers. It was surrounded by a sod wall with a gated entrance on the east side. The officers' tents were at the south end of the enclosure, and the enlisted men's were arranged in two facing rows at the north end.[17] The site is most notable for who commanded it: Lt. Col. Arthur MacArthur, father of Gen. Douglas MacArthur.

Camp Powell, or the Powder River Depot, a large field-supply depot associated with the summer campaign against the Lakota in 1876, was subjected to limited archaeological investigation.[18] Subsequent spatial analysis of the find locations, together with historical research, identified individual company areas, storage areas for rations and forage, a steamboat landing, a trader's or sutler's area, a large wagon park or storage area, and a fighting trench or earthwork.[19]

A Seventh Cavalry campsite associated with George Custer and the Little Bighorn has been investigated archaeologically. A June 23, 1876, rest stop on Rosebud Creek, the camp was associated with Custer's march from the Powder River Depot to the Little Bighorn.[20]

A limited initial archaeological reconnaissance yielded only a handful of artifacts: a .45-55 cartridge case, the back of a General Service button, a trouser button, a broken mess spoon, a crushed camp boiler, a badly rusted gallon can that might have held roasted coffee beans, a Burden horseshoe, and the tips of several horseshoe nails found near a fire pit. Taken together, these artifacts are the Seventh's camp equipage discarded or lost during a thirteen-hour overnight stay by more than six hundred men. The few artifacts were recovered in no definable pattern. Likely they represent items lost or discarded by the command. The only feature, a fire pit with clipped horseshoe-nail tips, suggests that a farrier probably reshod at least one horse before turning in for the evening.

Other short-term to long-term field camps in the Southwest, most associated with the 1885–86 Geronimo Campaign, have been investigated archaeologically. The usual finds include horseshoes, horseshoe nails, army cartridges, cartridges cases, buttons, glass bottles, and structural foundations. Artifact-deposition patterns have helped researchers identify each camp layout. For example, archaeological work located a Tenth Cavalry camp on flat ground west and north of the spring at Mescal Spring, Arizona. Rock foundations suggested that one or more semipermanent structures, possibly tent bases, existed at the north end of the campsite. Glass from wine or champagne bottles and brown beer bottles, found in a sheet midden in this same area, suggests that this might have been the officers' camp area. A concentration of horseshoes, worn horseshoe fragments, unused and clipped horseshoe nails, and cuttings from the heels of horseshoes at the south end of the camp near the edge of a wash suggests that a farrier or blacksmith worked there. Finds of large cut nails suggest that a corral or horse picket line might have been nearby to the west.[21]

Martyn Tagg and Mark Baumler, as well as Richard Ahlstrom, conducted archaeological investigations of another Tenth Cavalry camp of the Geronimo Campaign period at Bonita Canyon, Arizona.[22] There they found a variety of stone fireplaces and other stone features denoting tent locations for soldiers and officers, and they found features associated with blacksmithing and horse picket lines or corrals. The artifactual record—buttons, utensils, and bottles in middens—was extensive, and analysis reveals a lengthy occupation. The archaeologists also noted that the camp had been built up. Tents had rock sides or bases, indicating that the soldiers had time and either the inclination to make themselves more comfortable or officers who found things for the men to do to prevent boredom. The men also had time to erect a monument to the recently assassinated President James A. Garfield.

Charles Haecker and Eleanor King investigated a series of campsites used by African American units between the late 1860s and the early 1880s at Pine Springs in the Guadalupe Mountains of Texas.[23] There they found evidence of short- and long-term camping in the form of trash middens and tent pads with what King refers to as "hypocausts": underground heat ducts designed to warm tents in cold weather. (In military literature these are usually referred to as "Crimea ovens.") At one tent pad the team found an expedient tent peg that a blacksmith or farrier likely had made from iron-bar stock. The expedient tent peg nearly duplicates one recovered at Camp Alexis. Similar hand-forged tent pegs have also been found on sites associated with the Seventh Cavalry's Black Hills Expedition of 1874.[24] King describes fire hearths associated with the camps. A separate fire hearth associated with horseshoes and horseshoe nails is interpreted as a farrier's work area.

Other archaeological research in the Southwest includes Alan Skinner's archaeological investigations of a late-1860s infantry and cavalry camp. Camp Willow Grove, Arizona, has a layout similar to those at Bonito Canyon and Mescal Spring and is comparable to the Pine Springs camp. It appears that the men and officers followed standard camp-organization practices used by the army in the nineteenth century.[25]

With few exceptions the archaeological record demonstrates that camps—short or long term—are reflected in physical remains, including artifacts and tent foundations, deposited systematically across the landscape. One well-documented exception is Custer's June 22, 1876, camp on Rosebud Creek. That briefly-occupied campsite has been documented and surveyed but was found to contain no features or patterned distribution of artifacts, probably because the site was less a camp than an overnight stop to rest men and horses and was occupied for only hours. Many archaeologically investigated camps, however, have presented patterned material arrays.

Joseph Whitehorne defined the ideal military-camp organization from the late eighteenth century through 1865 and how it is reflected in the archaeological record.[26] He noted that the army continued to use Civil War-era camp organization through most of the nineteenth century. In western short- and long-term camps the generalized camp debris patterning found is consistent: horseshoeing areas and corrals or horse picket lines are isolated from the main camp and officer territory is separated from enlisted men's tents—as prescribed in Whitehorne's generalized prescriptions for Civil War camps.

Evidently General Sheridan wanted his camps organized and laid out according to current military fashion. He appears to have employed one or two hospital tents as dining and cooking facilities on his hunting forays, and he seems to have wanted the camps organized hierarchically, with senior officers' and dignitaries' tents in one area, enlisted personnel nearby but separate, and the horses, baggage train, and other impedimenta away from the dignitaries' space. Sheridan also insured that the senior officers' accommodations were clearly evident by placing a guidon at his tent to signify the commander's headquarters. According to his hunt chroniclers, Sheridan followed standard military protocol in camp selection, organization, and layout. And the archaeology of western camps associated with Sheridan demonstrates clearly that the army as a whole, at least in the West, followed the same protocol.

Picturing Camp Alexis: History, Photography, and Archaeology, a Holistic Approach

Modern computer programs afford an unparalleled ability to place Camp Alexis, and particularly its individual tents, on the modern landscape, enabling us to see the tents and the camp layout superimposed on modern photographic images and to compare them with the archaeological record. We employed two methods to "see" the tents and the camp layout on modern images. The first method, photographic superimposition, entails simply taking a detail of a historic image, laying it on a modern image of the site, and aligning the ridgelines and other comparable landscape features until the two "fit" together. To accomplish such a superimposition, we took digital images of the site from different positions with lenses ranging from 28 mm to 70 mm, creating a series of overlapping views, essentially panoramas of the site. Next we opened the images using Adobe PhotoShop CS® and, using the "Merge Images" command, placed the Eaton image of Custer and Spotted Tail at the dining tent on the image of the site. Employing the "Transform" function to adjust the scale and opacity of the Eaton image, we moved it around on the modern image until landscape features such as ridgelines and slopes were aligned. The result is a composite image showing the historic photograph superimposed on a modern image, a variation of the comparative or then-and-now photographic technique. Now we can see from a modern perspective where the tent stood on the landscape.

Figure 59. Eaton Number 6 (dining tent with Spotted Tail and George Custer) superimposed on the modern landscape. Graphics by Douglas Scott.

Figure 60. Eaton Number 3 (Grand Duke Alexis's tent with Adm. Constantine Possiet, Spotted Tail, and Lt. Paul Shouvalov) superimposed on the modern landscape. Graphics by Douglas Scott.

The second process employed Google SketchUp®, a three-dimensional computer-based drawing and modeling program available as a free download (the version we employed) or as a fee-based expanded version. A three-dimensional design and modeling environment allows users to draw the outline, or perimeter, of an object in a two-dimensional manner, similar to pencil and paper. Then editing tools can be used to push and pull the two-dimensional surface, modeling objects as they appear in three-dimensional space. We first employed the software to create scale drawings of 1870s-era army tents. After drawing the basic shapes, we extruded and shaded them, creating a model for each style of tent. Then we placed each model in a file that visually replicated its placement in each Eaton image in which that style of tent appears. Once the individual models had been placed, they were merged to create a single model of the camp, showing all tents in each image in which the same styles of tent appear. The three-dimensional character of the SketchUp® models allowed us to rotate a given model to match a view of the tents in the Eaton images and then to insert that model into a composite camp model.

One powerful feature of SketchUp® is its ability to import photographic images and GoogleEarth® landscapes. This function allows a properly scaled image of a specific place, such as the Red Willow Creek campsite, to be imported into the tent-layout model to determine if the archaeological find areas and the tent models are in concert. The three-dimensional and full-rotation capability of the program allows one to see if the landscape backgrounds in the Eaton images conform to the independently created three-dimensional tent-layout model. When the tent-layout model was placed on the aerial image, the match to visible landscape features was uncanny. And the fact that the layout of the tents matched the superimposed photographic images confirmed the validity of our techniques. Because the tent layout visible in the Eaton images could be placed on an image of the modern land surface, we were reasonably certain

Figure 61. Eaton Numbers 3 and 6 (the dining tent and Grand Duke Alexis's tent) overlaid on the modern landscape. The grand duke's tent is in a row behind the dining tent, which is foreshortened in the overlay. Graphics by Douglas Scott.

that what we saw is what Custer, Cody, Sheridan, and Grand Duke Alexis saw in 1872.

The stereographic photographs confirm that most of the hunting party, including the grand duke, and their escorts lived in army wall tents. The photograph of the interior of the grand duke's tent indicates that the tents were furnished simply. The grand duke's tent had a floor and a heating stove, but, contrary to some reports, no carpet is evident. The grand duke appears to have had his rank and status as a senior foreign dignitary honored by the placement of a U.S. cavalry guidon at his tent. At other camps, Sheridan used the guidon at his own tent to denote the senior commander's field headquarters, and he might have done so at Camp Alexis. The photographic superimposition indicates that the grand duke's tent was north and just west of the dining tents, in the line of tents with visible stovepipes. It seems likely that Sheridan's was the first tent in the line, that the Grand Duke's was second, and that at least three

Figure 62. Eaton Number 4 (Spotted Tail with his wife and daughter in front of their tent) overlaid on the modern landscape. Graphics by Douglas Scott.

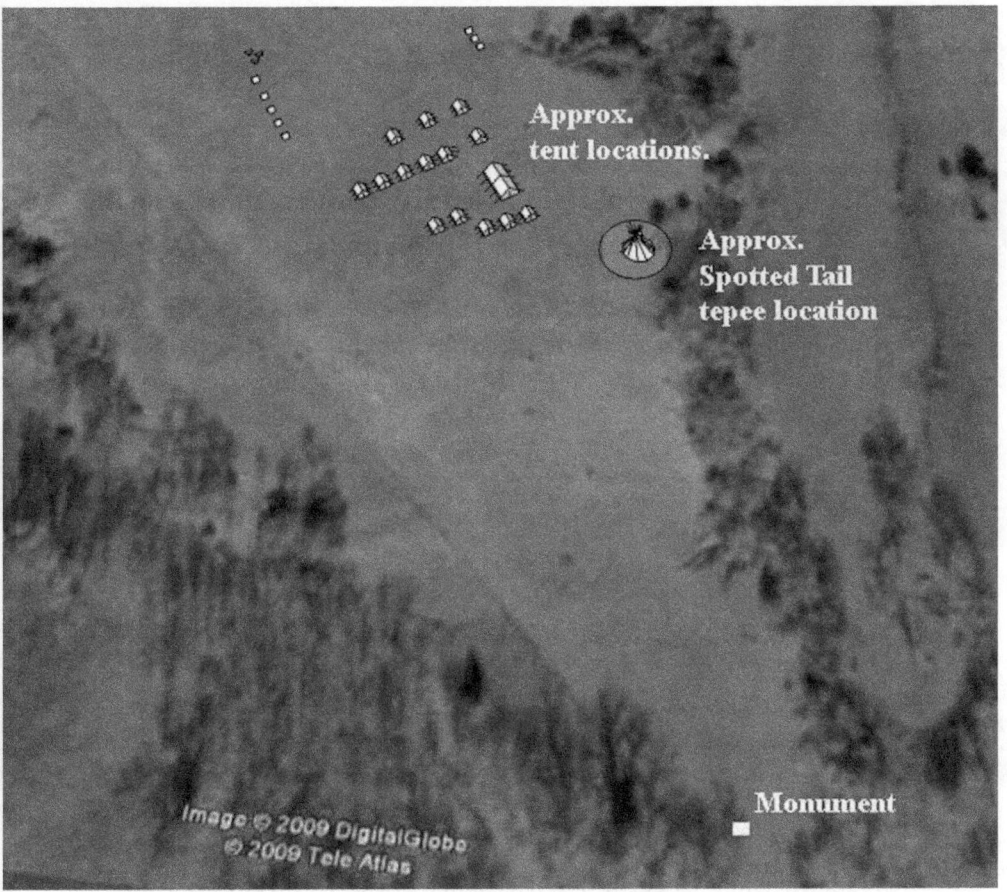

Figure 63. A three-dimensional model of the camp superimposed on a current aerial photograph. The tent locations are consistent with where archaeological artifact concentrations were found. Graphics by Stephen Damm and Douglas Scott.

other tents with stoves followed. The stovepipes are evidence that at least eight tents had stoves. The party's dining tent was two hospital tents set end to end that appear to have been warmed by two stoves. Perhaps one stove was for cooking and the second for warming the dining area.

The photographs show that the camp had an orderly arrangement. Four rows of wall tents appear to be oriented roughly east to west. The southern row appears to have at least three tents, perhaps for stewards, cooks, and the imperial party's servants. In the second row the double dining tent is on the east side, a wall tent beside it, and then at least one other tent is on the west end. The third row has at least five wall and "A" tents, each with a stove. And the north row has at least three "A" tents, the center one with a stove. Running perpendicular to the main line of large tents are two parallel rows of "A" tents set a some distance from the main cluster. The row on the east side appears to have a minimum of three tents, the row on the west side as many as four or five.

Thus there are at least two hospital tents and thirteen "A" tents arranged in four rows, likely housing the hunt-party dignitaries and officers. This is consistent with most descriptions of the officers' and the dignitaries' living arrangements as consisting of ten or twelve wall tents. The Eaton image of the standing party includes at least twenty-five individuals exclusive of Spotted Tail and other Indians. Some of the twenty-five might be enlisted soldiers, especially those posed in the background. Excluding them, the number of prominently featured individuals is about eighteen. Some important personages might not be in the image. Sheridan, for example, does not appear to be present. Nevertheless, the ten or twelve wall tents noted in the historic record, or approximately thirteen in the Eaton images, could easily house the twenty-five or so dignitaries and officers known to have inhabited the camp. The smaller "A" tents in the far background appear to run in a line perpendicular to that of the larger tents. They appear to be aligned north to south with two rows facing each other on opposite sides of the wall-tent alignment. These smaller tents are likely for the two cavalry companies and the band that provided logistical support and entertainment for the hunt party. If there were four enlisted men to a tent, about twenty-five would be need to accommodate the approximately one hundred men who made up the two cavalry companies and band. If each tent slept six men, only about seventeen tents would be required. These numbers are consistent with the total of thirty to forty other tents noted in the credible historic accounts.

The Eaton photographs do not record where all the enlisted personnel might have been housed. The visible tents in the enlisted line could not have accommodated the entire enlisted support contingent. Other tents likely were located outside the view of the camera when Eaton photographed the important party members and, coincidentally, captured the layout of the dignitaries' tents. The tent arrangement, officers and dignitaries on one end, enlisted tents in parallel lines running perpendicular to the officers' line, and wagons parked well off to the north indicates that the camp followed standard military protocol. The tent arrangement is also consistent with General Sheridan's known penchant for organizing camps in true military fashion and according to regulation.

William Illingworth took a sweeping photograph of one Seventh Cavalry camp during the 1874 Black Hills Expedition led by George Custer.[27] This image shows nearly the entire camp layout, and although it is much larger than Camp Alexis, the arrangement is remarkably similar. The Black Hills Expedition camp is sited next to a creek and arranged in a large open U shape. Hospital tents are visible at one end, and adjacent to them in parallel rows are wall and "A" tents that constitute officer country. Perpendicular to the officers' tents and running along each side of the camp are long lines of shelter tents for the enlisted men. At the open end of the U-shaped camp is a large, well-organized wagon park. Parked near the wagons is a blacksmith or farrier's forge cart. Some horses and mules, likely picketed, can be seen grazing near the enlisted tent rows. Camp Alexis was smaller, but various documentary and photographic sources suggest that it, too, was organized and laid out according to prevailing military regulations and guidance for field camps.

Analysis of the archaeological materials recovered during the investigations suggests that the area occupied by Camp Alexis has a long history of use. A few finds indicate that the area was used by prehistoric peoples and by American Indians early in the nineteenth century. The most intensive use of the site, which occurred long after the buffalo-hunt camp, were the commemorative picnics and associated softball and rodeo events in the first half of the twentieth century. But even this intermittent use has not obscured the remains of the 1872 campsite. The archaeological record is clear and distinct.

Artifacts from the campsite consist of U.S. Army general-service and cavalry uniform buttons, trouser buttons, 1870s-era tin-can fragments, iron tent stakes, an iron gimlet, and cartridges and bullets. The buttons and bullets recovered during the systematic work were scattered across the site in no apparent pattern except that the buttons cluster on the northeast side of the site.

The artifacts that present the richest detail about the camp are the cut nails, the fragments of beer, ale, wine, and champagne bottles, and the lead foil seals for the wine and champagne bottles. The

Figure 64. A Seventh Cavalry field camp during the 1874 Black Hills Expedition. The camp is far larger than Camp Alexis, but the general separation and arrangement of officers and enlisted tents as well as the wagon park mimic one another in large part, suggesting that Camp Alexis followed military guidelines for camp organization. Little Bighorn Battlefield National Monument.

seals were found clustered on the upper terrace. The liquor- and wine-bottle fragments and the lead foil seals tended to be scattered, but most were found west of the ephemeral drainage on the central part of the terrace. The cut nails were more widely distributed but also tended to be in the highest concentrations in this same area. The nails were grouped into three general sizes: small, medium, and large. The small nails, including one or two early wire nails, are likely the remains of packing boxes and crates used to transport goods to the site or, once their contents had been consumed, as temporary storage, ersatz seating, or even firewood. The medium-sized cut-nail group could have been from large crates or boxes but also might represent expedient tables, benches, and other items for camp use similar to that depicted in the dining-tent sketch of the 1867 Kansas hunt. The largest cut nails likely represent the remains of the three tent floors and other heavier construction. Most have lost their heads or are bent, likely the result of being pulled from lumber. Along with the fact that the majority of cut nails are clustered in one area, their condition suggests that they were discarded while the camp was being struck after the hunt party had departed. Thus the cut nails likely represent the disassembly of temporary wooden camp furniture and tent floors and the salvage of usable lumber. The distribution might reflect some of the various camp activities and perhaps the general location of the three floored tents: the dining tent, the grand duke's tent, and General Sheridan's tent. Most likely it represents the salvage of the lumber associated with those features.

The artifact distribution appears to indicate that wine and liquor consumption occurred in the vicinity of the dignitaries' tents, near the center of the upper terrace. Historical camp descriptions and photographic evidence place the dignitaries' tents and attendant features in the same location. The scatter of other artifacts, such as tin cans, a gimlet, blouse and trouser buttons from the clothing of enlisted men, a picket-pin loop, and horse-tack buckles, indicate that the lower ranks were located north and east of the dignitaries. This too is consistent with the historical and photographic record of the camp.

Spotted Tail's personal tent and the main camp of Indian participants in the 1872 hunt likely was in the Red Willow Creek valley immediately below the army camp. That area has suffered repeated flooding and is either degraded or alluviated to such a degree that available investigative techniques cannot locate any remains associated with the camp. Photographic evidence, presented in chapter 5, indicates that Spotted Tail's tepee was on the upper terrace near the army camp. Only one item appears to be associated with this location. That artifact is a silver dangle, likely from an earring. This ornament was found on the east side of the army camp, near the edge of the terrace and within ten meters of the site of Spotted Tail's tent as determined from photographic analysis. The dangle is a traditional type and might be associated with an earlier use of the site. But because it was found midway between the army tents and the place where the Spotted Tail family camped, it is most likely associated with the 1872 camp.

Historical documents and photographic evidence suggest that the 1872 camp was organized hierarchically, with dignitaries and officers segregated both from enlisted personnel and from the American Indian camp, and even from Spotted Tail's tepee. The archaeological materials and their distribution across the landscape are in full concert with the historical and photographic evidence. The several lines of evidence clearly demonstrate that Camp Alexis was organized according to the prevailing military-camp model. In one sense it was simply a small-scale version of a typical army field camp of the era. However, because it was intended for use by special dignitaries, it might also be considered unique. The archaeological record does not reveal at what time of year the camp was occupied, but it does show that unusual activities took place there over a short period. The number of personal and other artifacts recovered from Camp Alexis—low when compared to the numbers from longer-term military campsites—reveals its short-term use.

Historic documents and archaeological artifacts in many military camps reveal that wine, liquor, and beer consumption was relatively common. The concentration of bottle glass and lead-foil bottle seals; the presence of ceramic tableware fragments; and the concentrations of cut nails indicating the presence of wood flooring in a limited area, of packing boxes, and of lightly constructed tables and benches combine to indicate that Camp Alexis was socially stratified and that its use was noticeably different from that of other military campsites of its time.

Both the photographic and the historic record of the 1872 camp document a flagpole that we were unable to locate during archaeological investigations of the site. Likely a local tree cut and trimmed for the purpose and set in a dug hole, the flagpole was a prominent feature of the camp. According to the *New York Herald*, the first indication of the camp that the party saw on its arrival was "the Stars and Stripes . . . flying from a towering flagstaff on a broad plateau."[28] It seems unlikely that the flagstaff had much metal associated with it, perhaps a few nails to hold a pulley in place and a cleat to secure the rope, but whether these were salvaged or left in place is unknown. The Eaton photographic record, if we have interpreted the long shadow in the grand duke's tent image correctly, places the flagpole south and perhaps a little east of the southern line of tents.

During the field investigations we observed a depression approximately three feet in diameter in this general area. Metal detecting produced no results in or around the depression. At this point we cannot determine the flagpole position.

Archaeologically recovered nails, tin cans, wine-, champagne-, and lead-foil bottle seals, liquor-bottle glass, buttons, and cartridges were trash and lost items left following a three-day event in mid-January 1872. They are also the tangible evidence of that event. Placing the camp location precisely on the ground, documenting the camp and the hunt, they are the physical manifestation of where Custer, Cody, Sheridan, Grand Duke Alexis, and Spotted Tail once trod the ground in western Nebraska.

8

CAMP ALEXIS HISTORICAL ARCHAEOLOGY

Its Context and Meaning

In 1872, Grand Duke Alexis experienced the American frontier on the point of flat land to the north of Red Willow Creek. Ranchers, bronc riders, baseball players, and old settlers subsequently left their marks on the site. Today it is defined by barbed-wire fences, and a well-maintained road is less than a mile away. Even so, this spit retains a remarkably wild feel.

After carefully searching beyond intervening uses, we found material traces of the grand duke's 1872 visit. Those materials were not stridently apparent or immediately impressive, but as this volume tries to demonstrate, archaeological evidence—cut nails, fragments of bottle glass, lead-foil bottle seals, buttons, and bullets—does show where the grand duke camped. As we searched for archaeological evidence pinpointing the location of Camp Alexis, we realized that the archaeological record was but one of many sources of information—published accounts, photographic treatments, ephemera, and a surprisingly rich popular lore—on the grand duke's visit.

Searching the various sources of information made it clear that the grand duke's hunt has significance for scholars, collectors, and the general public. Finding what is important to each of these diverse audiences has been at least as challenging as finding the hunt's material residues. Perhaps the highest value of the artifact assemblage is as a basis of archaeological microhistory.

Ephemera offer clear evidence that the grand duke's visit to the United States generated immediate popular interest. The result was a variety of ephemera, and because disposable items intended for a single use rarely make it into archives, the challenge is to locate them. These items, mostly paper products, include ornate railroad timetables showing the date and time at which the special train would pass through each town; invitations to extravagant balls and dinners listing the cast of committee members, usually prominent locals, who planned the event; and copies of telegrams and letters sent to plan and execute the logistics of the visit. Photographs of the grand duke and other dignitaries, stereoscopic views taken at Camp Alexis, sheet music commemorating the visit—clearly these were meant as keepsakes. Regardless of the definition, nearly all are now rare, often one of a kind. Jim Crain said, "The great thing about pursuing the trail of ephemera for a subject such as this is that you never know what's going to turn up next."[1] He is right. Yet these bits of ephemera constitute the pictorial and written record of the royal visit, in essence the historical record of a roughly sixty-day visit to the United States. They are a certain and highly graphic reflection of the broad popular interest generated by the appearance and adventurous pursuits of a handsome young European nobleman in post-Civil War America. They provide historical context for more recent events and continuing interest in similar topics.

Photography was a well-established medium by the 1870s, so it is hardly surprising that the grand duke's visit was documented in photographs. What is remarkable is that the creative labors of Edric Eaton were so easily lost. Few Eaton images have survived, and reconstructing the events and individuals they illustrate is extremely difficult. The task is simplified somewhat by the availability of archaeological materials and the perspective of microhistory, but a full appreciation of Eaton's photographs of Camp Alexis involves analytical "excavation" fully comparable to the work involved in exposing archaeological deposits.

Written sources provide the fullest account of the grand duke's buffalo hunt, but measuring them against themselves and other sources discovered during this investigation reveals their shortcomings. Inconsistencies in accounts by major participants—most notably Buffalo Bill himself—suggest that from the beginning people have enjoyed wrapping the grand duke's hunt in the bunting of hyperbole and license. Did Cody himself drive the duke's wagon?

Did Sheridan really say, "Shake 'em up a little Bill, and give us some old-time stage driving"? Truly we cannot be sure, but hard archaeological evidence indicates that the grand duke and his host were richly feted at Camp Alexis. Travel to the jumping-off point at North Platte Station was in the best accommodations Victorian America could provide, the elegant Pullman palace car coupled to a steam locomotive. Once at North Platte the party took to horses and wagons, separating themselves from most trappings of civilization by traveling fifty miles over largely undeveloped trail to reach their camp on Red Willow Creek. They followed a trail rather than a road, and their facilities, though comfortable, were primitive. They ate and drank well. Witness the champagne foil and ale bottles. Indeed, no effort was spared to accommodate the grand duke, his entourage, and the senior U.S. Army officers who acted as hosts. But the group was housed in canvas army tents in the middle of winter. Even if luxurious by some standards, the experience was nevertheless primitive. The party was composed of socially prominent travelers with leisure time sufficient to experience the wide expanse of the Great Plains, to hunt buffalo, and to meet and experience the native inhabitants. In 1872 this was adventure tourism for the elite.

Both Grand Duke Alexis and General Sheridan recorded exuberant statements on the joy of the hunt and enjoyment of the wide-open spaces of the West. In this way they exemplified an early phase of America's tourism and vacation culture. Western tourism was still emergent in 1872, but the grand duke was following, and contributing to, a pattern by which tourists would relate to nature, isolation, and rustic living. That pattern constitutes yet another record that we had to consider in our effort to understand the archaeology of Camp Alexis.

Beginning with the grand duke's separation from his homeland as he and his entourage sailed from Russia, his world tour, and particularly his U.S. visit, exemplify William Hunt's anthropological/archaeological model of tourism. Alexis had many stages of adventure and sojourn as he made ports of call. In the United States he had many focal and destination points. Perhaps most memorable to him were the buffalo hunts he fondly recalled so often and for so many years. The sojourn at Camp Alexis exposed the grand duke—and the many Americans who followed popular accounts of his experiences—to a mystical place, the Great Plains, to mystical people, American Indians, and to mystical beasts, the American bison. That it was a romantic episode is clearly reflected in his personal communications with his family. Following his return, Alexis continued to regale friends and subordinates with stories about his experiences in and the wonders of the American West.

The buffalo hunt follows the general pattern of early adventure tourism, with most supplies being transported to the camp by army wagon from remote supply centers. The hunt might have been part of a diplomatic mission, but in showing him the young nation, his U.S. hosts entertained him in a primitive camp. From an anthropological perspective, Alexis's travels in the United States mirror those of most tourists or pilgrims of the same era. Clearly Alexis was conforming to broader cultural patterns. But because Alexis was on a diplomatic mission, railroads and telegraph were lifelines. Railroads and river steamers were an expedient and efficient means of transportation and to a certain extent dictated the grand duke's itinerary. Even the buffalo hunt took place near a rail line. And he relied on the telegraph not only as a means to stay in touch with his family, but also as a means to send and receive official state messages and instructions. The buffalo hunt and camp were the farthest he ranged from civilization, and even then he was able to communicate via messenger relay to the telegraph.

The combined historical and archaeological record of the camp shows that the grand duke and his hosts enjoyed special treatment, including flooring and rough furniture in their canvas accommodations. They were the elite, and they enjoyed not only the fruits of the hunt but also the trappings of status. They were supplied with fine wines and liquors, ceramic tableware, and other items that set them apart as special. Clearly the dignitaries at Camp Alexis fared well.

The historic record is nearly silent on the lifestyle of the men who established, maintained, and struck the camp and who transported the dignitaries between the camp and the railhead. It mentions only that the support groups were soldiers of the Second Cavalry and that they were housed in tents. The archaeological record of this part of Camp Alexis is limited, but it is there. Cartridges, a tool, and buttons from uniforms constitute some of the physical evidence of those who also served. Discarded tin cans suggest that they ate standard army rations, probably supplemented by bison meat. Photographs of the dignitaries include some common soldiers, and two images of the camp show the soldiers' tents in the far middle ground. Otherwise they are nearly absent. The common soldier left little behind, but he did leave some physical evidence of his presence and existence. The social elite are more prominent in the historic, photographic, and archaeological records, but the enlisted soldiers of the support units also left a record of their presence.

Short-term camps were a central feature of the army occupation of the American West. As troops moved across the frontier and into new territory, they lived in a series of short-term camps. The placement of these camps marked a strategy of western expansion, but because camps were ephemeral, they are hard to address archaeologically. Camp Alexis was the playground of a small, well-supported elite, but it was also a camp set up by common soldiers following regular military procedures. We might have hoped for better records and clearer images, but the sources available from Camp Alexis do constitute a basis for the exploration of frontier military encampments.

The one group nearly nonexistent in the archaeological record are the people in Spotted Tail's band who came to Camp Alexis to add color and entertainment. American Indians are not, however, absent from the archaeological record. Those who lived on the land before Camp Alexis was occupied left artifacts of stone and metal that attest to their presence. That the archaeological footprint of Spotted Tail's band is virtually nonexistent is perhaps explained by their choice of location in the Red Willow Creek valley and by changes at this location in the ensuing years. Few artifacts present tangible evidence that Spotted Tail and his band were at the camp, but the handsome silver ear bob found at the campsite must have been a real loss to its wearer.

Each social group occupying Camp Alexis—dignitaries, soldiers, and American Indians—left an archaeological record, but that record varies in scope and depth according to the social status of each group. The elite are most visible archaeologically, the soldiers are next, and the American Indians are least visible. Such a range of archaeological visibility is not uncommon in dealing with the material culture of social stratification. Those with the best and most leave us the richest archaeological record; those with the least often leave a small, almost imperceptible artifactual footprint. Thus, by looking holistically at material culture, historical documents, and ephemera, historical archaeology has built a more complete and accurate understanding of the story of Camp Alexis and the royal buffalo hunt.

Historical records give us a sense of who occupied the site and how it was used. The photographs are artifacts in the sense they provide us a glimpse into the camp layout, the relative status of its occupants, and the range of goods and materials used to support the hunt. But the archaeological record gives us the truly tangible remains of the site. The machine-cut nails were once part of crates and boxes that held foodstuffs, wine, champagne, beer, and other luxuries for the elite. They also likely held together the hardtack boxes and other containers needed to sustain the soldier escort, whose roles and responsibilities are not well recorded in the paper trail. Other nails once fastened boards that became the floors of the dining tent, the grand duke's tent, and probably General Sheridan's tent. And some might have fastened lumber to form seats and the table at which fancy foodstuffs and recently slaughtered buffalo were served.

These objects were last seen, used, or trod upon by the soldier escort, and the likes of Spotted Tail, the grand duke, Sheridan, Custer, and Cody in January 1872. The nails, glass bottle fragments, buttons, cartridges, ornaments, and other artifacts are a real and tangible link to our past, one that deserves recognition, protection, and preservation. The landscape of Camp Alexis is the only place the grand duke visited that has not been significantly altered by time and modern development. The landscape and the artifacts are our only remaining tangible link to an important, if ephemeral, event in American history, a time when Imperial Russia and the United States were friends.

Our dalliance with the site where the grand duke stayed while hunting buffalo in 1872 revealed a great many different records. We learned from artifacts, from papers and publications, from people, and from pictures. The details in each record required assessment. Each required peculiar treatment. Most had specific audiences, and often the records seemed to disagree. Each record also posed distinctive questions about how and why it deserved consideration. Every record posed unresolved questions. In the end the most permanent and direct record of the grand duke's visit to the United States is the archaeological record we have endeavored to elucidate. The slightly altered landscape itself—along with nails, wine- and champagne-bottle fragments, foil seals, army buttons, and other materials—is the hard evidence of the grand duke's buffalo-hunting adventure in Nebraska. Today that landscape is preserved and protected by two families whose ties to the land combine with their collective sense of history to protect not only the landscape but also the artifacts embedded in it.

NOTES

Preface

1. The compilation of papers published by Brooks, DeCorse, and Walton 2008 provides the best comprehensive overview of the theoretical and practical approaches to microhistory. More recent works, by Beaudry 2010 and Veit and Gall 2011, further develop the concepts.

2. For further discussion of the topic, see Brooks, DeCorse, and Walton 2008: 4.

3. In 1894, writing under the nom de plume "Buffalo Bill," William F. Cody published a short article on western hunting camps in *Cosmopolitan*. That article contains an image identified as Spotted Tail's campsite during the 1872 hunt.

Chapter 2

1. See Devore and Lee 1999 and Kelly 2007 for discussions of prehistoric and modern hunter-gatherer band organization and relationships.

2. Blackmore 1971 discusses the issue of elites in control of hunting resources in the early modern state.

3. See Paxson 1917 for an overview of the growth of leisure sport in the United States.

4. Paxson 1917:143–44 discusses the rise of sport hunting as a part of the leisure culture in the nineteenth century.

5. Bossenmaier 1976, MacDonald 1987, and McCorquodale 1997 all dis-

cuss the role of hunting in wildlife management during the latter half of the twentieth century.

6. James Hanson's 2011:33–53 study of firearms in the North American fur trade is the best modern treatment of the role of guns in the Americas.

7. Cramer's 2007:204–23 work is an excellent study of the proliferation of firearms in the United States.

8. Morris's biography of Theodore Roosevelt emphasizes his hunting and collecting safaris during his postpresidential years. Roosevelt epitomizes the dichotomy, which still exists, between hunting and conservation.

9. Merritt 1985.

10. McMurty 2002, 2003a, 2003b, and 2004.

11. B. Miles Gilbert 1986 and Wayne Gard 1960 discuss the role of bison by-products in industrial America.

12. Smits 1994 argues that the army deliberately destroyed the buffalo herds in an effort to impoverish American Indians and thereby force them to enter the reservation system for sustenance. See note 13.

13. William Dobak's 1995 argument that destroying the buffalo herds was not a policy of the U.S. army is accepted as having refuted Smits's 1994 argument.

14. Using an ecology-based argument, Isenberg 2000 shows that a combination of climate change, overhunting (by Indians as well as hide or meat hunters), and disease caused the near-extinction of the American Bison.

15. Letter to Gen. William Sherman July 3, 1871. Microfilm Reel 16, William T. Sherman Papers, Library of Congress (hereinafter Sherman Papers).

16. Andrews 2005 takes a socialist or Marxist postmodernist view of tourism: elites exploit the classes whose labor supports leisure tourism.

17. For historians' views on tourism, see Athearn 1953, Nevins 1948, Pomeroy 1990, and Wrobel and Long 2001.

18. Wrobel and Long 2001, Coles and Timothy 1998.

19. Rothman wrote extensively on tourism in the west. Much of his thinking is embodied in Rothman 1998:44.

20. Anthropological studies of tourism can be found in Bodine 1981, Nash 1981, and Crick 1989.

21. See Graburn 1989 for a discussion of stages of tourism.

22. William Hunt 2009 developed the first archaeological model of tourism for the West. Its focus is Yellowstone National Park, but it is applicable in other contexts.

23. Turner and Turner 1978 and Crick 1989 have developed a thoughtful model of the process of tourism.

24. See William Hunt 2009:9–11 for a more complete discussion of these anthropological tourism contexts.

25. Hunt 2009:1–74.

26. Buckley 2006 defines and develops the concepts of adventure tourism in some detail.

27. See Balicki 2010 for a full discussion of Civil War campsite typology.

28. The archaeological expression of Civil War campsites is the subject of abundant literature and extensive reports. See, for example, McBride and Sharp 1991, McBride 1994, Balicki 2000, McBride et al. 2003, and McBride and McBride 2006.

29. Nelson 2006 presents an overview of the vernacular forms these domiciles took.

30. See Balicki 2010 for a full discussion of the topic.

31. Corle and Balicki 2006 present a solid argument regarding the collaboration between collectors and professional archaeologists, noting that it is far too uncommon in the profession.

32. James Legg and Steve Smith 2007:227 make an evocative call for professional archaeologists to work more closely with amateur collectors to maximize the information potential on the sites they are investigating.

33. See Balicki 2010 for a full discussion of methods, and of the pitfalls of using inappropriate methods, on military sites.

34. Jones 1999, Buttafuso 2000, Sterling and Slaughter 2000, Espenshade et al. 2002, and Corle and Balicki 2006 provide ample examples of the failure of projects on Civil War sites when metal detectors are not employed. Likewise they provide excellent examples of the value of metal detecting as a tool in the archaeological study of historic sites.

Chapter 3

1. A Russian biography of Grand Duke Alexis describes his life and his world tour. Bleykova 2004.

2. See Ferrand 1995 and 1999 for details on Alexis's alleged marriage and his son.

3. Dumin 1999 and Bleykova 2004 discuss the granting of nobility to Alexis's son.

4. See Saul 1996a for an excellent summary of U.S.-Russian relationships through the nineteenth century.

5. The context for Alexis's trip to the United States and its effect on both countries is documented and discussed in contemporary accounts and modern scholarship, as are U.S. and Russian diplomatic ups and downs. See *New York Times* June 30, 1871, Saul 1996a:20–75, and Hanson 2005:132.

6. Throughout 1871, newspapers reported the progress of the plans and the course of the visit in great detail: "Grand Duke Alexis, His Departure for America in August," *New York Times* May 16, "Preparations for American Tour," *New York Times*, June 19, "Grand Duke Alexis, Departure of His Imperial Highness," *New York Times*, August 21, "Departure of the Russian Squadron for New York," *New York Times*, September 27, and "The Russian Reception," *New York Times*, October 29.

7. "The Coming Reception of Grand Duke Alexis," *New York Times* April 27, 1871, and Saul 1996a:20–75.

8. "On Board the *Mary Powell*, The Grand Duke's Reception by the Committee," *New York Times*, November 21, 1871, and "On Board the *Mary Powell*, The Grand Duke's Reception," *New York Times*, November 22, 1871, and McAlpine 1872:324.

9. Schmidt 2001.

10. The Frank Thomson Papers at Drexel University Archives (hereinafter Thomson Papers) contain more than sixty pieces of correspondence, Thomson's telegraph books, and railroad time cards for most legs of the journey across the United States. The correspondence makes clear that, although some railroads did charge the Russians for motive power and use of their roads, most did not. As transportation manager, Thomson sent a preprinted letter and circular (today's form letter) to each railroad asking that it supply an engine and a telegrapher for its leg of the trip. The correspondence indicates that most were eager to do so; in fact, there appears to have been spirited competition among some lines for the honor of conveying the royal party.

11. In a contemporary pamphlet the Pullman Company described a sleeping car as "containing twelve open sections of two double berths each, and two state rooms of two double berths each (in all twenty-eight berths) with conductor and porter, seventy-five dollars per day." The drawing-room [hotel] car was described as "containing two drawing rooms, as above described [for a sleeping car], one state-room having two berths, and six open sections of two double berths each (in all twenty-two berths), and having also, in one end, a kitchen fully equipped with every thing necessary for cooking and serving meals, with conductor, cook, and two waiters, eighty-five dollars per day." Nordhoff 1874:28–29, Bianculli 2002:53–60.

12. In a January 24, 1872, article entitled "Alexis at the Capital of Kansas!" the *Kansas State Record* notes that the train was made up of a "Pullman outfit," consisting of a baggage car, a commissary [dining car], a sleeper car [seats for day use were converted into beds at night—an early form of the classic Pullman sleeper], and a drawing-room (parlor) car for use by the grand duke. In addition, General Sheridan had two cars, including a sleeping car and a dining car. The circular that Thomson sent to the various railroad executives asking about transport on their lines says the train would be made of no more than five cars, which is consistent with the newspaper description (Thomson Papers, 1871–72 correspondence). Likewise a telegram dated November 30, 1871, from G. W. Barker of the Pennsylvania Railroad notes that the cars assigned to the trip are "PRR Baggage car, PRR Passenger car and Special car one hundred twenty." The telegram also asks if additional cars are required (Thomson Papers, 1871–72 correspondence). No response was found, but it seems likely that a commissary was added at that point. The passenger car is most likely the sleeper car mentioned in the newspaper account, and the special car is the drawing-room (parlor) car. The Thomson

Papers telegraph book contains a telegram to Albert Fink dated January 15, 1872, regarding transfer of the special train of five cars from St. Louis to the Louisville Northern Railway. In the telegram, Thomson states that the imperial train is made up of five Pullman cars, a baggage car, a commissary, two sleeping cars, and a drawing-room car. The car names are recorded in a January 25, 1872, *Leavenworth Weekly Times* article as *Geno* for the commissary car, *Manistee* and *Adelphi* for the sleeping cars, and *Adirondack* for the drawing-room car. The baggage car is unnamed.

13. Simon 1998:130–33, 146–53.

14. "The Grand Duke's Departure from New York," *New York Times*, November 23, 1871, and "The Grand Duke Pays His Respects to the President," *New York Times*, November 24, 1871.

15. "The City of Brooklyn, The Grand Naval Ball," *New York Times*, November 24, 1871, "The Grand Duke Visits the Federal Military Fortifications," *New York Times*, November 25, 1871, "A Quiet Sunday for the Grand Duke," *New York Times*, November 27, 1871, "The Grand Duke, His Movements Yesterday," *New York Times*, November 28, 1871, "Prince Alexis, Yesterday's Festivities," *New York Times*, November 29, 1871, and "How Alexis Passed the Day, A Shopping Excursion," *New York Times*, November 30, 1871, and "The Grand Duke's Visit, A Trip to West Point," *New York Times*, December 2, 1871, "NewYork City Reception for Grand Duke Alexis," *Frank Leslie's Illustrated Newspaper*, December 9, 1871, and "The Grand Duke Alexis," *Harper's Bazaar*, December 16, 1871.

16. Bradley 1990:111ff, 221, *Artillery Journal*, 1872, and Hatch 1956:117.

17. "The Grand Duke Alexis," *Springfield (Mass.) Daily Republican*, December 8, 1871, and Logan 1952.

18. Bradley 1990:114.

19. "Grand Duke Alexis, How He Passed His Time Yesterday," *New York Times*, December 3, 1871, "The Grand Duke, Reception at Philadelphia," *New York Times*, December 5, 1871, "Return of the Grand Duke," *New York Times*, December 6, 1871, "Duke Alexis in Boston," *New York Times*, December 9, 1871, "The Russian Prince, How He Passed His Second Day in Boston," *New York Times*, December 10, "Alexis Visits Boston Public Schools," *New York Times*, December 13, 1871, "Telegraphic Brevities," *New York Times*, December 15, 1871, and "Expense of the Ball in Honor of the Grand Duke," *New York Times*, December 20, 1871.

20. "The Grand Duke, Breakfast with the Mayor of Montreal," *New York Times*, December 16, 1871, "Reappearance of the Grand Duke," *New York Times*, December 23, 1871, "Royal Party at the Falls of Niagara," *New York Times*, December 25, 1871, and "Westward Progress of the Grand Duke," *New York Times*, December 27, 1871.

21. Frank Thomson, manager of transportation for Grand Duke Alexis and suite, was politically connected and well known to the Grant administration. During the Civil War he had served as chief assistant to Col.

Thomas Scott (president of the Union Pacific Railroad, 1871–74, and of the Pennsylvania Railroad, 1874–80), supervising the construction of railroads, bridges, and telegraph lines for the Union army. Thomson became president of Pennsylvania Railroad from 1897 until his death in 1899. "Frank Thomson," *New York Times*, February 28, 1897, and "Death of Frank Thomson," *New York Times*, June 6, 1899.

22. Some telegrams to Frank Thomson are in the possession of Jim Crain, who generously allowed us access to them.

23. *New York Times*, December 23 and 27, 1871, and "Chicago, the Grand Duke and the New Year," *New York Times*, January 4, 1872, and "The Grand Duke Alexis Arrives in Omaha," *New York Times*, January 13, 1872.

24. "Alexis Bound West," *New York Herald*, January 12, 1872, "Alexis in Omaha," *Beatrice (Nebraska) Express*, January 20, 1872, and "Grand Duke's Buffalo Hunt," *Rocky Mountain News*, January 16, 1872.

25. The Thomson Papers contain two books of telegrams that Thomson sent during his time as train manager. He sent more than seventy telegrams between December 13, 1871, and January 31, 1872. Six were from Camp Alexis regarding preparation for the trip to Cheyenne and Denver.

26. "Bos Americans the Imperial Shooting Party at Camp Alexis," *New York Herald*, January 18, 1872, telegram, John Evans to Frank Thomson, January 17, 1872 (Jim Crain collection), *New York Herald*, January 18, 1872, "Alexis, the Grand Duke," *Rocky Mountain News*, January 18, 1872, and telegram, Sheridan to Thomson, January 17, 1872 (Jim Crain collection).

27. "The Ducal Ball," *Rocky Mountain News*, January 19, 1872, "Alexis," *Chicago Tribune*, January 20, 1872, "Alexis' Visit to Denver," *Chicago Tribune*, January 21, 1872, and "Nimrod Alexis," *New York Herald*, January 22, 1872.

28. Gilbert et al. 2003:227–28, and Gard 1960:68–74.

29. *Returns from Regular Army Cavalry Regiments 1833–1916*. Sixth Cavalry, National Archives and Records Administration (hereinafter NARA) M744, and *Returns from U.S. Military Posts, 1800–1916*, Fort Wallace, December 1871–February 1872, NARA M617.

30. Otero 1935:50–56.

31. The Beeson account is transcribed in Connelly 1918. The Otero and Beeson hunt accounts were analyzed using forensic linguistic statement-analysis techniques (Olsson 2004). The analyses show that the veracity of both accounts is questionable, that their authors exaggerated and significantly embellished many areas. They attempted to inflate their own stature and worth by associating themselves with a famous event. Otero and Beeson may have been present at the Colorado hunt but certainly not in the roles they created for themselves.

32. "Nimrod Alexis," *New York Herald*, January 22, 1872.

33. Stewart 1980.

34. Telegram, Sheridan to Belknap, January 27, 1872. Microfilm Reel 3, Philip Henry Sheridan Papers, Library of Congress (hereinafter Sheridan Papers).

35. A telegram from the owners of the steamboat *Great Republic* to Custer—an apparent acknowledgment of his new position among the party—informed him that the boat was frozen in on the river and no longer available for use and offered the *Katie* instead. Thomson Papers, 1871–72 correspondence.

Eventually the party did get the *Great Republic* for the trip to Memphis. They contracted with James Howard and Company to provide the steamboat *James Howard* to convey them from Memphis to New Orleans. (January 31, 1872, telegram from B. R. Pegram to James Howard and Company, Thomson Papers, 1871–72 correspondence). The *Great Republic* and the *James Howard* were among the largest steamboats working the Mississippi River at the time, boasting 1,727 and 2,321 tons respectively. Hunter 1993:160, 607.

36. Saul 1996b:42.

37. Telegram, Sanford to Thomson, January 23, 1872. Jim Crain collection.

38. See Leckie 1993:134–36 for a description of Miss Sturgis and the Custers on the trip to New Orleans.

39. Custer's failure to invite Terry and the oversight by the grand duke's staff are reported in a February 9, 1872, letter from James Forsyth to Sheridan. James Forsyth Papers, Archives of William L. Clements Library, University of Michigan, Ann Arbor (hereinafter Forsyth Papers).

40. James Forsyth to Philip Sheridan, February 9, 1872. Forsyth Papers.

41. For the story of the New Orleans adventure, see "The Grand Duke Alexis Going to Louisville," *New York Times*, January 29, 1872, "The Grand Duke Alexis," January 30, 1872, "Movement of the Grand Duke Alexis," *New York Times*, February 2, 1872, "The Grand Duke at Vicksburg," *New York Times*, February 11, 1872, and "Arrival of the Grand Duke at the Crescent City," *New York Times*, February 13, 1872. Lee Farrow 2002 demystifies the story of the grand duke and the Rex parade.

42. "The Arrival of the Grand Duke and Suite at Havana," *New York Times* March 1, 1872, and "Alexis, the Grand Duke in Havana," *New York Times*, March 11, 1872.

43. "Cuba, the Progress of the War," *New York Times* March 3, 1872, "Alexis, the Grand Duke's Sojourn in Havana," *New York Times*, March 15, 1872, "Brazil," *New York Times*, July 23, 1872, "Arrival of the Grand Duke in Cape Town," *New York Times*, August 24, 1872, "South Africa," *New York Times*, September 6, "Arrival of the Grand Duke Alexis at Hong Kong," *New York Times*, September 18, 1872, September 26, 1872, "China, the Movements of the Grand Duke," *New York Times*, October 13, 1872, and "China, the Grand Duke Alexis," *New York Times*, November 16, 1872.

44. "Japan, Reception of the Grand Duke," *New York Times*, December 17, 1872.

45. Bleykova 2004.

46. "The Epiphany Ceremony on the Russian Vessel Svetlana," *Frank Leslie's Illustrated Newspaper*, 3 March 1877.

47. Nunes 2001, 2002.

48. Grand Duke Alexander 1932:41, 138–39.

Chapter 4

1. Saul 1996b:242.

2. Buecker 1982 and Adamson 1910.

3. Cody 1978 and 1923.

4. See Paul Andrew Hutton 1985 for a description of the October 1871 hunt. Cody said Sheridan told him of the upcoming hunt with the grand duke during the October hunt (MS6.1321.02, Grand Duke Alexis's Buffalo Hunt, undated manuscript page, McCracken Research Library, Buffalo Bill Research Center, Cody, Wyoming). Cody also noted that he first met Sheridan in 1867 when Sheridan employed him as a scout and that he had met Custer at Fort Hays earlier in 1867, while acting as a courier and scout. Cody, 1908:91–94, 166–76.

5. William Warren Tucker 1872:7 and Jeff Dykes 1972:7.

6. Bleykova 2004.

7. "The Grand Duke Alexis of Russia," *Frank Leslie's Illustrated Newspaper*, May 13, 1871. See Saul 1996a:23–26, 55 for discussions of the trip derived from research in the Russian State Archives.

8. Telegram, Bierstadt to General Dix, April 13, 1871. Jim Crain collection.

9. Saul 1996b:28.

10. Microfilm Reel 16, Sherman Papers; Belknap to Bierstadt August 7, 1871, from a private collection, cited in Hendricks, 1974:207; and Anderson and Ferber, 1991:220–23.

11. Saul 1996a:55.

12. "The Grand Duke Alexis," *Harper's Weekly*, October 14, 1871.

13. Sherman 1889:426.

14. Belknap to Sherman, November 1, 1871, Microfilm 666, Roll 36, RG94, Letters Received 1871–80, National Archives and Records Administration, Records of the Adjutant General's Office (hereinafter AGO 1871).

15. Sherman to Sheridan, November 1, 1871, AGO 1871.

16. Secretary of War to Secretary of State, November 2, 1871, AGO 1871.

17. Hendricks 1974:207–208.

18. Sheridan to Bierstadt, November 25, 1871, from a private collection, cited in Hendricks 1974:208.

19. Sheridan to Bierstadt, November 25, 1871 from a private collection, cited in Hendricks 1974:208.

20. Sheridan to Townsend, November 22, 1871, AGO 1871, and Adjutant General to Secretary of State, November 24, 1871, AGO 1871.

21. Hyde 1987:194–95.

22. Hyde 1987:195–96.

23. Telegram, December 24, 1871, AGO 1871.

24. Telegram, December 20, 1871, AGO 1871.

25. Frost 1964:107 and telegram from Sheridan to Custer, January 2, 1872. Jim Crain collection.

26. See Millbrook 1975, Dippie 1980, Frost 1985, and Grafe and Horsted 2002 for more information on Custer's interest in hunting and his hunting parties.

27. Dippie 1980:9–12.

28. Millbrook 1975:434–37 and Frost 1986.

29. Telegram, January 3, 1872, AGO 1871.

30. Letter, Delano to Secretary of War Belknap, January 4, 1872, AGO 1871.

31. M21, Reel 103, Letters Sent 1821–81, Office of Indian Affairs.

32. Frank Thomson sent at least seven telegrams between January 1 and 3 announcing the change of plans and asking various sources to help implement the change. Thomson Papers, correspondence 1871–72 and telegraph books.

33. Telegrams, Sickels to Thomson, January 5 and 10, 1872. Jim Crain collection.

34. Cody 1917. Cody's accounts of the hunt and the "shake 'em up Bill" ride were subjected to forensic linguistic statement analysis (Olsson 2004) and, like those of Otero and Beeson, found to be exaggerated and lacking veracity.

35. Cody 1917. The account of the royal buffalo hunt in Cody 1908:166–76 is far less embellished than are those in the posthumous "autobiographies." Portions of the 1908 buffalo-hunt chapter were published April 1, 1909, in the *Hazel Green Herald* (Wolfe County, Kentucky) as "The Plains Greatest Hunt." Clipping in the McCracken Research Library, Buffalo Bill Historical Center.

36. Tucker 1972:150.

37. *Returns from Regular Army Cavalry Regiments 1833–1916*, Second Cavalry, January 1872, NARA M744, Roll 19, and Fifth Cavalry Regimental Returns, January 1872, NARA M744, Roll 54.

38. Receipt, AGO 1871.

39. Vaughn 1966, Rodenbough 1875, Fleming 1911, and Thrapp 1991: 454–55.

40. "Alexis Bound West," *New York Herald*, January 12, "The Alexis Buffalo Hunt," *New York Herald*, January 13, 1872, and "Alexis at the Capital of Kansas!" *Kansas State Record*, January 24, 1872.

41. "The Alexis Buffalo Hunt," *New York Herald*, January 13, 1872.

42. *Beatrice (Nebraska) Express*, January 20, 1872. Clarke and Dickey might have traveled with the main hunt party in the Pullman sleeper, or they might have added a separate car for this leg of the journey. Their presence is reported in "Recollections of a Royal Buffalo Hunt," *Denver Times*, March 31, 1899.

43. Accounts of the arrival at North Platte Station and the trip to the camp are found in *Rocky Mountain News*, January 16, 1872, "Our Royal Guest," *Chicago Tribune*, January 15, 1872, "The Imperial Buffalo Hunter," *New York Herald*, January 16, 1872, "The Grand Duke and His Party Arrived This Morning," *Lincoln (Nebraska) Daily State Journal*, January 16, 1872, and "The Russian Prince," *Omaha Tribune and Republican*, January 15, 1872.

44. "The Weather along the Union Pacific," *Omaha Tribune and Republican*, January 13, 1872.

45. Saul (1996a:37, 56) lists the Russian party members.

46. See Heitman 1903:920 for Steever's service record. *Returns from U.S. Military Posts, 1800–1916*, Fort McPherson, Nebraska, January 1866–December 1872, January 1872, Roll 708, NARA M617, and Second Cavalry Regimental Returns, January 1872, Roll 19, NARA M744.

47. *Returns from U.S. Military Posts, 1800–1916*, Fort McPherson, Nebraska, January 1872, NARA M617, Roll 708, and letter, Capt. James Eagan to Lt. Edward Hayes, January 20, 1872, Letters and Endorsements copy book, NARA RG393 Part V, Vol. 2, North Platte Station, Nebraska.

48. See Broome 2009 for a detailed account and maps of the 1867 route.

49. Broome 2000 and Johnson and Allan 1999.

50. NARA RG33, U.S. Army Continental Commands, Department of the Platte Records, 1858–95, S61, Microfilm Roll 3, War Department Map of the Yellowstone and Missouri Rivers, 1876.

51. General Land Office (GLO) cadastral survey maps also show the trail running southward from Fort McPherson (GLO plat map for Township 12 North and Range 28 West, dated January 19, 1870), and the GLO map encompassing the Camp Alexis site (Township 7 North, Range 32 West), surveyed in July and August 1872, shows one trail trending southwesterly that would run about one mile below the campsite. Hutton 1985.

52. The trip to the camp and the story of the broken-down conveyance is cited in "The Imperial Buffalo Hunter," *New York Herald*, January 16, 1872, "The Imperial Buffalo Hunt," *New York Times*, January 16, 1872, "The Buffalo Hunt," *Chicago Tribune*, January 19, 1872, "Alexis among the Buffaloes," *Cleveland Morning Daily Herald*, January 20, 1872, and "The Grand Duke's Buffalo Hunt," *Lincoln (Nebraska) Daily State Journal*, January 17, 1872.

53. *New York Herald*, January 16, 1872, and *New York Times*, January 16, 1872. Clippings of unattributed newspaper articles regarding the progress of the hunt are also found in the Gustavus Vasa Fox collection in the archival

collections at the Museum of American History, Smithsonian Institution, old catalog number No. 255641 USNM.

54. *New York Herald*, January 16, 1872, and *New York Times*, January 16, 1872.

55. *New York Herald*, January 16, 1872.

56. *New York Herald*, January 16, 1872.

57. *New York Herald*, January 16, 1872, and "Alexis Hunting the Buffalo," *San Francisco Chronicle*, January 16, 1872. In a January 14, 1872, telegram, Frank Thomson reported to Lewis Parsons that they "have had a splendid time. The Grand Duke killed five Buffalo today in fine style." Thomson Papers, telegraph books.

58. "Alexis' Grand Hunt," *New York Herald*, January 17, 1872, "The Second Day's Hunt," *Nebraska Intelligencer*, January 17, 1872, "The Second Day's Hunt," *Chicago Tribune*, January 19, 1872, "Miscellaneous," *Lincoln (Nebraska) Daily State Journal* January 18, 1872, and "Camp Alexis," *Omaha Tribune and Republican*, January 17, 1872.

59. "Alexis' Grand Hunt," *New York Herald*, January 17, 1872, and "The Second Day's Hunt," *Nebraska Intelligencer*, January 17, 1872.

60. Dykes 1972:170.

61. "Bos Americans the Imperial Shooting Party at Camp Alexis," *New York Herald*, January 18, 1872, "Telegraphic Brevities," *Chicago Tribune*, January 21, 1872, and "The Grand Duke's Second Hunt," *Cleveland Morning Daily Herald*, January 22, 1872.

62. "Alexis' Grand Hunt," *New York Herald*, January 17, 1872, and Dykes 1972:168–69.

63. Lying partway between Moscow and St. Petersburg, Tver' is home to at least four museums. In July 2009, Stephen Damm visited Tver' in an attempt to track down the artifacts. One museum is an art gallery in a former palace of Catherine the Great; another is essentially a historical marker for Mikhail Yevgrafovich Saltykov-Shchedrin, a famous writer from Tver'. The other two museums are the Tver' State Museum and the Tver' Museum of Culture. Museums in Russia are focused on defining and creating a city identity and establishing its connections to famous or important (including royal) personages. Inquiries always seem to be welcome. Unfortunately the artifacts were not on exhibit in the museums visited. When we inquired, the museum staff and administrators expressed great interest but were unaware of such objects in the collections. Administrators made an inquiry on our behalf at another museum but discovered nothing. In the tumultuous events of the early twentieth century the items could have been lost or destroyed. The overthrow of the czarist regime certainly made associations with them much less popular. By way of comparison, in the nearby town of Vladimir, a statue of Czar Alexander II, Grand Duke Alexis's father, was torn down almost immediately after its completion in 1917 and replaced by a statue of Vladimir Lenin, which still stands today. Alternatively, they might have been lost during the Second World War. Perhaps they never were

in Tver'—or never existed. Certainly the museum staff in Tver' had never heard of them.

64. Allen 1988:235.

65. "A Grand Duke's Book on America," *Appleton's Journal* 1874 11(251):55.

66. Russian State Naval Archives Fond 1247, inventory 1, files 40–41.

67. Russian State Naval Archives Fond 1297, inventory 1, file 40, pp. 82 and 83.

68. Russian State Naval Archives File 40, pp. 146. 147, 148, and 149.

69. Russian State Naval Archives File 40, pp. 158, 159, 160, and 161.

70. Russian State Archives, January 1872 letter from Alexis to Maria Alexandrovna, Fond 641, inventory 1, file 34, p. 110.

71. Russian State Archives Fond 642, inventory 1, file 768, p. 10.

72. Russian State Archives Fond 652, inventory 1, file 385, pp. 7–9.

73. Russian State Archives Fond 678, inventory 1, file 739, p. 206.

74. Russian State Naval Archives, Fond 31, inventory 2, file 2, pp. 39 (back)–40.

75. Saul 1996a:55–70.

76. For American attitudes toward Russian nobility, see Saul, 1996:589.

77. *New York Herald*, January 18, 1872.

78. Telegram, January 16, 1872, AGO 1871.

79. *Lincoln (Nebraska) Daily Sate Journal*, January 18, 1872. "Sheridan and a Few Other Americans Have Been Decorated by the Czar," *Pueblo Colorado Chieftain*, May 12, 1872, laments that Cody was not "decorated by the Czar" as were Sheridan and other hunt-party members. Apparently the editor was unaware of Grand Duke Alexis's gifts to Cody. One gift, depicted in a circa 1879 Buffalo Bill poster or show bill in the Buffalo Bill Historical Center collections, is a gold cross-pattée medal. Also depicted, at the bottom of the poster, is a fanciful scene of the royal buffalo hunt featuring Cody in the center, a mounted George Custer amongst some uniformed Russians to the far left, and U.S. Army troops to the right. The dismounted Cody appears to be introducing Grand Duke Alexis to General Sheridan. Given that the hunt scene is imaginary, the depiction of the medal is suspect as well.

80. Cody 1917.

81. *New York Herald*, January 18, 1872, and *Lincoln (Nebraska) Daily State Journal*, January 18, 1872. The earliest citation of the "shake'em up Bill" story that we located is in "Sheridan and Buffalo Bill," *Sioux County Herald*, September 27, 1888, of Orange City, Iowa, found in the McCracken Research Library, Buffalo Bill Historical Center, Cody, Wyoming.

82. Blackstone 1986:81and Dean, 1975:3.

83. Cody with Cooper 1919:215.

84. "William McDonald Pioneer Recollections," *North Platte Telegraph-Bulletin*, January 13, 1958.

85. Yost 1979:57.

86. Yost 1979:57–58.
87. Smith 2003:25.
88. Miles and Bratt 1894:23.
89. Paine 1935:158 and Faulkner 1957:53.
90. For example, Breternitz 1931, Parry 1948, McDonald 1958, Tarsaidze 1958, White 1972, Louis Steinwedel 1961, Zornow 1961, Yost 1979, Dixon 1994, Sprague 1967:95–117, and Carter 2000.
91. Compare with Massie 1984a, 1984b.
92. Logan 152:37–42.
93. Pate 2006:223–25.
94. Hatch 1956:113–17.
95. Drummond 1923:349–50, and 421–22 and Hadley 1908.
96. Lee et al. 1915.
97. See Farrow 2002.
98. The alleged Thompson and Barrett associations were accessed on the Internet on November 8, 2011, at www.myspace.com/ixionburlesque/blog/454504002.
99. General Land Office Land Tract Book 54, Section 14, Range 32W, Township 7N, NARA RG509 GLO Series 3, Microfilm Roll 16.
100. Mintling 2004:8.
101. "Second Annual Picnic Drew a Record Breaking Throng," *Hayes Center Times Republican* August 18, 1932.
102. "The Famous Hunt of Grand Duke Alexis," *Hayes Center Times Republican* September 15, 22, and 29 and October 6, 13, and 20, 1932.
103. Paine 1932 and 1935 and "The Famous Buffalo Hunt of Grand Duke Alexis," *Cambridge (Nebraska) Clarion* June 28, 1934.
104. Compare with Cody 1917, 1923, and 1978,
105. Weiland 1932. Compare with "Buffalo Hunt Provided Sport for Russian Royalty," *Columbus Daily Telegram* April 29, 1931.
106. Mintling 2004:8, Smith 2009:174–76, and Anonymous 1977:2. David Frank Neiswanger arrived in Saline County, Nebraska, about 1875 and settled in the town of Cambridge in 1883, where he became a barber. With an abiding sense of history and stonecutting skills learned from his father as a boy in Iowa, he began marking historic sites in western Nebraska. He placed roughly thirty markers at such places as Camp Alexis and the highwater mark of the 1935 Republican River flood. In 1938 Elbert Taylor wrote a tribute to Neiswanger that is found in the Neiswanger Family File, Nebraska State Historical Society, Lincoln. Images of some of Neiswanger's commemorative marks are found in T239 in the NSHS photographic collections.
107. Paine 1932:25–27.
108. Paine 1935:164–83.
109. Mintling 2004:8.
110. *Jewels of the Romanovs.*

111. In "The Tsar and the President: Alexander II and Abraham Lincoln," Suzanne Massie reprises her earlier articles on the grand duke in the United States.

112. Mintling 2004:47.

CHAPTER 5

1. "Alexis at the Capital of Kansas!" *Kansas State Record*, January 24, 1872, and Katz 1985:92–93.

2. Katz 1985:94.

3. "Alexis at the Capital of Kansas!" *Kansas State Record*, January 24, 1872.

4. Piston and Sweeney 2009:3–4.

5. Katz 1985:95–99.

6. Dykes 1972:163.

7. Dustin 1980:24–25.

8. Savage and Bell 1894:142.

9. "Returned, Mr. E. L. Eaton," *Omaha Daily Telegraph*, March 28, 1861.

10. Edmunds 1871:461.

11. Andreas 1882 and Wakeley 1917:95.

12. Dyer 1994.

13. Palmquist and Kailbourn 2005:225–27, Mautz 2000:299, and Andreas 1882.

14. "Photography, Mr. Eaton," *Omaha Daily Herald*, February 12, 1867.

15. Jackson 1940, Blaurock 1975, and Forsee 1964.

16. Edmunds 1871.

17. "Anderson Studio out at Wahoo Oldest One in Nebraska," *Omaha World Herald*, November 13, 1927.

18. "Photographic,"*Omaha Bee*, June 28, 1872, and "For Views of Omaha [Edric Eaton Adviertisement]," August 8 and 10, 1872.

19. "Photographs, Now Is the Time [Edric Eaton Advertisement]," *Omaha Bee*, June 21, 1891.

20. "Deaths, Eaton," *Chicago Tribune*, April 2, 1909.

21. Mace 1990:94–101 and Darrah, 1981:13–14.

22. Robert N. Dennis Collection of Stereographic Views (hereinafter Dennis Collection), MFY Dennis Coll G90–F388–003F.

23. Greene 1989:221.

24. Dennis Collection, MFY Dennis Coll G90–F388–004F.

25. Nelson 2006:179.

26. E. B. Custer 1893:347–48.

27. George Allen Collection, NAA, INV 09878.

28. Dennis Collection, MFY Dennis Coll G90–F388–005F.

29. U.S. Army 1882.

30. Neuman 2010:241–50.
31. Crain 2000:24.
32. Ward 1948:176.
33. Ward 1948:167–70.
34. Edmunds 1871.
35. Cody 1978.
36. Letter, James Forsyth to Phil Sheridan, February 9, 1872. The letter mentions Cody's layover in Chicago, where he resided in Sheridan's home. Forsyth's letter says, "Prof. Ward, the buffalo bone man, went east with him [Cody]." The description of Ward as the buffalo bone man suggests that Sheridan knew who Ward was. Forsyth Papers.
37. *Omaha Tribune and Republican*, January 15, 1872.
38. Nebraska State Historical Society, RG3004–10.
39. Katz 1985:91.
40. New York Public Library Photographic Collections, Dennis Collection, MFY, G90–F388–006F.
41. "Ward and Cody," A.W23, Photographs Box 1:1:2, Henry August Ward Papers, Rare Books Special Collections and Preservation Collections, Rush Rhees Library, University of Rochester, Rochester, N.Y.
42. Haynes 1995.
43. McChristian 2000.
44. Greene 1986: 202–205.
45. Greene 1986: 209–15.
46. Scott and Bleed 2002.
47. E. B. Custer 1893:342–44.
48. E. B. Custer 1893:345.
49. Taft 1946:264. Berghaus revised Henry Wornall's sketches of the grand duke's hunt, creating caricatures that were published in *Leslie's Weekly*.

Chapter 6

1. We decided to employ metal detecting as the most effective identification technique based on investigations by Connor and Scott 1998, David 2006, Graham 1995, and Takasaki et al. 2006.
2. Metal-detecting methods were adapted from Connor and Scott 1998 and Scott et al. 1989.
3. Mintling 2004 published his research on the site. He recorded many oral traditions associated with the site and its history.
4. Tucker first published his embellished compilation of newspaper accounts in 1872.
5. Hanson 1975:82 and Karklins 1992:104. Karklins' source book contains an excellent overview of silver usage among indigenous Canadian people in the eighteenth and nineteenth centuries.
6. Tice 1997 contains extensive research on uniform buttons.

7. Greene 1986:95 illustrates these simple button types.

8. Dorsey (1984) researched Army waist belts extensively.

9. Basic construction-nail descriptions and identifications are found in Nelson 1968.

10. Bealer 1972 explains the function of historic tools.

11. See Greene's (1986:vii) introduction to the quartermaster catalog.

12. See Welsh 1966 and Sloane 1964 for identification and discussions of historic tools.

13. Horsted et al. 2009:266–67 and King and Dunnavant 2008 describe and identify the context for the discovery of these expedient tent pins. The fact that the pins have been recovered from multiple sites indicates that the form was known to many blacksmiths and farriers.

14. A republished carriage and wagon supply catalog, Spivey 1979:81, identifies this artifact.

15. See Thomas and Thomas 2007:11 for identical bullets.

16. See Pitman 1990:24 and 28 and Pate 2006:202, and 320–37 for discussions of the Richards conversion of the Colt Model 1860 and its associated ammunition.

17. See Farrington 2004:97–99 for a listing of arms used by troops at this time.

18. Farrington 2004:76.

19. One of the best bottle-identification sites is maintained by the Society for Historical Archaeology, http://www.sha.org/bottle.

20. See Harding 2006:59–66 for descriptions and dating of Eley Brothers cartridges.

21. Herskovitz 1978.

22. American Indian adoption of the metal projectile point is found in Hanson 1972 and Russell 1967.

23. Lyle and Porter 1882. See Steffen 1978 for identification of army horse tack.

24. See Tice 1997 for button identification.

Chapter 7

1. United States War Department, 1980 reprint.

2. Balicki et al. 2002a and 2004, Balicki 2006a, Reeves 2006, and Whithorne 2006.

3. Geier et al. 2006:11.

4. Balicki 2000.

5. Jensen 2000.

6. Balicki 2000.

7. Hutton 1985:16–19.

8. *Returns from U.S. Military Posts, 1800–1916,* Fort McPherson, Nebraska, January 1866–December 1872, NARA M617, Roll 708.

9. Davies 1985:78.
10. Davies 1985:78.
11. Strong 1960:9–11.
12. Geier et al. 2006.
13. Fesler et al. 2006:232–34.
14. Jolley 2008.
15. Geier et al. 2006 and Fesler et al. 2006.
16. Clark 1995 and Garrow et al. 2000 and 2005.
17. Watson 1999.
18. Clark to Scott, personal communications, November 20, 1981, March 26 and November 11, 1986, January 29 and March 5, 1989, and Clark to Altizer, personal communications, March 20 and 30, 2006.
19. Heski 2003.
20. Scott 2000.
21. Scott 2008.
22. Tagg and Baumler 1987 and Ahlstrom 1988.
23. King 2006 and 2008 and King and Dunnavant 2008.
24. Horsted et al. 2009.
25. Skinner 1968.
26. Whitehorne 2006: 28–50.
27. Horsted et al. 2009:68.
28. *New York Herald,* January 16, 1872.

Chapter 8

1. Crain 2005:10.

REFERENCES

Adamson, Archibald R.
    1910 "North Platte and Its Associations." North Platte, Neb.: *North Platte Evening Telegraph.*

Allen, Robert V.
    1988 *Russia Looks at America: The View to 1917.* Washington, D.C.: Library of Congress.

Anderson, Nancy K., and Linda S. Ferber
    1991 *Albert Bierstadt: Art and Enterprise.* New York: Hudson Hills Press.

Andreas, A. T.
    1882 *History of the State of Nebraska.* Chicago: Western Historical Company.

Andrews, Thomas A.
    2005 "'Made by Toile'? Tourism, Labor, and Construction of the Colorado Landscape, 1858–1917." *Journal of American History* 92(3):857–63.

Anonymous
    1885 *The Official State Atlas of Nebraska, Compiled from Government Surveys, County Records and Personal Investigations.* Philadelphia, Pa.: Everts and Kirk.
    1977 *Hayes County Heritage Book: 100 Years of Progress, 1877–1977.* No publisher or place.

Athearn, Robert G.
    1953 *Westward the Briton.* New York: Charles Scribner's Sons.

Balicki, Joseph
    2000   "Defending the Capital: The Civil War Garrison at Fort C. F. Smith." In *Archaeological Perspectives on the American Civil War*, edited by Clarence R. Geier and Stephen R. Potter, 125–47. Gainesville: University Press of Florida.
    2006a   "'Masterly Inactivity': The Confederate Cantonment Supporting the 1861–1862 Potomac River Blockade, Evansport, Virginia." In *Huts and History: The Historical Archaeology of Military Encampment during the American Civil War*, edited by Clarence Geier, David Orr, and Mathew Reeves, 97–136. Gainesville: University Press of Florida.
    2006b   "Supplemental Metal Detection Investigations Associated with Structural Landscape Enhancements, Blenheim Estate." Report prepared for the City of Fairfax, Virginia. Alexandria, Va.: John Milner Associates.
    2007   "The Confederate Cantonment at Evansport, Virginia." In *Fields of Conflict: Battlefield Archaeology from the Roman Empire to the Korean War*, edited by Douglas Scott, Lawrence Babits, and Charles Haecker, 2:255–77. Westport, Conn.: Praeger Security International.
    2010   "The Watch-Fires of a Hundred Circling Camps: Theoretical and Practical Approaches to Investigating Civil War Campsites." In *Method and Topic in the Historical Archaeology of Military Sites*, edited by Clarence R. Geier, Lawrence Babits, Douglas Scott, and David Orr, 57–74. College Station: Texas A&M University Press.

Balicki, Joseph, Bryan Corle, and Sarah Goode
    2004   "Multiple Cultural Resources Investigations at Eight Locations and along Five TankTrails, Marine Corps Base Quantico, Prince William, Stafford, and Fauquier Counties, Virginia." Report to EDAW, Inc., Alexandria, Va. Alexandria, Va.: John Milner Associates.

Balicki, Joseph, Kerri Culhane, Walton H. Owen II, and Donna J. Seifert
    2002   "Fairfax County Civil War Sites Inventory, Technical Report Version." Report to Fairfax County Park Authority, Fairfax, Va. Alexandria, Va.: John Milner Associates.

Baumler, Mark F., and Richard V. N. Ahlstrom
    1988   The Garfield Monument: An 1886 Memorial of the Buffalo Soldiers in Arizona. *Cochise County Quarterly* 18(1):3–34.

Bealer, Alex W.
    1972.   *Old Ways of Woodworking*. Barre, Mass.: Barre Publishers.

Beaudry, Mary C.
    2010   "Stitching Women's Lives: Interpreting the Artifacts of Sewing and Needlework." In *Interpreting the Early Modern World:*

Transatlantic Perspectives, edited by Mary C. Beaudry and James Symonds, 143–58. New York: Springer.

Bianculli, Anthony J.
2002 *Cars.* Vol. 2 of *Trains and Technology: The American Railroad in the Nineteenth Century.* Dover: University of Delaware Press.

Blackmore, Howard L.
2000 *Hunting Weapons from the Middle Ages to the Twentieth Century.* Mineola, N.Y.: Dover Publications.

Blackstone, Sarah J.
1986 *Buckskins, Bullets, and Business: A History of Buffalo Bill's Wild West.* Santa Barbara, Calif.: Greenwood Press.

Bland, Roger
2005. "Rescuing Our Neglected Heritage: The Evolution of the Government's Policy on Portable Antiquities in England and Wales." *Cultural Trends* 14(56):257–96.

Blaurock, Carl
1975 "William Henry Jackson, Pioneer Photographer." *Denver Westerners Roundup* 31(4):391–408.

Bleykova, Zoia
2004 *Grand Duke Alexis Alexandrovich: For and Against.* Saint Petersburg (Russia): Logos (translated by Stephen Damm).

Bodine, J. J.
1981 "Comment on Tourism as an Anthropological Subject by Dennison Nash." *Current Anthropology* 22(5):469.

Bossenmaier, Eugene F.
1976 "Ecological Awareness and Sport Hunting: A Viewpoint." *Wildlife Society Bulletin* 4(3):127–28.

Bradly, Joseph
1990 *Guns for the Tsar: American Technology and the Small Arms Industry in Nineteenth Century Russia.* DeKalb: Northern Illinois University Press.

Brooks, James. F., Christopher R. N. DeCorse, and John Walton (Editors)
2008 *Small Worlds: Method, Meaning, and Narrative in Microhistory.* Santa Fe, N.M.: School for Advanced Research Press.

Broome, Jeff
2000 "On Locating the Kidder Massacre Site of 1867." *Denver Westerners Roundup* 56(4):4–33.
2009 *Custer into the West with the Journal and Maps of Lieutenant Henry Jackson.* El Segundo, Calif.: Upton and Sons.

Breternitz, Louis A.
1931 "The Settlement and Economic Development of Lincoln County, Nebraska." M.A. thesis, Department of History, University of Colorado, Boulder.

Buckley, Ralf
    2006   *Adventure Tourism.* Wallingford, U.K.: CABI.
Buecker, Thomas R.
    1982   "The Post of North Platte Station, 1867–1878." *Nebraska History* 63(3):381–98.
"Buffalo Bill" [Cody, William F.]
    1894   "Famous Hunting Parties of the Plains." *The Cosmopolitan* 17(2):132–43.
    1908   *True Tales of the Plains.* New York: Cupples and Sons.
Buttafuso, Robert A.
    2000   *Civil War Relic Hunting A to Z.* Ann Arbor, Mich.: Sheridan Books.
Carter, Robert A.
    2000   *Buffalo Bill Cody: The Man Behind the Legend.* New York: John Wiley Sons.
Clark, Caven P.
    1995   *Archaeological Investigations at Camp Lincoln (23CT355), Carter County, Missouri.* Van Buren, Mo.: Ozark National Scenic Riverways, National Park Service.
Cody, Louisa Frederick, with Courtney Ryley Cooper
    1919   *Memories of Buffalo Bill.* New York: Appleton.
Cody, William F.
    1917   *Life and Adventures of "Buffalo Bill."* Chicago: Stanton and Van Vliet.
    1923   *An Autobiography of Buffalo Bill.* Rahway, N.J.: Cosmopolitan Book.
    1978   *The Life of Hon. William F. Cody, Known as Buffalo Bill.* Lincoln: University of Nebraska Press. (First published in 1878.)
Coles, Tim, and Dallen J. Timothy
    1998   *Tourism, Diasporas and Space.* New York: Routledge.
Connelly, William
    1918   *A Standard History of Kansas and Kansans.* Chicago: Lewis Publishing.
Connor, Melissa, and Douglas Scott
    1998   Metal Detector Use in Archaeology: An Introduction. *Historical Archaeology* 32(4):76–85.
Corcoran Gallery of Art
    1997   *Jewels of the Romanovs: Treasures of the Russian Imperial Court.* Washington, D.C.: Corcoran Gallery of Art.
Corle, Bryan, and Joseph Balicki
    2006   "Finding Civil War Sites: What Relic Hunters Know; What Archeologists Should and Need to Know." In *Huts and History: The Historical Archaeology of Military Encampment during the American Civil War,* edited by Clarence R. Geier, David G. Orr,

and Mathew B. Reeves, 55–73. Gainesville: University Press of Florida.

Crain, Jim
   2000   "The Royal Buffalo Hunt." *Stereo World: The Magazine of 3-D Images, Past and Present* 27(5):18–30.
   2005   "From Society Balls to Buffalo Tails: *Ephemera* Traces the Grand Duke's Tour." *Ephemera News* 23(4):1, 10–17.

Cramer, Clayton E.
   2007   *Armed America: The Remarkable Story of How and Why Guns Became as American as Apple Pie.* Nashville, Tenn.: Thomas Nelson.

Crick, M.
   1989   "Representations of International Tourism in the Social Sciences: Sun, Sex, Sights, Savings, and Servility." *Annual Review of Anthropology* 18:307–44.

Custer, Elizabeth B.
   1893   *Tenting on the Plains or Gen'l Custer in Kansas and Texas.* New York.: Charles L. Webster.

Custer, Elizabeth B. (Edited by John S. Manion, Jr.)
   1990   "Custer, Cody, and the Grand Duke Alexis." *Research Review, Journal of the Little Big Horn Associates* 4(1):2–14, 31–32.

Darrah, William C.
   1981   *Cartes de Visite in Nineteenth Century Photography.* Gettysburg, Pa.: Privately published by the author.

David, Andrew
   2006   "Finding Sites." In *Archaeology in Practice: A Student Guide to Archaeological Analyses*, edited by Jane Balme and Alistair Paterson, 1–38. Malden, Mass.: Blackwell Publishing.

Davies, Henry E. (Edited by Paul Andrew Hutton)
   1985   *Ten Days on the Plains.* Dallas, Tex.: Southern Methodist University Press.

Dean, Frank
   1975   *Trick and Fancy Riders.* Caldwell, Id.: Caxton Printers.

Devore, Irven, and Richard Lee
   1999   *Man the Hunter.* Hawthorne, N.Y.: Aldine De Gruyter.

Dippie, Brian
   1980   *Nomad: George A. Custer in Turf, Field and Farm.* Austin: University of Texas Press.

Dixon, David
   1994   *Hero of Beecher Island: The Life and Military Career of George A. Forsyth.* Lincoln: University of Nebraska Press.

Dobak, William A.
   1995   "The Army and the Buffalo: A Demur." *Western History Quarterly* 26(2):197–203.

Dorsey, R. Stephen
   1984   *American Military Belts and Related Equipment*. Union City, Tenn.: Pioneer Press.

Drummond, T. F.
   1923   "A Famous Buffalo Hunt." *Field and Stream*, July, 349–50, 421–22.

Dumin, Stanislaw
   1999   "Les Romanoff et leurs Mariages après le 1917." In *Russie et autres pays du Monde: Liens Généalogiques*, 29.XI–4.XII, 11–15. Moscow: I Colloque International de Généalogie.

Dustin, Dorothy Devereux
   1980   *Omaha and Douglas County: A Panoramic History*. Woodland Hills, Calif.: Windsor Publications.

Dyer, Frederick H.
   1994   *Regimental Histories*. Vol. 2 of *A Compendium of the War of the Rebellion*, Dayton, Ohio: Broadfoot Publishing, Morningside Press. (First published in 1908.)

Dykes, Jeff C. (editor)
   1972   *The Grand Duke Alexis in the United States of America*. New York: Interland Publishing. (First published anonymously in 1872 by Riverside Press, Cambridge, Mass., as *His Imperial Highness the Grand Duke Alexis in the United States of America during the Winter of 1871–72*.)

Edmunds, A. C.
   1871   *Pen Sketches of Nebraskans*. Lincoln, Neb.: Tribune and Republican Publishers.

Espenshade, Christopher T., Robert L. Jolley, and James B. Legg.
   2002   "The Value and Treatment of Civil War Military Sites." *North American Archeologist* 23(1):39–67.

Farrington, Dusan P.
   2004   *Arming and Equipping the United States Cavalry, 1865–1902*. Lincoln, R.I.: Andrew Mowbray Publishers.

Farrow, Lee A.
   2002   "Grand Duke Alexei and the Origins of Rex, 1872: Myth, Public Memory, and the Distortion of History." *Gulf South Historical Review* 18(1): 6–30.

Faulkner, Virginia (Editor)
   1957   *Roundup: A Nebraska Reader*. Lincoln: University of Nebraska Press.

Ferrand, Jacques
   1995   *Descendances Naturelles des Souverains et Grand-Ducs de Russie de 1762 à 1910: Répertoire Généalogique*. Paris: Jacques Ferrand.

1999 *Les Familles Comtales de l'Ancien Empire de Russie: Répertoire Généalogique.* Paris: Jacques Ferrand.

Fesler, Garrett R., Matthew R. Laird, and Hank D. Lutton
2006 "'Beautiful Confusion': The Archaeology of Civil War Camp Life in an Urban Context." In *Huts and History: The Historical Archaeology of Military Encampment during the American Civil War*, edited by Clarence R. Geier, David G. Orr, and Matthew B. Reeves, 216–43. Gainesville: University Press of Florida.

Fleming, David L.
1911 *From Everglade to Cañon with the Second Dragoons. A Commemorative Address.* Governors Island, N.Y.: Journal Military Service Institution.

Forsee, Aylsea
1964 *William Henry Jackson: Pioneer Photographer of the West.* New York: Viking,

Frost, Lawrence A.
1964 *The Custer Album: A Pictorial Biography of General George A. Custer.* Seattle, Wash.: Superior Publishing.
1986 *Custer's 7th Cavalry and the Campaign of 1873.* El Segundo, Calif.: Upton and Sons.

Gard, Wayne
1960 *The Great Buffalo Hunt: Its History and Drama, and Its Role in the Opening of the West.* New York: Knopf.

Garrow, Patrick H., Jeffery L. Holland, and Larissa A. Thomas
2000 *Camp Lincoln of the Army of Southeastern Missouri: Historical and Archaeological Studies of 23CT355, Van Buren, Missouri.* Atlanta, Ga.: TRC Garrow Associates.

Garrow, Patrick, and Jeffery L. Holland
2005 "Camp Lincoln and the Army of Southeastern Missouri." *Missouri Archaeologist* 66:93–118.

Geier, Clarence R., David G. Orr, and Matthew B. Reeves
2006 *Huts and History: The Historical Archaeology of Military Encampment during the American Civil War.* Gainesville: University Press of Florida.

Gilbert, Miles
1986 *Getting a Stand.* Tempe, Ariz.: Hal Green Printing.

Gilbert, Miles, Leo Remiger, and Sharon Cunningham
2003 *Encyclopedia of Buffalo Hunters and Skinners*, vol. 1. Union City, Tenn.: Pioneer Press.

Graburn, N. H.
1989 "Tourism: The Sacred Journey." In *Hosts and Guests: The Anthropology of Tourism*, edited by V. L. Smith, 21–36. Philadelphia: University of Pennsylvania Press.

Grafe, Ernest, and Paul Horsted
    2002   *Exploring with Custer: The 1874 Black Hills Expedition.* Custer, S.Dak.: Golden Valley Press.
Graham, Richard K.
    1995   "Metal Detection: The Crime Scene's Best Kept Secret." *FBI Law Enforcement Bulletin* 64(2):10–16.
Green, Thomas L.
    1954   "Notes on a Buffalo Hunt: The Diary of Mordecai Bartman." *Nebraska History* 35(8):193–222.
Greene, Jerome (Editor)
    1986   *U.S. Army Uniforms and Equipment, 1889.* Lincoln, Neb.: Bison Books.
Greene, Jerome A., and Douglas D. Scott
    2004   *Finding Sand Creek: History, Archeology, and the 1864 Massacre Site.* Norman: University of Oklahoma Press.
Hadley, James Albert
    1908   "A Royal Buffalo Hunt." *Kansas State Historical Collections* 10:564–80.
Hanson, James
    1972   "Upper Missouri Arrow Points." *Museum of the Fur Trade Quarterly* 8(4):2–8.
    1975   *Metal Weapons, Tools, and Ornaments of the Teton Dakota Indians.* Lincoln: University of Nebraska Press.
    2005   *When Skins Were Money: A History of the Fur Trade.* Chadron, Neb.: Museum of the Fur Trade.
    2011   *Firearms.* Vol. 1 of *The Encyclopedia of Trade Goods*, Chadron, Neb.: Museum of the Fur Trade.
Harding, C. W.
    2006   *Eley Cartridges: A History of the Silversmiths and Ammunition Manufacturers.* Shrewsbury, U.K.: Quiller Press.
Hatch, Alden
    1956   *Remington Arms in American History.* New York: Rinehart and Company.
Haynes, C. Vance, Jr.
    1995   *General Custer and His Sporting Rifles.* Tucson, Ariz.: Westernlore Press.
Heitman, Francis E.
    1903   *Historical Register and Dictionary of the United States Army, from its Organization, September 29, 1789, to March 2, 1903,* vol. 1. Washington: Government Printing Office.
Hendricks, Gordon
    1974   *Albert Bierstadt: Painter of the American West.* New York: Harry N. Abrams and the Amon Carter Museum of Western Art.

Herskovitz, Robert M.
　　1978　"Fort Bowie Material Culture." Anthropological Papers of the University of Arizona Tucson, No. 31.
Heski, Thomas M.
　　2001　"Camp Powell: The Powder River Supply Depot." *Research Review: The Journal of the Little Big Horn Associates* 17(1):13–24.
Holloway, W. L.
　　1891　*Wild Life on the Plains and Horrors of Indian Warfare.* St. Louis, Mo.: Royal Publishing.
Horsted, Paul, Ernest Graffe, and Jon Nelson
　　2009　*Crossing the Plains with Custer.* Custer, S.D.: Golden Valley Press.
Hunt, William J.
　　2009　"A Model of Tourism as Context for Historical Sites: An Example of Historical Archaeology in Yellowstone National Park." In *Historical Archaeology of Tourism in Yellowstone National Park*, edited by Annalise Corbin and Matthew Russell, 1–74. New York: Springer.
Hunter, Louis C.
　　1993　*Steamboats on the Western Rivers: An Economic and Technological History.* New York: Dover Publications.
Hutton, Paul Andrew (Editor)
　　1985　"Introduction." In *Ten Days on the Plains*, by Henry E. Davies. Dallas: Southern Methodist University Press.
Hyde, George E.
　　1987　*Spotted Tail's Folk: A History of the Brulé Sioux.* Norman: University of Oklahoma Press.
Isenberg, Andrew C.
　　2000　*The Destruction of the Buffalo: An Environmental History, 1750–1920.* Cambridge, U.K.: Cambridge University Press.
Israel, Fred L.
　　1968　Sears Roebuck Catalogue No. 104. New York: Chelsea House Publishers. (Reprint of 1894 catalog.)
Iwacha, Henry
　　1979　"The Use of Metal Detectors in Archaeology." *Manitoba Archaeological Quarterly* 3(2):13–16.
Jackson, William H.
　　1940　*Time Exposure.* New York: Putnam.
Jensen, Todd L.
　　2000　"'Gimmie Shelter': Union Shelters of the Civil War: A Preliminary Archaeological Typology." M.A. thesis, Department of Anthropology, College of William and Mary.
Johnson, Randy, and Nancy Allan
　　1999　*A Dispatch to Custer: The Tragedy of Lieutenant Kidder.* Missoula, Mont.: Mountain Press.

Jolley, Robert L.
  2008 "An Archaeological Survey of an 1864 Union Earthwork and Encampment (44FFK111), Frederick County, Virginia." *Quarterly Bulletin of the Archeological Society of Virginia* 63(1): 18–39.

Jones, Joe B.
  1999 "'Our brigade has never been in winter quarters, but always in tents & moving about. . . . ' Lessons Learned from the Archeological Evaluation of Camp Mason, An Early Confederate Winter Encampment near Winchester, Virginia." *Quarterly Bulletin of the Archeological Society of Virginia* 54 (1): 20–35.

Karklins, Karlis
  1992 *Trade Ornament Usage Among the Native Peoples of Canada: A Source Book.* Ottawa, Ont.: National Historic Sites, Park Service, Environment Canada.

Katz, D. Mark
  1985 *Custer in Photographs.* Gettysburg, Pa.: Yo-Mark Production.

Kelly, Robert L.
  2007 *The Foraging Spectrum: Diversity in Hunter-Gatherer Lifeways.* Clinton Corners, N.Y.: Eliot Werner Publications.

Kelsey, D. M.
  1901 *History of Our Wild West and Stories of Pioneer Life from Experiences of Buffalo Bill, Wild Bill, Kit Carson, Davy Crockett, Sam Houston, Daniel Boone, and Others.* Chicago: Thompson and Thomas.

Kennedy, Martha H.
  1991 "Nebraska's Women Photographers." *Nebraska History* 72(2): 62–79.

King, Eleanor M.
  2006 "Archeology and the Warriors Project: Exploring Buffalo Soldier Campsite in the Guadalupe Mountains of Texas." In *People Places and Parks, Proceedings of the 2005 George Wright Society Conference on Parks, Protected Areas, and Cultural Sites*, edited by David Harmon, 475–81. Hancock, Mich.: The George Wright Society.
  2008 "Buffalo Soldiers, Apaches, and Cultural Heritage Education." *Heritage Management* 1(2):219–41.

King, Eleanor M., and Justin Dunnavant
  2008 "Buffalo Soldiers and Apaches in the Guadalupe Mountains: A Review of Research at Pine Springs Camp." *Bulletin of the Texas Archeological Society* 79:87–94.

Leckie, Shirley A.
  1993 *Elizabeth Bacon Custer and the Making of a Myth.* Norman: University of Oklahoma Press.

Lee, Willis T., Ralph W. Stone, and Hoyt S. Gale
    1915   *Guidebook of the Western United States, Part B., The Overland Route with a Side Trip to Yellowstone Park.* Bulletin 612, United States Geological Survey, Department of the Interior. Washington, D.C.: Government Printing Office.

Lees, William B.
    1986   *Jotham Meeker's Farmstead: Historical Archaeology at the Ottawa Baptist Mission, Kansas.* Anthropological Series Number 13. Topeka: Kansas State Historical Society.

Legg, James B., and Steven D. Smith
    2007   "Camden: Salvaging Data from a Heavily Collected Battlefield." In *Fields of Conflict: Battlefield Archaeology from the Roman Empire to the Korean War,* edited by Douglas Scott, Lawrence Babits, and Charles Haecker, 1:208–33. Westport, Conn.: Praeger Security International.

Logan, Herschel C.
    1952   "Royal Buffalo Hunt." *American Rifleman,* October 37–42.

Lyle, D. A., and Samuel W. Porter
    1882   *Report on the Manufacture and Issue of Files and Rasps.* Executive Documents of the House of Representatives, 47th Congress, Appendix 35 to Ordnance Reports No. 1, part 2, vol. 3, pp. 320–85. Washington, D.C.: Government Printing Office.

Mace, O. Henry
    1990   *Collector's Guide to Early Photographs.* Radnor, Pa.: Wallace-Homestead Book.

MacDonald, Duncan
    1987   Hunting: An Exercise in Pluralistic Democracy. *Wildlife Society Bulletin* 15(3):463–65.

Massie, Suzanne
    1984a   "The Grand Duke Alexis in the U.S.A., Part 1." *The Gilcrease Magazine of American History and Art* 6(3):1–5.
    1984b   "The Grand Duke Alexis in the U.S.A., Part 2: From Buffalo Bill to the Mardi Gras." *The Gilcrease Magazine of American History and Art* 6(4):6–24.
    2008   "A Royal Visit: The Grand Duke Alexis in the United States." In *The Tsar and the President: Alexander II and Abraham Lincoln,* 59–66. Washington, D.C.: American-Russian Cultural Cooperation Foundation.

Mautz, Carl
    2000   *Biographies of Western Photographers: A Reference Guide to Photographers Working in the 19th Century American West.* Nevada City, Calif.: Carl Mautz Publishing.

McAlpine, R. W.
    1872   *The Life and Times of Col. James Fisk, Jr.* New York: The New York Book Company.

McBride, W. Stephen
    1994   "Civil War Material Culture and Camp Life in Central Kentucky." In *Look to the Earth: Historical Archaeology and the American Civil War*, edited by Clarence R. Geier, Jr., and Susan E. Winter, 130–57. Knoxville: University of Tennessee Press.

McBride, W. Stephen, and Kim A. McBride
    2006   "Archaeological Investigations of Fort Donnally." *Journal of the Greenbrier Historical Society* 8(2):21–36.

McBride, W. Stephen, and William E. Sharp
    1991   "Archaeological Investigations at Camp Nelson: A Union Quartermaster Depot and Hospital in Jessamine County, Kentucky." Archaeological Report 241, University of Kentucky Program for Cultural Resource Assessment.

McBride, Steven W., Susan C. Andrews, J. Howard Beverly, and Tracey A. Sandefur
    2003   *From Supply Depot to Emancipation Center, the Archaeology of Camp Nelson, Kentucky*. Lexington, Ky.: Wilbur Smith Associates.

McChristian, Douglas C.
    2000   "Plainsman—or Showman? George A. Custer's Buckskins." *Military Collector and Historian* 52(1):2–13.

McCorquodale, Scott M.
    1997   "Cultural Contexts of Recreational Hunting and Native Subsistence and Ceremonial Hunting: Their Significance for Wildlife Management." *Wildlife Society Bulletin* 25(2):568–73.

McDonald, Jack
    1958   "Buffalos and Champagne." *Tradition*, December, 15–30.

McLeod, K. David
    1985   "Metal Detecting and Archaeology: An Example from EbLf-12." *Manitoba Archaeological Quarterly* 9(2):20–31.

McMurty, Larry
    2002   *Sin Killer*. New York: Simon & Schuster.
    2003a *The Wandering Hill*. New York: Simon & Schuster
    2003b *By Sorrow's River*. New York: Simon & Schuster.
    2004   *Folly and Glory*. New York: Simon & Schuster.

Merritt, John I.
    1985   *Baronets and Buffalo: The British Sportsman in the American West, 1833–1881*. Missoula: Montana Press Publishing.

Mikhailovich, Grand Duke Alexander
    1932   *Once a Grand Duke*. New York: Farrar and Rinehart.

Millbrook, Minnie Dubbs
    1975   "Big Game Hunting with the Custers, 1869–1870." *Kansas Historical Quarterly* 41(4):429–53.

Miles, W. H., and John Bratt
   1894   *Early History and Reminiscence of Frontier County, Nebraska.* Maywood, Neb.: N. H. Brogue.
Mintling, Wayne L.
   2004   "The Last Great Buffalo Hunt: A Grand Hunt For A Grand Duke." Privately published by the author, no place given.
Morris, Edmund
   2010   *Colonel Roosevelt.* New York: Random House.
Nash, D.
   1981   "Tourism as an Anthropological Subject." *Current Anthropology* 22(5):461–68.
Nelson, Dean E.
   2006   "'Right Nice Little House[s]': Winter Camp Architecture of the American Civil War." In *Huts and History: The Historical Archaeology of Military Encampment during the American Civil War,* edited by Clarence R. Geier, David G. Orr, and Matthew B. Reeves, 177–93. Gainesville: University Press of Florida.
Nelson, Lee H.
   1968   "Nail Chronology as an Aid in Dating Old Buildings." Technical Leaflet 48, American Association for State and Local History.
Neuman, Robert W.
   2010   "North American Indian Encampments: Tipi Rings, Wooden Wall Anchors, and Windbreaks." *Plains Anthropologist* 55(215): 241–50.
Nevins, Allan
   1948   *America through British Eyes.* New York: Oxford University Press.
Nordhoff, Charles
   1874   *California: For Health, Pleasure, and Residence, A Book for Travellers and Settlers.* New York: Harper and Brothers.
Nunes, Pepsi
   2001   "The Evolution of the Imperial Russian Navy and the Grand Dukes 1850–1917." *Atlantis* 2(3, 4):16–24.
   2002   "The Evolution of the Imperial Russian Navy and the Grand Dukes 1850–1917." *Atlantis* 3(1):7–15.
Office of Indian Affairs
   1872   Letters Sent 1821–81. Microfilm 21, Roll 103, National Archives and Records Administration.
Official State Atlas of Nebraska
   1885   *Official State Atlas of Nebraska.* Philadelphia, Everts and Kirk Publishers.
Olsson, John
   2004   *Forensic Linguistics: An Introduction to Language, Crime, and the Law.* New York: Continuum Press.

Otero, Miguel Antonio
 1935 *My Life on the Frontier, 1864–1882: Incidents and Characters of the Period when Kansas, Colorado, and New Mexico were passing through the last of their Wild and Romantic Years.* New York: The Press of Pioneers.

Paine, Bayard H.
 1932 *The Famous Buffalo Hunt of the Grand Duke Alexis of Russia As Given at the Second Annual Picnic Held at Camp Duke Alexis, Hayes County, Nebraska.* Lincoln: Nebraska State Historical Society Archives.
 1935 *Pioneers, Indians and Buffaloes.* Curtis, Neb.: The Curtis Enterprise.

Palmer, Robert G.
 1995 "Colorado's Odd Couple: The 1872 Visit of Grand Duke Alexis and Gen. George A. Custer to the Mile High City." *The Denver Westerners Golden Anniversary Brand Book* 32: 221–43.
 2003 "Custer and the Grand Duke." *Greasy Grass* 19:24–30.

Palmquist, Peter E., and Thomas R. Kailbourn
 2005 *Pioneer Photographers from the Mississippi to the Continental Divide: A Biographical Dictionary, 1839–1865.* Stanford, Calif.: Stanford University Press.

Parker, James
 2003 *The Old Army: Memories 1872–1918.* Mechanicsburg, Pa.: Stackpole Books. (Reprint of 1929 edition.)

Parry, Albert
 1948 "The Grand Duke Comes to America." *American Mercury* 67(297):334–41.

Pate, Charles W.
 2006 *Smith and Wesson American Model in U.S. and Foreign Service.* Woonsocket, R.I.: Andrew Mowbray Publishers.

Paxson, Frederic L.
 1917 "The Rise of Sport." *Mississippi Valley Historical Review* 4(2):143–68.

Perry, John Curtis, and Constantine Pleshakov
 1999 *The Flight of the Romanovs, A Family Saga.* New York: Basic Books.

Piston, William Garrett, and Thomas P. Sweeney
 2009 *Portraits of Conflict: A Photographic History of Missouri in the Civil War.* Fayetteville: University of Arkansas Press.

Pitman, John
 1990 *The Pitman Notes on U.S. Martial Small Arms and Ammunition, 1776–1933.* Vol. 2, *Revolvers and Automatic Pistols.* Gettysburg, Pa.: Thomas Publications.

Pomeroy, Earl
    1990   *In Search of the Golden West: The Tourist in Western America.* Lincoln: University of Nebraska Press.

Records of the Adjutant General's Office
    1871   Letters Received, 1871–80. RG94, Microfilm 666, Roll 36, National Archives and Records Administration.

Records of U.S. Army Continental Commands
    1876   Department of the Platte Records, 1858–95. RG33, Microfilm S3, Roll 3, National Archives and Records Administration.
    1872   North Platte Station, Letters and Endorsements copy book. RG393, Part V. Vol. 2, National Archives and Records Administration.

Reeves, Matthew B.
    2001   "Dropped and Fired: Archeological Patterns of Militaria from two Civil War Battles, Manassas National Battlefield Park." Occasional Report No. 15, Regional Archaeology Program. National Capital Region. Washington, D.C.: National Park Service U.S. Department of the Interior.
    2006   "Under the Forest Floor: Excavations at a Confederate Winter Encampment, Orange, Virginia." In *Huts and History: The Historical Archaeology of Military Encampment during the American Civil War,* edited by Clarence Geier, David Orr, and Mathew Reeves, 194–216. Gainesville: University Press of Florida.

Returns of Regular Army Cavalry Regiments
    1872   Second Cavalry, 1833–1916. Microfilm 744, Roll 19, National Archives and Records Administration.
    1872   Fifth Cavalry, 1833–1916. Microfilm 744, Roll 54, National Archives and Records Administration.
    1872   Sixth Cavalry, 1833–1916. Microfilm 744, Roll 59, National Archives and Records Administration.

Returns from U.S. Military Posts
    1872   Fort McPherson, Nebraska. Microfilm 617, Roll 708, National Archives and Records Administration.
    1871–72   Fort Wallace, Kansas. Microfilm 617, Roll 1339, National Archives and Records Administration.

Rodenbough, T. F. (Compiler)
    1875   *From Everglade to Cañon with the Second Dragoons: An Account of Service in Florida, Mexico, Virginia and the Indian Country. With an Appendix, Containing Orders, Reports, etc. from 1836–1875.* New York: D. Van Nostrand.

Rosa, Joseph P.
    1996   *Wild Bill Hickok: The Man and the Myth.* Lawrence: University of Kansas Press.

2005 "Wild Bill Hickok, Buffalo Bill Cody, and the Grand Buffalo Hunt at Niagara Falls." *Nebraska History* 86(2):14–25.

Rothman, Hal K.
1998 *Devil's Bargains: Tourism in the Twentieth-Century American West*. Lawrence: University Press of Kansas.

Russell, Carl P.
1967 *Firearms, Traps, and Tools of the Mountain Men*. New York: Alfred A. Knopf.

Russell, Don
1960 *The Lives and Legends of Buffalo Bill*. Norman: University of Oklahoma Press.

Russian State Archives
1871–72 Romanov Family Records, Fond 641, Inventory 1, File 34.
1871–72 Romanov Family Records, Fond 642, Inventory 1, File 768.
1871–72 Romanov Family Records, Fond 652, Inventory 1, File 385.
1871–72 Romanov Family Records, Fond 678, Inventory 1, File 739.

Russian State Naval Archives
1872 Warrant Officer V. K. Ienesh, Fond 31, Inventory 2, File 2.
1871–72 Admiral K. N. Possiet Diaries and Letters, Fond 1247, Inventory 1, File 40.

Saul, Norman E.
1996a *Concord and Conflict: The United States and Russia, 1867–1914*. Lawrence: University Press of Kansas.
1996b Grand Duke Alexis and the American West. *Prairie Scout* 6:23–42.

Savage, James Woodruff, and John T. Bell
1894 *History of Omaha*. New York, Munsell and Co.

Schmidt, James M.
2001 "Tredegar 'Mosby Cannon' on View at Oklahoma 45th Infantry Museum." *The Artilleryman* 22(4):3–6.

Scott, Douglas D.
2000 "Archeological Investigations of Custer's June 23, 1876 Campsite, Rosebud County, Montana." Ms on file, Midwest Archeological Center, Lincoln, Neb.
2008 "A Gunfight in the Whetstones: The Archaeology of a Conflict Site, Mescal Springs, Cochise County, Arizona." Department of Anthropology and Geography, University of Nebraska, Lincoln.

Scott, Douglas D., and Peter Bleed
2002 "Custer and the Grand Duke in Nebraska, 1872: Some Insights from New Photographic Evidence." In *Custer and His Times*, Book 4, edited by John P. Hart, 94–109. La Grange, Ill.: Little Bighorn Associates.

Scott, Douglas D., Richard A. Fox, Jr., Melissa A. Connor, and Dick Harmon
1989 *Archaeological Perspectives on the Battle of the Little Bighorn*. Norman: University of Oklahoma Press.

Sherman, William T.
　1889　*Memoirs of William T. Sherman.* Vol. 2. New York: D. Appleton.
Simon, John Y. (Editor)
　1998　*The Papers of Ulysses S. Grant.* Vol. 22, *June 1, 1871–January 31, 1872.* Carbondale: Southern Illinois University Press.
Skinner, S. Alan
　1968　"Camp Willow Grove, Arizona Territory." *Plateau* 41(1):1–13.
Sloane, Eric
　1964　*A Museum of Early American Tools.* New York: Ballantine Books.
Smith, D. Jean
　2003　*Medicine Creek Journals: Ena and the Plainsmen.* North Platte, Neb.: The Old 101 Press.
　2009　*Wolf's Rest and Other Tales of Southwest Nebraska.* Charleston, S.C.: Create Space Publishing.
Smith, J. Greg
　1962　The Duke Alexis Hunt. *Outdoor Nebraska* 40(4):6–7, 29–30.
Smits, David D.
　1994　"The Frontier Army and the Destruction of the Buffalo: 1865–1883." *Western Historical Quarterly* 25(3):313–40.
Spivey, Towana
　1979　*A Historical Guide to Wagon Hardware & Blacksmith Supplies.* Lawton, Okla.: Museum of the Great Plains.
Sprague, Marshall
　1967　*A Gallery of Dudes.* Boston: Little Brown.
Steffen, Randy
　1979　*The Horse Soldier, 1776–1943.* Vol. 2, *The Frontier, The Mexican War, The Civil War, The Indian Wars, 1851–1880.* Norman: University of Oklahoma Press.
Steinwedel, Louis William
　1961　"Royal Russian Buffalo Hunt." *True West* 9(1):12–13, 72.
Sterling, Bruce B., and Bernard W. Slaughter
　2000　"Surveying the Civil War." In *Archeological Perspectives on the American Civil War,* edited by Clarence R. Geier and Stephen Potter, 305–22. Gainesville: University of Florida Press.
　1980　*Revised Regulations for the Army of the United States, 1861.* Harrisburg, Pa.: The National Historical Society. (Originally published in 1861 by the U.S. War Department.)
Stewart, Byron
　1980　"The Meeting of Two Bears: Grand Duke Alexis at the Missouri Legislature." *Missouri Historical Review* 75(2):166–89.
Strong, William E.
　1960　*Canadian River Hunt.* Norman: University of Oklahoma Press.
Tagg, Martyn D.
　1987　"The Camp at Bonita Cañon, A Buffalo Soldiers Camp in Chiricahua National Monument." Arizona. Publications in Anthro-

pology No. 42. Tucson, Ariz.: Western Archeological and Conservation Center.

Takasaki, Kymberly C., W. Andy Martin, Victor F. Medina, and Joseph R. Marsh
    2006   "A Metal Detector Study to Locate Inactive Small Arms Range Impact Areas." *Soil and Sediment Contamination* 15:379–86.

Tarsaidze, Alexandre
    1958   *Czars and Presidents: The Story of a Forgotten Friendship*. New York: McDowell Obolensky.

Thomas, James E., and Dean S. Thomas
    2007   *A Handbook of Civil War Bullets and Cartridges*. Gettysburg, Pa.: Thomas Publications.

Thrapp, Dan L.
    1991   *Encyclopedia of Frontier Biography*, Vol. 1. Lincoln, Neb.: Bison Books.

Tice, Warren K.
    1997   *Uniform Buttons of the United States, 1776–1865*. Gettysburg, Pa.: Thomas Publications.
    2003   *Dating Buttons: A Chronology of Button Types, Makers, Retailers and Their Backmarks*. Gettysburg, Pa.: Thomas Publications.

Tucker, William Warren
    1872   *His Imperial Highness the Grand Duke Alexis in the United States of America During the Winter of 1871–1872*. Cambridge, Mass.: Riverside Press.

Turner, V., and E. Turner
    1978   *Image and Pilgrimage in Christian Culture: Anthropological Perspectives*, New York: Columbia University Press.

Tutherly, Herbert E.
    1898   *Elementary Treatise on Military Science and the Art of War*, 2nd ed. Burlington, Vt.: Free Press Association.

U.S. Army
    1882   *Specifications for Means of Transportation, Paulins, Stoves, and Ranges, and Lamps and Fixtures for Use in the United States Army*. Washington, D.C.: Government Printing Office.

Vaughn, J. W.
    1996   "Captain James Egan." *The Westerners Brand Book, New York Posse* 13(1):1–7, 18.

Veit, Richard, and Michael J. Gall
    2011   "Patriots, Tories, Inebriates, and Hussies: The Historical Archaeology of the Abraham Staats House, as a Case Study in Microhistory." *Northeast Historical Archaeology* 38:49–69.

Wakeley, Arthur C.
    1917   *Omaha: The Gate City and Douglas County Nebraska*, Vol. 1. Chicago, Ill.: S. J. Clarke.

Ward, Eric
    2002   *Army Life in Virginia: The Civil War Letters of George G. Benedict*. Mechanicsburg, Pa.: Stackpole Books.

Ward, Roswell
    1948   *Henry A. Ward: Museum Builder to America*. Rochester, N.Y.: The Rochester Historical Society.

War Department
    1862   *Revised Regulation of the Army of the United States, 1861*. Philadelphia, George W. Childs.

Warren, Louis
    2005   *Buffalo Bill's America: William Cody and the Wild West Show*. New York: Knopf.

Watson, Danial
    1999   "Special Order No. 75: '. . . Opposite Beauvais' Ranche.' An Archaeological Investigation of an 1867 Military Camp in the South Platte River Valley." Nebraska Archaeological Survey Technical Report 99–04. Lincoln: University of Nebraska State Museum.

Weiland, F. N.
    1932   "The Southwestern Nebraska Historical Society." Typescript of a presentation given to the Annual Meeting of the State Historical Society, 1932. Copy on file Nebraska State Historical Society, Lincoln.

Welsh, Peter C.
    1966   *Woodworking Tools 1600–1900*. Contributions from the Museum of History and Technology Paper 51 of United States National Museum, Bulletin 241.Washington, D.C.: Smithsonian Institution.

Wetmore, Helen Cody
    1903   *The Last of the Great Scouts, The Life Story of Col. William F. Cody (Buffalo Bill)*. London, U.K.: Partington Advertising.
    1965   *Buffalo Bill: Last of the Great Scouts*. Lincoln: University of Nebraska Press. (Reprint of 1899 edition, by Duluth Press.)

Wetmore, Helen Cody, and Zane Grey
    1918   *Last of the Great Scouts (Buffalo Bill)*. New York: Grosset and Dunlap.

White, John I.
    1972   "Red Carpet for a Romanoff." *American West* 9(1): 5–9.

Whitehorne, Joseph W. A.
    2006   "Blueprint for Nineteenth Century Camps: Castramentation, 1778–1865." In *Huts and History: The Historical Archaeology of Military Encampment during the American Civil War* by Clarence R. Geier, David G. Orr, and Matthew B. Reeves, pp 28–50. Gainesville: University Press of Florida.

Wolfe, J. M. and Company
- 1871 *Wolfe's Omaha City Directory 1870–1871.* Omaha, Neb.: J. M. Wolfe and Co.

Wrobel, David M., and Patrick T. Long (Editors)
- 2001 *Seeing and Being Seen: Tourism in the American West.* Lawrence: University Press of Kansas.

Yost, Nellie Snyder
- 1979 *Buffalo Bill: His Family, Friends, Fame, Failures, and Fortunes.* Chicago, Ill.: Sage Books.

Zornow, William
- 1961 "When the Czar and Grant Were Friends." *Mid-America Historical Review* 43(3):164–81.

INDEX

Accouterments. *See* Artifacts
Alexis. *See* Grand Duke Alexis
Alexis, son of Grand Duke Alexis, 24
Ammunition. *See* Firearms
Arrowheads. *See under* Artifacts
Artifacts: arrowheads, 132; awl, 116; bottle, ale, 129–30; buttons, 119, 132; cans, 125; ceramics, 126; cooking pot, 126; glass, 126; horse equipment, 124–25, 132; horseshoe and horseshoe nail, 125, 133; lead-foil bottle seals, 126, 132–33; nails and tacks, 120–22, 132; ornaments, 116–18; pocket knife, 132; prehistoric lithic, 115, 132; saber belt stud, 119; scraper blade, 112, 116, 117; screws, 122, 124; suspender grip, 132; tent pins, iron expedient, 122; tools, 122
Asch, Morris (surgeon), 48, 52, 56, 68, 80, 134, 138
Aspinwall, William Henry, 24

Bache, A. B., Lt., 138
Baroness Seggiano. *See* Zhukovskaya, Alexandra
Barrett, Lawrence, 71
Beeson, Chalkley, hunt account questioned, 34, 71
Belknap, William, Sec. of War, 41–42, 44, 66, 137
Bennett, James Gordon, Jr., 138
Berghaus, Albert, 105
Bierstadt, Albert, 15, 24, 40–43
Bodisco, Waldemar, 47, 56, 60, 68, 80, 89, 91
Brown, William, Capt., 138
"Buffalo Bill." *See* Cody, William F. "Buffalo Bill"

Camp Alexis, 5–6, 9, 12, 15, 21, 52, 107, 109, 141, 156–57, 160–61; archaeology of, 110–29, 144–55; collecting at, 129–33; description of, 58; flagpole at, 58, 94–95, 154; monument at, 8; tents at, 87–104, 144–55

Camps: archaeological expression of, 19–21, 136–37, 140–44; idealized organization, 134–36; theoretical microhistory approach, 156–57
Carr, Eugene, Maj., 57
Catacazy, Constatin, 28, 40
Chalfant, David, 130–32
Clark, Ben (scout), 139
Clark, William Philo, 1st Lt., 56
Clarke, S. H. H., 54
Clifford, Mark, 72
Clifford, Scott, 72
Clifford, William, 8, 72
Clothing, types worn in camp, 80, 89–90, 93, 99, 101, 102. *See also under Artifacts for archaeological data on types of clothing*
Clum, H. R., Acting Indian Commissioner, 52
Cody, Louisa, 69
Cody, William F. "Buffalo Bill", 4, 6, 8, 11, 48, 70–71, 77, 86, 94, 134, 137–38, 155–58, 161; account of return to North Platte Station, 67–68; account of role in hunt questioned, 76; hunt camp location, 74; photographs at Camp Alexis, 82, 89, 91; photograph by E. L. Eaton, 85, 98–101; scout on Neb. hunt, 38, 55, 66
Confederate Mountain Rifle, key to New York City made from, 27
Count Belevsky. *See* Alexis, son of Grand Duke Alexis
Crain, Jim, 157
Crook, George, Gen., 139
Crosby, John S., 138
Custer, Elizabeth, 6, 95, 105
Custer, George Armstrong, Lt. Col., 4, 6, 8, 12, 32–33, 38, 45, 77, 80–81, 101, 142 144, 151, 155, 161; flirtation with Spotted Tail's daughter, 68; with hunt party, 53–54, 56, 58–61; photograph of at Camp Alexis, 82, 89–90, 101–104
Czar Alexander II, 3, 10, 22–23, 63, 77
Czar Alexander III (Alexander Alexandrovich), 63, 66
Czarina Maria Alexandrovna, 22, 63

Davies, Henry E., 138
Delano, Charles, Sec. of Interior, 47
Dickey, J. J., 54
Dix, John Adams, Gen., 24
Dodge, Henry, Gen., 24
Drummond, T. F., 71
Dunning, John, finding relics at campsite, 74–75

Eaton, Edric L. (photographer), 4, 7; biography of, 82–85; photographs taken at Camp Alexis, 81–105, 157
Egan, James, Capt., 52–53
Emory, William, Col., 138
Evans, John, 32

Farragut, David, Adm., 24
Field, Cyrus, 24
Firearms, at hunt: bullets, 127–28, 130–31; cartridge cases, 128–31; Colt, 128–30; Remington, Rolling Block, 98–99, 129–30; Sharps, 129–30; Smith and Wesson, 128; Springfield, Cody's M1866 "Lucretia Borgia," 94; Springfield, sporting rifle, 101; Winchester, M1866, 98
Fish, Hamilton, Sec. of State, 42–43
Fitzhugh, Charles L., Gen., 138
Forsyth, George A., Lt. Col., 48, 52–53, 56, 80, 91
Forsyth, James, Lt. Col., 53, 56, 80, 89
Fort Hays, Kans., 11, 57, 138–39

INDEX

Fort McPherson, Neb., 5, 11, 43, 47, 50, 52, 57, 69, 74, 99, 138–39
Fort Riley, Kans., 53
Fort Wallace, Kans., 33, 57
Fowler, Joshua L., 1st Lt., 52, 57
Frank, William, Pvt., 102

Godon, S. W., R. Adm., 24
Gorchakov, Alexander, 40
Gorlov, Alexander, Col., 30
Grand Duchess Maria Fyodorovna, 64
Grand Duke Alexis (Aleksei Alexandrovich Romanov), 3, 8, 10, 15, 18–19, 22, 24, 44, 77, 80, 137, 155–56; gifts to and from Spotted Tail, 61; hunting in Colorado, 33–34; hunt origin and planning, 40–44; later life and death, 36–37; Nebraska hunt and camp, 56–66; photographs of at Camp Alexis, 82, 88, 90; received by President Grant, 28; visit to Bridgeport, Conn., 30; visit to Louisville, Ky., and Mamouth Cave, 35–36; visit to New Orleans, La., and Mardis Gras, 36, 71; visit to Springfield, Mass., 31
Grand Duke Vladimir Alexandrovich, 64
Grant, Frederick, Lt. Col., 139
Grant, Ulysses S., 28
Grinnell, Moses H., 24

Hancock, Winfield Scott, Gen., 57
Hayes, Edward M., Capt., 44, 48, 52; with hunt party, 56
Hearst, William Randolph, 69
Heckscher, John G., 138
Hutchens, Lyle, 130–32

Ienesh, V. K., Warrant Officer, 65–66
Illingworth, William, 151

Jackson, Henry, Lt., 57
Jackson, William Henry, 84
Jerome, Lawrence R., 138
Jerome, Leonard W., 138
Johnson, Andrew, 10
Johnson, Samuel, 138
Johnston, John Taylor, 24

Kidder, Lyman, Lt., 57
Kit Carson, Colo., second hunt at, 32, 34, 63
Knight, J. Lee, 78, 81
Koudrin, Vladimir, Dr., 6, 80, 90, 93

Langford, Mayme Watts, 69
Lee, Samuel Phillips, Adm., 24
Lincoln, Abraham, 10, 77
Livingston, Carroll, 138
Longnecker, Mrs. John, hunt camp location, 74

Machin, William T. V., 56, 80
McArthur, Arthur, Lt. Col., 141
McArthur, Douglas, Gen., 141
McChristian, Douglas, 102
McDonald, William, 69
McDowell, Irwin, Gen., 24
Microhistory, theoretical use. See Camps, theoretical microhistory approach
Miles, William "Paddy", 70
Mintling, John, 72
Mintling, Rufus, 7, 72
Mintling, Wayne, 72
Moore, Thomas, Col., 139
Mosby, John Singleton, Col., 27
Morse, Samuel F. B., 24
Myers, Edward, Lt., 57

Neiswanger, David F., hunt site monument, 72–74
North Platte, Neb., 3, 138
North Platte Station, Neb., 11, 32, 52, 54, 138, 158

Olsenfieff, Count Alexander, 56, 80, 90
Ord, E. O. C., Gen., 56, 58, 89, 99, 134
Otero, Miguel, hunt account questioned, 34, 70

Palmer, Innis N., Col., 52, 56, 58, 60, 134
Palmer, W. H., *See* Miles, William "Paddy"
Paine, Bayard, 70, 72, 74–76
Possiet, Constantine Nikolayevich, V. Adm., 22, 24, 44, 56, 61–63, 66, 80, 89, 90
Pullman railroad cars, use of by Grand Duke Alexis, 3, 4, 27–28, 54, 158

Randall, Todd, Indian Agent, 44–45, 47, 52
Red Willow Creek, Neb., 57; campsite on, 5, 7, 44, 48, 74, 156, 160; possible photograph of, 86–87
Rogers, M. Edward, 138
Roosevelt, Theodore, 14
Roosevelt, Theodore, Sr., 24
Rowan, Stephen Clegg, V. Adm., 24
Rucker, David, Col., 138

Sanford, E. S., Adams Express Co., 31, 47
Saunders, Alvin, Gov. Neb., 31–32, 54
Scholten, James A., 80–81
Second Cavalry, escort, 5, 53
Seventh Cavalry, 57
Sickles, Theophilus E. (Union Pacific Railroad), 47
Sixth Cavalry, 33
Sheridan, Michael, Lt. Col., 53, 56, 60, 80, 138
Sheridan, Philip, Lt. Gen., 4, 8, 11–12, 15, 32–34, 38, 77, 80, 134, 137–40, 144, 150, 153, 155, 161;

with hunt party, 53–56, 60–62, 66–67; Indian Territory hunt, 139–40; "millionaires" hunt, 137–39; photographs of at Camp Alexis, 82, 89; planning of hunt, 42, 44–45, 48
Sherman, William, Gen., 15; hunt origin with, 40; planning of hunt, 42
Shirkoff, Vladimir, 56
Shouvalov, Paul, Lt., 56, 80, 89, 91
Sioux Indians, party at hunt, 59
Smith & Wesson: firearms gifts to royal party, 31; pistol used in hunt, 59, 69, 71
Sport hunting as context for royal buffalo hunt, 12–15
Spotted Tail (Brulé Sioux), 5, 8, 38, 43, 47, 50–52, 77, 90, 150, 155; camp of, 87, 96–98, 153–54; at hunt, 59–60, 69, 160–61; photograph of at Camp Alexis, 94–96, 101–104
Stager, Anson, 138
Steever, Edgar Zell, 2nd Lt., 56
Stevens, Lt. *See* Steever, Edgar Zell, 2nd Lt.
Stover, Lt. *See* Steever, Edgar Zell, 2nd Lt.
Stoves and stovepipes, use in Camp Alexis, 94–95, 104, 107, 139, 148, 149, 150
Strong, William, 139–40
Sweeney, Harry, Lt., 139
Sweitzer, Nelson, Maj. 56, 80, 90

Teller, Henry, 32
Third Infantry, 33
Thomson, Frank (railroad transportation manager), 4, 31–32, 47–48, 56, 80
Thompson, Lydia, 71
Tourism: archaeological model of, 17–19; hunt as part of nascent tourism, 15–19

Townsend, Edward D., Adj. Gen., 43–45
Tudeer, Karl, Lt., 56, 68, 80
Twain, Mark (Samuel Clemens), 24
Two Lance, Brulé Sioux, 60–61

Union Pacific Railroad, 3

War Bonnet (Brulé Sioux), 60
Ward, Henry Augustus, 98–99
Washburn, J. M. (Indian Agent), 44
Wetmore, Helen Cody, 69–70, 76
Wham, James (Indian Agent), 44

Whipple, William, Asst. Adj. Gen., 139
Whistler (Brulé Sioux), 60
Wilson, Charles L., 138

Yates, Stephen (Indian trader), 44
Yellowstone National Park, 17–19

Zhukovskaya, Alexandra, 23; title conferred, 23
Zhukovsky, Vasily Andreyevich (father of Alexandra), 23

www.ingramcontent.com/pod-product-compliance
Lightning Source LLC
Chambersburg PA
CBHW032250150426
43195CB00008BA/401